Bon Papa

Other Books by Bernard Diederich

Papa Doc: The Truth about Haiti Today (with Al Burt). McGraw-Hill, 1968.

Trujillo: Death of the Goat. Little-Brown, 1978.

Somoza: The Legacy of U.S. Involvement in Central America. E.P. Dutton, 1981.

The Ghosts of Makara. Xlibris, 2002.

Una camera testigo de la historia; published in Spanish by Fundación Global Democracia y desarrolla, 2004, and in the Dominican Republic by Fundación Cultural Dominicana.

Le Prix du Sang: La résistance du people haïtien à la tyrannie. Vol. 1: François [Papa Doc] Duvalier, 1957-1971. Editions Antillia, Port-au-Prince, Haiti, 2005.

Teenage Heir to Dictatorship—Baby Doc. Book 2: 1971-1986. Presently being translated into French.

Bon Papa

Haiti's Golden Years

BERNARD DIEDERICH

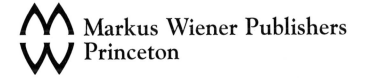

Markus Wiener Publishers
Princeton

Photo credits: All photographs not otherwise attributed are from the
collection of the *Haiti Sun*.

Cover bust of Gen. President Paul E. Magloire, courtesy of *Time* magazine.
Cover designed by Jean-Bernard Diederich.

For information, write to Markus Wiener Publishers
231 Nassau Street, Princeton, NJ 08542
www.markuswiener.com

Library of Congress Cataloging-in-Publication Data

Diederich, Bernard
        Bon Papa: Haiti's golden years / Bernard Diederich
        p. cm
        ISBN 978-1-55876-464-4 (hc : alk. paper)
        ISBN 978-1-55876-465-1 (pbk. : alk. paper)
1. Haiti—History—1934-1986. 2. Diederich, Bernard.
3. Visitors, Foreign—Haiti. 4. Journalists—Haiti. I. Title
    F1928.D54 2008
    972.94'06—dc22

                                        2008002903

Markus Wiener Publishers books are printed in the United States of America
on acid-free paper, and meet the guidelines for permanence and durability
of the Committee on Production Guidelines for Book Longevity of the
Council on Library Resources.

CONTENTS

This book is dedicated to the youth of Haiti, who may not recognize the Haiti of this book, with the hope they will one day help to make Haiti stand tall and proud among nations again.

ACKNOWLEDGMENTS

This is a work of nonfiction drawn mostly from the author's own experiences and from his newspaper, the *Haiti Sun*, during the years 1950-1956. The motto of the newspaper: "Reporting the truth to the best of our ability."

***** *

With thanks to my relatives, Pierre-André (Pierrot) Sajous and Josiane Hudicourt-Barnes, who gave generously of their time to critique this book. To Samantha Jacob, who knows more about photo editing on the computer than I ever want to know. To my wife, Ginette, who is the best copyeditor in the family, and to our talented son, Jean-Bernard, who designed yet another of my book covers. I am also grateful for the encouragement of my old colleague at *Time*, Bruce (Bouqui) Henderson.

AUTHOR'S NOTE

It has been said that in order to face the future we must first understand the past. My weekly newspaper, the *Haiti Sun*, was my effort to help enhance the future of a nation with an extraordinary past, and what seemed like a great potential. In the process I grew to love the Haitian people and their westernmost part of Hispaniola, the second-largest Caribbean island.

Those early years of my sojourn in Haiti were a magical time. Every Haitians, it seemed was a poet or painter. My peasant neighbors at Frères, then a rural, hilly, corn-growing community, where I lived before I went to prison under Papa Doc Duvalier, had wonderful Roman names such as Mercius, Alcius and Brisius.

Until 1956, under the popular *Bon Papa*, Gen. Paul E. Magloire, Haiti passed though a "golden age", and then things began going down hill. In a country in which leaders were too often self-proclaimed and all-powerful, the people again became secondary, like the imported second-hand clothing and shoes they later were to wear. Political parties were created only as vehicles for the brief ride to the National Palace. By 1957 it was pitiful to watch politicians believing only in themselves tear the country asunder leading it into bankruptcy, civil war and anarchy. This produced one of the strangest and most fearful dictatorships, the reign of Dr. Francois "Papa Doc" Duvalier.

Once the sugar bowl of Europe, Haiti produced untold wealth based on the sweat and blood of African slaves. With the heroic, if devastating, war that led to independence 200 years ago, a Black orphan nation came into being, feared and hated by its colonial slave-owning neighbors.

Today sugar is imported. Coffee is no longer a major export. Tourism is dead. For Haiti the list is full of superlative negatives: The poorest country in the Western Hemisphere, the highest child mortality rate. It also has a high birth rate that makes its 10,700 square miles the most heavily populated piece of land outside of Monaco. And much of that land is mountainous and eroded, no longer fit for agriculture. Farmers penetrated so high on steep mountains, they often fell out of their gardens.

For me Haiti proved to be not only an exhilarating experience, it was my University. For half a century I have reported and done my best to document its progress, and lack of progress and suffered its pain. Even today I miss the wheezing of my old flatbed Kelly press, the clanging of the linotype, and the strong odor of newsprint meeting ink.

This is my story of operating a newspaper in Haiti from 1950 until 1963. The first volume tells the story of what some call, Haiti's Golden Years, from 1950 to 1956.

The other volumes tell the story of man's inhumanity to man—and of a nation's decline from creativity and promise into the void of bloody dictatorships.

End of the Sun

It churned in the pit of my stomach and throbbed unceasingly through my head. It was a combination of anguish and fear more excruciating than any physical pain. My terror was not for my own fate but that of my young wife and our 40-day-old son. They were in grave danger. Nobody was safe in Port-au-Prince during those late-April nights in 1963 when Papa Doc's goons and military had turned the Haitian capital into a human killing field. I feared that the *Tontons Makouts** would return to my home and take my wife and infant son away, adding them to the lengthening roster of the "disappeared".

I myself was in a tiny bare cell in the National Penitentiary, having been summarily arrested for my reporting as the resident correspondent for several major international media outlets. It was the end of the *Haiti Sun*! The prison was strangely silent. There were occasional gunshots but no human sounds. Where were all those I had seen arrested by the rampaging *Makouts*? Physical torture, a beating, would have almost been a relief. This was the worst kind of torture, not knowing what was going on outside the ancient walls of Haiti's legendary prison, especially concerning the fate of my wife and child. The dread and isolation gave new meaning to solitary confinement. In my anguish I prayed to my old God, to Jesus Christ, and to every *Vodou* deity in the Haitian supernatural pantheon for my family.

Mentally exhausted and feverish, I could not sleep; nor could I force myself to think of anything other than my wife and baby boy. Even the odyssey that had brought me naked, except for underpants, to this bare concrete cell floor was far from my mind.

---

*   The *Tontons Makouts* were equal opportunity thugs who would attack and spirit away anyone accused of being an enemy of Papa Doc, along with their families. The *Makouts* were composed not only of armed civilians with their intimidating dark sun glasses but were also drawn from Papa Doc's army and paramilitary militia.

CHAPTER 1

Drums of Destiny

On October 12, 1949, we departed Halifax. Our destination was the South Pacific. Our Nova Scotia shipyard worker friends who had watch us for three months making the 36-year-old India-built ketch sea worthy, had laughed and placed bets that we wouldn't make it to Boston, our first port of call. Not particularly great under sail, the *Culver,* nevertheless was a tough, reliable 128-foot ketch. After riding out one storm after another, we arrived on October 17 in East Boston. The trip on to New York City was uneventful until, chugging along the East River, our vintage Thornycraft diesel engine suddenly quit. The current was dragging us swiftly toward an outcropping of jagged rocks. Minutes away from being wrecked within view of the Manhattan skyline, we were saved when the motor coughed back to life.

A wealthy New Yorker whose avocation was observing the River with binoculars from his penthouse apartment came down to the dock at 34th Street adjacent to Bellevue Hospital, where we berthed. He wanted to know how we had escaped being wrecked on the rocks. He then offered us a drink from his elaborate bar in his station wagon and toasted the *Culver's* old British-made engine.

As always, New York City was special. One evening before we sailed away an elderly couple strolling along the East River dock paused alongside as I paced on deck to keep warm.

"Are you headed for Palestine?" the man asked. It was the second time in New York, because of my black beard and black navy coat, that I had been mistaken for a rabbi. The couple asked a lot of concerned questions. Did we have a radio, medical supplies, plenty of food? Our not being able to afford these essentials shocked them and they admonished me in parental tones that we young men should not take such chances. Conversing with each other with serious miens they returned to their parked car and suddenly large objects flew through the air and landed with thuds on our wooden deck. They were giant salami sausages. This kind-hearted Jewish couple, I subsequently learned, owned a delicatessen in Brooklyn. They had provided food supplies that proved vital on the next leg of our trip, to Miami.

Finding it impossible to shelter our ketch adequately at a dock on Brooklyn's Sheepshead Bay, we decided to put to sea in a winter storm. I was at the helm when Peter was knocked overboard by a swinging spar. The *Culver* was not the type of boat to maneuver in rough seas. Alex and I could see Peter's red pompom beret popping up like a cork. Holiday fishermen heading home to Brooklyn spotted Peter. After several tries they managed to pluck him from the freezing cold water and return him aboard. Peter was blue with cold and needed some slapping around to stir his body's circulation.

For nearly a week the *Culver* rode out the mountainous waves of a storm off Cape Hatteras. We had little to eat. The entrance to our galley was under water much of the time as the *Culver's* bow bucked through the huge waves. In reinforcing our new cargo hatch we had closed off the galley from below deck, but food had lost its importance in that storm.

Heaven finally arrived in the form of the warming Gulf Stream, which had rejuvenating effects on us all. We could cook again. Each of us took turns in preparing meals. My masterpieces were a marathon stew. It continued to boil day after day and each day its taste improved. I added whatever ingredient was immediately available. It was a wholesome if eclectic dish. Our diet was to change for the better as the lights of Miami beckoned.

To avoid paying for a harbor pilot—as we were classified as a cargo-carrying vessel—we decided to sneak into a yacht anchorage during the night. Unbeknown to us a sandbar at the entrance to Biscayne Bay stood in our way. We went aground. Endeavoring to pull the *Culver* off the sandbar we used the old method of kedging. The Nova Scotia dory we kept on deck was lowered into the water, and the anchor into it. The idea was to "row" the anchor out a distance into deeper water and drop it. With the anchor firmly caught on the sea bottom we were to return aboard and all hands would heave in the anchor and free the *Culver*. But the anchor proved too heavy and Alex and I sank a hundred yards from the *Culver*. As we managed to untangle ourselves from the towrope, anchor and dory we heard Peter hailing us that the *Culver* was afloat. The incoming tide had freed the ship. The long journey from New York ended in laughter swimming in Biscayne Bay.

Our green-painted hull and red sails made us conspicuous among the mostly white designer pleasure craft in the Diner Key yacht basin off Coconut Grove. Deep-water sea yarns were a meal ticket to dine aboard the larger luxury yachts. (No invitations were forthcoming after I shaved off my beard.) Rumors began to circulate that we were smuggling Chinese into South Florida—the illegal aliens of the day. Peter gave an interview to the *Miami News* explaining our true free-lance voyage, and in response we were offered a $400 fee to carry a cargo destined for a place called Haiti.

We moved to the Port of Miami docks to load our cargo. Marked, "Glass, Silvera, El Rancho," the cases were suspiciously heavy. We requested that they be opened to make sure they were not guns. They were glass window jalousies. A *Monsieur* Albert Silvera needed them delivered in Port-au-Prince immediately as he was rushing to complete Haiti's first luxury hotel, which would become known as El Rancho.

A man identifying himself as a dry-cleaner came aboard shouting, "Dry-cleaning! Same-day service!" and took away my best Bond Street suit. It was the last I saw of my suit. As we sailed away from Miami with our cargo of glass jalousies, Haiti was to be only a stop en route to the Panama Canal. I was anxious to get to the Pacific.

———

The mountains reared up from the Haitian shoreline, their steep slopes towering over our approaching sailing vessel. Like fireflies, the peasants' *tèt gridap* lamps (tiny tin lamps) flickered against the cliff outline etched into sharp relief by the setting sun. Much later I identified the tangy perfume carried on the evening breeze as the aroma of *gayak*, a precious hardwood being slowly burned into charcoal under mounds of fresh earth. Charcoal farming had long since edged out sugar cane as the scent of Haiti. It was slowly devastating the countryside as trees were felled to provide cheap fuel for villages and towns. Resulting erosion was shredding the denuded farmland.

I also recall the rhythmic beat of drums, their magnetic percussion drifting out to sea. Those drums from the coastal darkness of the Caribbean republic proved mysteriously bewitching. (I mistakenly thought that, as in Africa, they were a medium of communication. I later learned that the drumbeats were dedicated to *Vodou*.)

I had only recently read the historical novel *Lydia Bailey* by Kenneth Roberts. The story was set in the time of Henri Christophe, King of North Haiti, during the nation's bloody birth from the only successful slave revolt in history. In a 13-year war Haiti's slaves had wrested control of France's richest colony by defeating Napoléon Bonaparte's legions. For me, not only were the drums a magnet but so were the people whose ancestors had accomplished such a seemingly impossible feat.

Looking back to that night in December 1949, I like to think that the drums' hypnotic beat was beckoning me to Haiti.

We sailed into Port-au-Prince the next morning amidst a fleet of small coastal craft with colorful patched sails. Behind the sparkling blue bay the city stretched like a mosaic of color against the green hills. The city climbed up the hills. The twin-towered peach-colored cathedral, the glistening white National Palace, was our landmarks. The name of the Haitian capital, we were told, came from *Le Prince*, the first European ship to arrive here in 1680.

The population of Port-au-Prince when we arrived in 1949 was 180,000. Our harbor duties and wharfage fees were extremely high and quickly swallowed up our profit from the $400 cargo fee. The police officer, who cleared us to enter the port on December 21, 1949, was chubby Lt. Jean (he preferred to be called John) Beauvoir. The first two nights ashore I spent in the barrel of Rum Barbancourt. To give their exhibition originality at the Bicentennial fair Barbancourt had built a bar in the form of giant barrel. It was located in the *Aux Palmistes* section of the fair, so-called because of the huge royal palms surrounding it.(Rhum Barbancourt 3-star $1 a bottle, superior cognac-style 5-star was $2 a bottle. 1-star excellent in rum punches was .50 cents a bottle.)

There was magic in the air not only because of the excellent local rum—the country's distinctive culture had awakened my curiosity. Ti Roro, a famous Haitian drummer, provided a background beat nearby at the open-air *Théatre de Verdure,* which featured the country's National Folkloric troupe. Relaxing with five-cent shots of rum, I was intrigued listening to members of Haiti's bourgeoisie discussing why their country's president should be dumped. Politics, I learned, was a major preoccupation of everyone. Their very lives seemed to depend on politics, which was divided along class lines. The upper class, oligarchy, or aristocracy referred to itself as the Elite. They were also referred to as the bourgeoisie. The middle-class referred to simply as *La Classe* was small and searching for its space. The peasant class—I was shocked at their title—was more numerous and the president had decreed that they had to wear shoes in the city. No matter what their class, the Haitians were all friendly.

However, my love affair with Haiti actually began in anger. The night after we docked at the wharf in the capital of Port-au-Prince, thieves managed to slip aboard and steal my precious Zeiss Icon camera. The loss of my watch and several other belongings, which were also pilfered, hardly mattered by comparison. My still camera on the other hand was critically important. I had hoped to produce a photo essay on what remained of the huge American military bases I had visited during World War II in the Pacific. A *LIFE Magazine* editor whom I had approached in New York with my story idea had given me film and agreed to look at my picture story.

That night we moved the *Culver* away from the pier and anchored directly across from Captain Ace's seaside restaurant. It was not long before water-borne thieves came aboard that same night. We rushed on deck but they managed to escape by jumping into the water to disappear into the inky darkness.

I couldn't sleep; Peter had prepared an evil-looking green turtle soup, which he bragged would cost a fortune in the best restaurant in the States. He had purchased the turtle from a fisherman for "peanuts." That night I decided I had had enough of turtle soup and the *Culver*. Moreover, Peter had wanted to turn the ship into a cargo carrying business that didn't interest me. Suddenly I was tired of escapism and found myself yearning for a more meaningful existence.

However, the War had changed my life forever. I could not bring myself to return to my childhood life in New Zealand. My country was the most beautiful Little England in the South Pacific, socialist and dull. One could chart their life from cradle to grave worrying only about the price of wool. With a population of nearly three million humans and 70 million sheep it was then a very conformist society. Europe too now seemed less than inviting. I had spent much of my time there in search of a vocation, even at one point considering the church. But most callings, including establishment religion, seemed trivial, boring, and without real meaning.

The next morning I made my decision known. I gave up the ship in sadness. My shipmates sailed off to more mishaps. I went in search of my camera, preparing at that initial juncture to return to Europe. I never did find my camera. I did however find Haiti.

Alex and Peter Bolton eventually crossed the Pacific, making one of the longest sailing trips on record from Costa Rica's Pacific coast to Christmas Island (139 days). They ran out of food after 90 days to be saved from starvation by an army of hundreds upon hundreds of tuna. The big fish stayed with them for three weeks providing the ketch with daily fresh steak. They had run out of vegetable oil and cooked their tuna steaks with salt.

(The ketch was eventually sold and sank in a typhoon in the Pacific off Ponape, a mountainous island in the central Carolinas. Alex went on to serve in the U.S. Navy during the Korean War and now lives in Hawaii having retired as vice president of the Madison Shipping Line. I met up with Peter, a senior pilot for the Panama Canal, again in 1977 when I interviewed him while working on a *Time Magazine* cover story on the Panama Canal treaty.)

I did feel a little like Willems in Joseph Conrad's An *Outcast of the Island*. But Haiti was not the Far East. Conrad* had written: "He was baffled, repelled, almost frightened by the intensity of that tropical life which wants the sunshine but works the gloom; which seems to be all grace and of color and form, all brilliance, all smiles, but is only the blossoming of the dead; whose mystery holds the promise of joy and beauty, yet contains nothing but poison and decay."

Ashore in Port-au-Prince I sought out the British ambassador. "Not such a problem," he said, "You'll need a Haitian visitor's visa, and I'll fix it." He had no suggestions as to where I should look for my stolen camera. He believed it a lost cause. He was right. There didn't appear to be a thieves market. The landmark Iron Market on the Grand Rue was a bustling bazaar that appeared to sell everything. I spread the word as best as I could that a *blan*—foreigner—wanted to buy old Kodaks. I had learned that the Haitian word for all cameras was Kodak. I did see an interesting collection of ancient unworkable cameras but my German-made Zeiss was not among them.

Port-au-Prince sparkled even more than usual as the celebration of its bicentennial was in full swing. Lodged at the Mon Rêve, a lovely gingerbread 15-room pension on the Champ de Mars close to the Paramount cinema, I wired to New Zealand for money only to learn that Haiti was a dollar country and therefore my country, which like Britain was a sterling country, and under strict monetary controls. Thus no money was forthcoming from home in a hurry. Cabling friends in the U.S. also entailed a long wait. The Mon Rêve, was $5 a day with meals so I moved for a brief period to L'Avenir an even smaller gingerbread mansion squeezed in between houses at the bottom of Avenue John Brown. The price was right: $1 a day with meals and corpulent *Kè Pòpòz* was a wonderful host.

A congenial commercial attaché at the U.S. embassy introduced me to some Americans who ran the part-government-owned new *Casino National*. One of the Americans, the Casino manager, said he needed someone with a smattering of French to impress his clientele and to control the booze. He created a temporary job as "*maitre d'*

---

* (As a young man in 1876, Conrad, had visited Haiti on the *Saint-Antoine*. He and the first mate of the ship went off and did a spot of gunrunning to Central America while the *Saint-Antoine* remained in Haiti awaiting a cargo. From this trip to the Caribbean and Venezuela came one of his great works *Nostromo* which is certainly a Latin American masterpiece. Having spent those war years at sea I found a kinship with the Polish-born sailor turned writer and recall the deep impression *Nostromo* had made on me. I only hoped that the Latin American state he named Costaguana was not based on Haiti. Conrad professed interest only in "The truth of life," and in *Nostromo* he reflected the depressing spiritual emptiness of politics and politicians.)

booze". Outfitted in a tropical dinner suit by Coles, the city's top tailor, I could liberally dispense the Casino's beverages to gambling visitors and newly made friends alike. As I wrote to Sir Philip Williams and family back in England, "The job frightened me at first, but I soon realized how advantageous it is." Part of the Casino was a nightclub with dancing until the wee hours. In no time at all I knew the community's movers and shakers, at the top of Haiti's strange, color-coded social pyramid. The upper class was not rich by American or British standards. And many of the habitual gamblers were not Haitian but resident Syrian textile importers.

With authority to dispense drinks to select customers free of charge, I soon had a lot of new friends who didn't even gamble. French was of limited use so I enrolled in Créole classes at the Haitian-American Institute where I befriended the American and Haitian teachers who became my guests on weekends at the Casino. Some of the more interesting expatriates, including Horace Ashton, were connected with the Institute. Ashton had come to Haiti as the Institute director during the war and stayed. Sympathetic to and knowledgeable about all things Haitian, he brought up his family in the country and died there at an advanced age.

The Casino operators were Damon Runyon types whose gravelly voices could have come right out of *Guys and Dolls*. When the Casino closed in the early morning hours, these Americans—professional gamblers all—would take off their dinner jackets and sit down to play poker among themselves until breakfast. One morning Haiti's President Dumarsais Estimé happened by on an inspection trip. The American Casino operators panicked and ordered me to lock them in the beverage room. The President didn't bother to enter the Casino and his bodyguards, after sniffing the stale air of the gaming room, quickly left. For nearly half an hour I was in full control of the Casino with the management under lock and key—and I held the keys. But they were a friendly lot even though some local lore had it that they were members of the Mafia.

One beautiful evening I felt like walking home to my small hotel. The streets were empty or so it seemed as I passed the huge alabaster triple-domed National Palace. Suddenly I furthered my Créole lessons. Into my ears came the words, *"Annou wè."* It was the Créole term, which I quickly learned that night meant, "Let's go." A rifle barrel prodding the small of my back stressed the meaning of the term, and the soldier who was forcing me across the street and onto a grassy area kept repeating it. I had been distracted by the magnificence of Haiti's ghost-like National Palace and not noticed the soldier who had taken me prisoner. As he kept pronouncing the phrase very persistently I thought, "Damn! I'm going to be shot like a dog and I don't know why!" The soldier was almost half my size and somehow that made me angrier. Then I made out other soldiers lurking behind bushes, rifles at the ready.

Delivered to Police Headquarters, a short distance from the palace, I was greeted by the duty officer, a lanky Lieut. Lanor Augustin who knew me from the Casino. He laughed and explained that there was an alert: opponents of President Dumarsais Estimé were plotting some mischief. Walking so close to the palace so late at night was not a good idea, Augustin advised. He dismissed the soldier and called me a taxi, which returned me to my resident hotel. The next day I learned that the neighboring dictator, Generalissimo Rafael Leonidas Trujillo Molina of the Dominican Republic, was helping a group of Haitians try to topple Estimé. Later over drinks at the Casino Lieutenant Augustin told me that the threat from Trujillo was serious and that Haitian authorities had information about movements of guns and men to assassinate Haiti's top military as well as President Estimé.

It was the first of many run-ins with guns in Haiti. My knowledge of Caribbean politics had been limited to wartime crossings of the Panama Canal to load fuel oil in romantic Curacao and Cartagena, Colombia. Now there was much to learn. I became a regular customer at Port-au-Prince's *La Caravelle* bookshop and began compiling what, over the years, became an extensive library on Haiti in English, French, and Créole.

Haitians I found almost universally friendly and helpful. Despite the imbalance in their society I encountered no anger or envy as I had experienced in some poor countries I had visited. The passivity of the poor was offset by their dignity. Their capacity to laugh at adversity made them even more special. Such qualities among the peasant class made it easy at first to shrug off the arrogance of those at the top of the social ladder. In the countryside there was something deeply spiritual about the people. Their salutations were those of an equal in the divine scheme of things. I was to hear "*Bondye bon*"—"God is good", so many times that I thought it was a daily prayer instead of a familiar excuse.

There was another attraction that tugged at me, the *Centre d'Art*. Haitian artists were at work in every nook and cranny of the old white building downtown Port-au-Prince. The Center had been opened five years earlier by a California artist named DeWitt Peters. He was a gentle, almost shy, man who seemed more of a coat-and-tie business manager than an artist. And he had put away his own brushes to discover, cultivate, and aid Haitian artists. Of medium height and with a heavy mustache, Peters was then 48 and giving impetus to a movement that fifty years later would make art one of Haiti's major money-earners.

Particularly interesting was the fact that the best artists came out of the *oungfò*, or *Vodou* temple. Unfortunately Peters' major discovery, *oungan* (*Vodou* priest) Hector Hyppolite, had died two years earlier. Hyppolite's works, produced during a short period of three years under Peters' guidance, were to fetch extraordinary prices. How had this Caribbean Island nation produced so many gifted artists? I concluded it was because of the Haitians, exceptional spiritual dimension, namely *Vodou*.

Peters related to me that he had come to Haiti in February 1943, sent by the United States Government, to teach English to Haitians, and had got the idea of the art center during his first vacation from teaching English at the *Lycée Alexandre Pétion*. Working at first with Horace Ashton at the Haitian-American Institute, Peters opened an art branch at the Institute and finally in 1944 persuaded the Haitian and U.S. governments to participate in establishing the Art Center with a monthly budget of $400.

By this time, enthralled with Haiti, I had given up the search for my camera and was actively seeking to understand this complex new land. But my time had run out. Lieut. Lucien Scott, in charge of the immigration police, stopped me in the street. "Your papers are not in order. You must leave. You had 24 hours to leave the country and as I couldn't find you, your time is up." I had been in Haiti five weeks without a visa. The British ambassador had fixed nothing. So infuriated was I at being booted out of Haiti that I stubbornly decided to return. Had I not been so ignominiously deported I might have left Haiti voluntarily and returned to England as planned. I sought legal advice from Jean-Claude Léger, a young lawyer I had befriended, saying, "I would like to spend a little more time here." He suggested that I apply for a Haitian visa in Jamaica.

Arriving in Kingston on February 2, 1950, I shared the little Melrose hotel at the top of Duke Street in the Jamaican capital with actor Errol Flynn's father who was visiting from Tasmania on a study trip. (Nine years later, in January 1959, I was to meet Errol Flynn himself, who was marooned in Santiago de Cuba where he was trying to make a documentary film on the Cuban revolution. The Fidelistas were not sympathetic to Flynn because he reportedly spent much of his time inebriated.) The Haitian consul in Kingston telegraphed a request for my visa and I was surprised to receive it. I flew back to Port-au-Prince by Pan American Clipper on February 9, 1950. In my pocket was my passport with the proper Haitian visa and money from my family back home in New Zealand.

On my return attorney Jean-Claude Léger introduced me to an American, Allan Benson. The tall, well-built New Yorker explained that he had been a shoe salesman during the war as he had been medically unfit for service. For reasons that escaped me, he had decided to launch a daily English-language newspaper in Haiti. Money was no problem, he said, as his savings amounted to ten thousand dollars, which he had brought with him. Newspapering was more to my calling than dispensing libations in a casino, so I accepted his invitation to work with him in launching the paper. There would be no salary, but he would provide room and board and give me an interest in the newspaper. Rising before dawn each morning I traveled across town in a wartime Jeep to *Le Matin,* the morning French-language daily where we job-printed the new *Port-au-Prince Times.* I loved the work. Benson loved to relax at the El Rancho hotel and date pretty tourists.

Franck Magloire, proprietor of *Le Matin,* could be as smooth as glass one moment, screaming and cantankerous as a mad man the next. He reminded me in his white suit, Panama hat and black and white shoes of the type that peopled the films in which actor George Raft appeared. The editor of *Le Matin* at the time was Félix Morisseau-Leroy, an amiable writer and poet, graduate of Columbia University (with a degree in education) in New York. He had taken up wearing a bow tie when Harry Truman (a bow-tie aficionado) was the U.S. President. Franck's father, Clément Magloire, had founded *Le Matin* on April 1, 1907. In his large scrawl Morisseau wrote his editorials with pen or pencil on whatever piece of newsprint he could find and handed it to the linotyptist. His sense of humor was constant and infectious but he also could write with a caustic and sharp wit. Our friendship lasted his lifetime and I did what I could to help him with his principal avocation—promoting Créole as the accepted language of Haiti.

The major evening paper *Le Nouvelliste,* was *Le Matin's* competitor and the country's oldest daily, having been founded on August 4, 1899. When I arrived *Le Nouvelliste* was being published by Ernest Chauvet. Amiable with ready laugh Chauvet had done his newspaper apprenticeship abroad at the *Brooklyn Eagle*. U.S. Marine Corps Captain John H. Craig, who had been Port-au-Prince police chief during the U.S. occupation of Haiti, writes glowingly of "the good humored Chauvet" in his infelicitously entitled book, *Cannibal Cousins* (New York, Milton Balch, 1934.). In his book the American Marine police chief recounts his embarrassment when he was ordered by Haitian then-President Louis Borno to arrest his newspaper friend, Chauvet, for some small infraction of the Occupation's draconian press laws.

(There was also the Roman Catholic newspaper, *La Phalange,* founded in 1939, Well-equipped with modern printing equipment it was highly successful. (I later purchased a huge "guillotine"—paper cutter—from *La Phalange* which weighed several tons.) *Haiti Journal,* which had been started in 1930 by Stenio Vincent, was still publishing but was in perpetual decline. There were any numbers of small weekly that came and went depending on politics of the moment. Compared with other countries, Haiti's dailies were a sad reflection of the country's high illiteracy. Their circulation while extremely limited did have an impact on Haitian politics. Publishers didn't become wealthy from their newspaper but from Haitian politics. Government assistance and often a government sinecure supplemented their circulation and advertisements. The French-language dailies, despite their small circulation were well read by the powers that be. What the papers printed and didn't print was important. They were essentially journals of opinion, or as the French say, "*engagé.*" Aspiring writers, poets and politicians begged—and some paid—to be published in them. Many books began as articles in the French-language dailies since authors had to self-publish. (It was only after the Duvalier dictatorship ended in 1986 that the trade-book publishers Henri Deschamps Fils of Port-au-Prince began to publish books in Haiti. Deschamps' first such book published in Haïti was *Papa Doc et les Tonton Macoutes* which I had authored with Al Burt, then of the *Miami Herald*, in 1969.)

I'll never forget the roar that brought us running that morning in early May 1950 from the print shop where I was proofreading the day's edition of the *Port-au-Prince Times*. It was the rumbling of a human avalanche. A gesticulating and chanting mob had literally exploded down the *Rue Américaine* before *Le Matin*. It was my introduction to a Haitian mob in action. It was not, the linotypist informed me as we surveyed the spectacle, the famous, organized *rouleau compresseur* (steamroller) of loyal partisans of opposition politician Professor Daniel Fignolé. This sea of prancing protesters were that day defenders of incumbent President Estimé. They sang the Créole song of the moment: "*Kenbe, oo, pa lage.*" ("Hold on tight, don't let go.") followed by the chant, "*God in heaven sent us this president . . .*"

I caught up with the mob as they were literally tearing apart the Senate. On the preceding April 18th, the Haitian Senate had rejected the Lower House's motion to change the constitution and permit Estimé to succeed himself as president. The political invective had moved to the streets. As I drove up in my jeep the mob, mistakenly recognized me as a diplomat, and courteously made way to allow me to enter the once-stately gingerbread mansion. Looters burdened down with desks and chairs stood aside as an escort who, proudly showed off their handiwork. The Senate lay in ruins. It was not considered looting but *dechoukaj* (Créole for "uprooting",) a tradition older than the Republic.

It was a prelude to the coup d'état to come. President Estimé publicly congratulated his mob for its "eloquent attitude" and "political maturity." He then formally dissolved the now furniture less Senate, which had refused to do his bidding. By this act however he had signed his fate: dismissal and exile. A military cabal was waiting impatiently in the wings to once again step onto center stage as a ruling junta. Early the next day following Estimé's decree my publisher Allan Benson emerged from the office of Franck Magloire carrying a brown envelope. Benson asked me to drive him to the Caserne Dessalines. Benson returned to the Jeep all smiles after delivering the envelope to Col. Paul E. Magloire, the leader of the impatient military group. The envelope contained, I later learned, a copy of the official government gazette, *Le Moniteur* with Estimé damming decree. Franck Magloire, who had obtained a copy of *Le Moniteur* from the Government Printing office, subsequently liked to boast that he had placed Colonel Magloire (no relation) in the palace.

After the army started to move against Estimé, the mob was back in the streets but this time their chant had changed to "*A bas Estimé!*" ("Down with Estimé") It was another important lesson in Haitian politics: Don't believe everything you hear or see. There was nothing spontaneous or menacing about this mob even though a few participants' dutifully brandished machetes. This mob had been paid in advance and orchestrated.

The only way any ordinary Haitian who cared could rationalize his country's politics was to place it, like most things, on a religious plane under the fatalistic philosophy: "What God gives, God takes." Estimé was shipped off to France were his children were studying.

———

I liked Estimé personally even though he was dour and acerbic. His groceress, my future mother-in-law (whose store was named Bazar du Champ de Mars), described her friend and customer Estimé, or "Titime" as he was known, as having a very delicate stomach. He was the embodiment of the Haitian political dream. Born in 1900 in Verrettes, a small town in the Artibonite Valley, he had been raised by an uncle. Well educated, Estimé became a professor of mathematics at the prestigious Lycée Alexandre Pétion in Port-au-Prince until he lost his position when he joined a strike against President Louis Borno during the U.S. Marine occupation. Estimé went on to become a congressman, president of the Chamber of Deputies, and a cabinet minister in the post-occupation government of President Sténio Vincent. Estimé was later elected by the Senate to become Haiti's first black president, after four mulatto presidents who served during the 19-year U.S. Marine occupation. An intrinsically good man, he was soon portrayed as a genuine representative of the "masses" as the country people were known.

Estimé sought to be a reformer who did what he could within the realities and constraints of Haitian politics. He brought blacks into the government bureaucracy. His "World's Fair," celebrating Port-au-Prince's bicentennial, converted the capital's unsightly waterfront into a beautiful, spacious, modern area with an expansive sea drive named to honor U.S. President, Harry S. Truman. This downtown renewal project gave a perfectly timed impetus to Haiti's newly developing postwar tourist industry.

Estimé made mistakes and there was a certain amount of corruption, but he was not known to be personally corrupt. However like the majority of his predecessors, he became heavy-handed and sought to prolong his mandate. Haitians often speculated that all of their presidents eventually fell under a spell, which like a magnet held the president to the presidential chair. No matter how well meaning a new president might be, at the end of his term, because of this particular spell (as well as his newly inflated ego) he had to be dragged out of the chair by force. The Haitian version of Lord Acton's: "Power tends to corrupt, and absolute power corrupts absolutely." On May 10, 1950, Estimé overthrown by the military was forcibly shipped into exile abroad. The black army colonel, member of the three-member Military Junta stepped in to replace a black president. Col. Paul Eugène Magloire, U.S. Marine Corps-trained, was to usher in what was quite frankly a happy pause in the country's turbulent civilian politics, and Haiti once again could challenge Cuba as a *Pearl of the Antilles*. The Caribbean Black Republic of Haiti appeared literally aglow with promise, and hope soared. The colonel vowed to continue Estimé's important structural changes—bringing his fellow blacks into the bureaucracy and fostering the nascent tourist industry. It was the question of color that puzzled me. Wasn't this the Black Republic? Shouldn't blacks of every hue—dark, mulatto, light—be considered equal? Why should there even be a question of differences in color? I soon learned that degrees of blackness, as well as education, class, language and religion, divided this small country into a land of many separate cultural majions.

President Dumarsais Estimé, chief of state 1946-1950. Builder of Port-au-Prince's World Fair commemorating the capital's bicentennial, President Estimé can be considered the father of tourism. *Titime*, as he was known, converted the unsightly waterfront into the Expositions grounds. The songs of the day were: *Kawolin a Kawo, Panama'm Tombé* and *Papa Guedé bel gason*.
(Collection Estimé family)

Author with Roger Dorsainville, who had encouraged him to launch the *Haiti Sun*. Dorsainville's accomplishments were impressive, an Army officer, teacher, journalist and prolific author. President Estimé's *chef de cabinet*, Consul in New York, one of the architect of Duvalier's campaign in 1957, he was exiled, and spent twenty years in Liberia and Senegal. Returning home in 1986, and despite his blindness, he produced a number of important books before he died Jan.12 1992.

Friend Emmanuel (Manno) Ambroise who became an advertiser in the *Sun* had also encouraged the editor to launch the paper in 1950.

Once the printing and distribution of the *Port-au-Prince Times* over, my job entailed distributing it to the hotels and other tourist centers and selling advertising. And it was in listening to my own sales pitch that I realized what kind of paper I really wanted to sell. To hell with daily news reports of the outside world and its problems in English. Haiti's problems had suddenly become much more important to me. I envisioned a newspaper that would contribute to the Haitian community and help establish communications between the haves and have-nots. I had no axe to grind other than to help a people to whom I had formed a very strong attachment. New friends Roger Dorsainville, a remarkable Haitian who had been Estimé's chief of Cabinet and later Consul in New York and his friend Emmanuel (Manno) Ambroise a storeowner dared me to try.

After four month I was fed up with Benson and the newspaper and quit. I reported home that, "at least I felt every minute was rich in experience."

A retired American admiral invited me to spend a few days at his experimental kanaf plantation in the Artibonite Valley. (The cultivation of kanaf, a plant that produces a fiber used for rope-making collapsed when nylon came onto the market.) Through this flat valley ran Haiti's major river, the Artibonite. Scattered around the plain were *lakous* (family compounds like in Africa). It was in one of these *lakous*, near the river, that I witnessed my first *Vodou* ceremony. There seemed nothing evil about the ritual. Indeed it appeared to be a joyous occasion, with spectacular drumming and dancing. While I had no knowledge at the time of the various rites, I did discern that they were a family affair honoring a member of the *lakou* who had died. *Vodou*, I learned, was still as essential to the *lakou* as were the wooden *pilon*, and *pestle* used to crush corn and coffee.

Returning from the Artibonite I focused again on my newspaper vision. It was at the Thorland Club, four miles south of the capital that Paul Vrooman had turned into a chic hotel, that the *Haiti Sun* was born. Architect Albert Mangones who had made the renovations at Thorland believed in my publishing dream and helped me turn it into a reality. We met during the lunch hour and evening in a bungalow at Thorland with painter Roland Dorcely who worked on decorating the new Thorland. Dorcely helped design the *Haiti Sun*. The social column we named *The Beachcomber*. To entice the literate rich their names would appear, along with their birthdays, baptisms, receptions, and weddings illustrated by photos of the event. Their travels would be noted and scandals would be carefully hinted at to satisfy the community's born gossips. A page would be devoted to book and art review commentary, while *Personality of the Week* would be a column about people of merit—common people as well as the well known, their trades, their misfortunes, their glories. The *Sun* would interview them, let them speak in their own way, give them a voice, present their biographies and publish their picture. *Vodou* would also find a home with tutorials from legitimate *oungans*. Other columns would follow but there would be no editorials, at least to start with. As a foreigner I didn't wish to be so presumptuous as to tell Haitians how to run their lives and their country.

Meanwhile publisher Franck Magloire and Allan Benson had had a fallen out. Given Franck's volatile temperament it was predictable. Vindictive to the extreme Franck was not above using *Le Matin* to personally attack his so-called "enemies". Benson found another printing outlet for the *Port-au-Prince Times*, and as I was still on Franck's good side he was more than happy to allow me the use of his printing plant. He saw the *Haiti Sun* as direct competition to Benson's paper and even called the *Sun* his own until we also quarreled and parted.

There were few rules governing the opening of a newspaper in Haiti. The newspaper was required to have a Haitian *Gérant Responsable,* who technically was responsible for whatever was printed and would be responsible to the law if there was a problem. The name of the *Gérant Responsable* had to be prominently displayed in the newspaper. Among the *Haiti Sun's* distinguished *Gérant Responsable* over the years was Paul Najac who wrote a regular column of Haitian folktales for the *Sun*. (In 1960 as the Duvalier dictatorship became more oppressive, one of the *Sun's* capable delivery men, Mauclair Labissière, volunteered his name as *Gérant Responsable*.) Another requirement was to send three free copies of each edition to respectively, the Interior Ministry, Army headquarters, and Police as well as the National Palace.

Neither the taxes or printing costs were exorbitant; in fact they were ridiculously low and Franck Magloire out of spite for Benson gave me three months' free printing. Franck's mother ran *Le Matin's* accounts, as best she could, given Franck's habit of bartering advertising for whatever he wished to buy at the moment.

Franck's half-brother, the surrealist poet Clément Magloire St Aude and I became friends. I had known bohemian poets in London but in Port-au-Prince Magloire St. Aude took his eccentric way of life to the extreme. During the rainy season I once noticed the poet's head peeping above water. He had fallen into a deep flood drain near *Le Matin*. Happy as a lark he embraced me slobbering mud and *kleren* (rum) from a bottle he still held in one hand. He was still holding his battered briefcase in the other. Often Magloire St. Aude passed by to see Mrs. Clément who was sympathetic and generous when she could be, even though he was her husband's *pitit deyò* (illegitimate son). It was a surprise just how many Haitians were related through their father's children born out of wedlock. Often it was only when they were grown-up did friends learn that they were first cousins.

———

On Saturday near midnight, September 16th, 1950, the first issue rolled off the flatbed press, and the next morning Haiti had a new Sunday newspaper: the English-language weekly, the *Haiti Sun*.

It was the beginning of my love affair with Haiti and, as all such affairs; it had its ups and downs, its challenges and disappointments. It was also a learning experience and I never ceased to learn. Haiti had become my school. Not exactly the London School of Economics, but for me the equivalent.

An opportunity to pursue a youthful dream—that of publishing my own weekly newspaper. Only those who know the reward of doing one's own reporting, writing, editing, printing, and publishing the old-fashioned way, can understand the joy of air permeated with the aroma of printer's ink, the clanging of the old flatbed press as it presses page after page. This after the Linotypist turns one's words into hot lead. Proofreading type upside-down becomes second nature after page-setting. This all takes me back to my days as a small boy when I loved to linger at the Wellington *Evening Post* to watch the huge press run before sprinting to my appointed corner to hawk the afternoon daily after school with a distinctive yodel.

"It is a devil of a job publishing my paper, [but] I absolutely love it and am going to make a success of it," I wrote home from Port-au-Prince to New Zealand. Drawing on my modest savings to finance my endeavor, I had given my experiment six months to succeed. It did, and was to last thirteen years.

The one-man enterprise soon had collaborators and over the years some noted visitors, offered themselves as guest writers. To keep expenses at a minimum I slept, in those early days, in my office, which I rented in the new Baboun building. I didn't need a watch. Lieut. Georges (*Ti Pouce*) Elie would drill his firemen, members of the Army, outside my window at the break of dawn. Later in the day I would drive out to the Thorland Club to shower and swim and if I had time, a game of tennis.

Appearing each Sunday morning, the *Sun* contained first twelve and then sixteen crisply printed, large-size pages. Its monthly subscription was 50 cents U.S., *Haiti Sun* delivered, or 5 cents per newsstand copy. The paper soon reflected the broad local interests of the community, and circulation ultimately reached a total of 1,500 Readers consisted mainly of Haitians and members of the foreign community. Eventually the *Sun* had overseas subscribers in the U.S. Canada, Jamaica and Cuba.

Despite my limited budget, the paper served up a cornucopia of features and local "hard news". One area of domestic, growing interest was the tourist industry. Haitian poet Jean Brierre had moved from his position as undersecretary of state for tourism to director of the newly formed National Office of Tourism. Foreign visitors included U.S. sailors on shore leave from warships, even a submarine; tourists from the occasional transatlantic passenger vessel; and much later, from the many cruise ships. In that first issue of the *Haiti Sun* the United States Lines advertised a trip to Europe on the *SS America* from $160, and Pan American World Airways took a half-page ad offering a 60-day special round trip from Port-au-Prince to Miami, with stops at Montego Bay and Kingston, Jamaica, for a grand total of $100 and we campaigned against the excessive prices of air travel.

Nor was advertising lacking from local tourism-geared businesses. Among the *Sun's* first advertisers was Austrian-born Kurt Fisher, who with his father ran the "Art and Curio Shop" on *Rue du Quai*; there was Paquin and Gaetjen's Gift Shop; Madame James Ewald's *La Perle des Antilles* jewelry shop; Dorismond and Meinberg's store which sold a variety of handcrafted articles including those fashioned from sisal; and Al Noustas's modern *La Belle Créole*, billed as Haiti's only department store. Factory advertisers included those producing Haiti's popular mahogany salad bowls and other items. Fritz and Huguette Mev's had established their mahogany factory in Turgeau at the bottom of Port-au-Prince's Babiole Hill in the former chic Bellevue Club. Georges Deslandes operated his factory on *Rue du Peuple*.

There were the Syrian (Lebanese and sometimes Jews were all known as Syrians) shops selling textiles by the yard. They didn't need to advertise but Toya Boulos, André Saieh, the Babouns, Elie Joseph and Cassis were always ready to chat.

A new dress shop that soon had customers was that of beautiful Mrs. Lorraine Perigord Dora. Lorriane hailed from California and was later to marry Mike Wallace of CBS. She sharing her shop on Rue Dantès Destouches near the Cathedral St-Trinité with artist Angel Botello-Barro. Haiti was also famous for its dressmakers.

Artist Roland Dorcely had designed an appealing Haitian drummer-and-roosters logo inviting readers to "Look"—"*gade pa boule gé*", it said in Créole ("It doesn't hurt the eyes")—as a standing heading for restaurant advertising. Haitian food was, as always, special and didn't need any elaborate praise. Restaurants that chose to promote themselves in the *Sun* ranged from the *Chatelet des Fleurs* in Kenscoff above Port-au-Prince; to the Voodoo Club south of the capital in the neighborhood of Carrefour; the

Higgins Bar downtown; Sylvio Cator's *Savoy* restaurant on the *Champ de Mars*; *Club Tabou* in nearby Petionville; and *Captain Aces* in Martissant overlooking the Bay of Port-au-Prince. Captain Ace later sold his restaurant and the new owners called it *Ki Pi*. As for the hotels, each had its special evening featuring folklore shows and its particular local cuisine—all announced in the *Haiti Sun*.

The *Sun* also won non-tourism foreign advertisers. Firestone advertised its automobile batteries and refrigerators, while Deschamps offered to meet "Your printing needs" and school books. Why anyone wanted to drink Scotch whisky when Haiti had the world's finest rum, seemed unpatriotic but Scotch importer were good advertisers as was Barbancourt Rhum. *Haig* followed *Grant* scotch whisky as Jean Desquiron and Théodore (Toto) Donner of Haiti Trading Company located on the Exposition grounds were modern businessmen and understood the need to advertise. Each week I would photograph a pretty baby and hand the infant a bottle of Grant Scotch whisky as the winner of the *Haiti Sun's*, "Most beautiful baby of the week" contest. Haiti's lone brewery had been packed up and shipped away after the beer-swigging U.S. Marine Corps departed in 1934, ending their 15-year occupation. Unluckily the brewery's components were sunk by a German submarine during the World War II while being transported on the deck of a freighter to Puerto Rico. The *Sun's* main beer advertisement was for the American beer Schlitz. Its distributor was also the distributor for Coca-Cola. The last page contained classified ads a list of church services, as well as the week's coming attractions and a horoscope which the editor compiled. The current movies at Paramount and Rex were listed. It was much later that the *Sun* offered advice to the lovelorn.

Perhaps my personal favorite regular column was the "Sun Library", which featured weekly book reviews prepared in conjunctions with the *La Caravelle* book shop. The first review was of *Black Majesty: The Life of Christophe, King of Haiti*, by John W. Vandercook. Price: $2.75. Another of my favorite weekly features was the "Art" column. There was also a "Poet's Corner". The "Beachcomber" gossip column was the icing on the cake to attract readers. Weddings, engagements, fetes, births, travels were important happenings and rivaled the *Sun's* sports column in popularity.

The *Centre d'Art* was my favorite spare-time haunt, and also a rich source of news. Haitian artist Jean Chenet (he became a contributor) had become art director of another art center, the *Foyer des Arts Plastiques* and in early September 1950 he organized a highly successful showing at the *Palais des Beaux Arts*, located on the Port-au-Prince exposition grounds. Featured in the exhibit—duly reported in the *Haiti Sun*—were works by painters Brice, Depas, Lapier, Lazarre, Jacob, Yolette Magloire, Edgad Francois, Jeanty, Boucard, and Malebranche Pinchinat, plus sculptures by André Lafontant and ceramics by Dorcely, Pinchinat, and Racine. All of the artists presented were Haitians, and they were so well known throughout the local art world there was no need to use first names.

There was of course room in the paper for "fillers", as they are called in the publishing trade—small items used to fill out column space. In the Sept. 24, 1950, issue, for example, the *Sun*'s fillers noted that: "Karl Berhman's motorboat caught fire while it was being repaired Thursday at Bizoton. The fire was extinguished without serious damage." And: "Tuesday afternoon an elderly man was found at the bottom of the Bois de Chêne ravine. Hospitalized he refused to give his name to attendants at the General Hospital until [he was] paid 3 cents."

In fact Haiti was like a small town. Everyone in Port-au-Prince knew everyone else. They knew each others' automobiles and didn't need a directory to recall their friends' four-digit telephone numbers. Few people bothered to carry money as hotels, restaurants, and grocery shops extended monthly credit. There was a Haitian Chamber of Commerce, whose president was agronomist (and later failed presidential candidate) Louis Déjoie, but business was based as much on handshakes as on written contracts. There was trust.

Eventually, total strangers brought me news tidbits. Those I came to know more closely provided tips, political background, and of course the latest from the *télédjol*, Haiti's highly efficient word-of-mouth grapevine.

Indeed, the Caribbean republic of Haiti in 1950—was not rife with poverty and other forms of deprivation—was alive and vibrant. There was hope.

Little did we know at the time, neither foreign residents nor Haitians, that only seven years later, everything would change—with the rise to power of the late François (Papa) Doc Duvalier, whose horrendous, ghostly presence, and barbaric legacy, still overshadow the little country.

*   *   *

R.C. Board, a cigar-chomping ex-Marine who had stayed in Haiti after the Marine occupation ended in 1934, became one of the first to be featured as the *Sun*'s "Personality of the Week." Over coffee in his café on Rue Pavée, (best sandwiches in town) "RCB" as he was known (his full name was Russel C. Board) warned me several times that first year, "You can miss too many boats, I did." A *bon vivant,* he had married a Haitian lady, and, unlike his wealthy fellow business expatriates who remained aloof as members of the exclusive American club, "RCB" entertained Haitian friends at a log cabin he had built in Carrefour on the banks of the *Rivière Froide.*

It was Board who introduced me to "stringing" for U.S. news media. He had become tired of filing stories for what was then the *International News Service* (INS). (Later part of United Press International, or UPI) In no time I had also picked up as "clients" the *Associated Press, The New York Times, NBC News* and eventually in 1956 the *Time-Life News Service,* plus a few daily newspapers in London that requested that I "string"—do non-staff reporting—for them.

In this manner when advertising was thin or the business community later boycotted my weekly because I was perceived as against their candidate for the presidency in 1957, I could continue surviving financially. (I refused any form of subsidy from the government. Such refusal guaranteed my independence.)

On Sunday April 1, 1951: *Personality of the Week*.

"The story of Russell C. Board, familiarly known as "RCB" and his stay in Haiti is the story of the U.S. Marine Corps Occupation, and the organization and development of the *Garde d'Haiti*. Mr. Board arrived in Haiti in 1923 on detached duty from the Marine Corps to what was, at that time, the Haitian Army. A number of Marine personnel were attached to the Army of Haiti, then known as the *Gendermerie d'Haiti*, for the purpose of training officer and enlisted material to the end that Haiti would have a combined Army and Police Force capable of keeping order in the country. The training of the Army had started in 1917 but no real progress was not made until the late 20's. Board was commissioned an officer with the Army by the President of Haiti and continued with that organization for about 12 years, until the Occupation ended in 1934. He was the last of the Occupation Force to leave Haiti departing about 15 days after the last man had left aboard the Navy Transport. His delay in leaving Haiti was caused by several Code Books that had been in use in Haiti and had to be delivered to Naval Intelligence in person.

The last three years of Board's time as an officer in the Army of Haiti was spent at Headquarters in charge of (G-2) Intelligence, and assisting in compiling a History of the *Garde d'Haiti*. This History was completed prior to the departure of the Occupation and is considered one of the most interesting outlines on the *Garde d'Haiti* from its early days to the final departure of the Occupation in 1934. In addition to his duties as Intelligence Officer Board was for some time attached to the Staff of the Adjutant and Inspector. This detail took him into almost every city, town and village in the Republic and his stories about these trips; particularly the one of "Impersonating the Archbishop" is a classic. Mr. Board has received the Distinguished Service Medal, and the Medal of Honor and Merit in the garde of Chevalier for services rendered Haiti, in addition to a number of Medals issued for service in the Marine Corps. Board retired from the service and took up residence in Haiti with an occasional trip to the States to break the monotony and to prevent the whispers we hear about a few who stayed too long "He Missed Too Many Boats."

Invitations to Board's log cabin at Carrefour for Rice and Beans every Saturday night are much in demand and the parties there have become famous not only for the characters who attend but for the lies that are told. Walking across the Wooden Bridge after a party without falling in the River is considered quite a feat. However, Board takes pretty good care of his guests and not many fall in the water.

"Board has on several occasions threatened to write of his experiences in Haiti and 'expose' some of the antics of his good friends in the "Old Days" but on second thought it is perhaps better to let well enough alone. Incidentally he was born in Detroit U.S.A. in the last century".

Another Personality *of the Week*, a year after the *Sun* was launched was a 27-year-old newsman for *Le Nouvelliste*, Aubelin Jolicoeur. He hailed from the lovely seaport town of Jacmel and we often met covering stories. In 1951 we were practically the only two local journalists who bothered to do any reporting. Editors of the other papers expected the news articles to be brought to them usually by those involved in the news story. Jolicoeur we noted in our story in the September 23, 1951 issue of the *Sun* was "a spry, trim figure", who could, "be seen darting along the Grand Rue at the speed seldom witnessed in this part of the tropics. In his hand, you can be sure to find a rolled-up manuscript. It's as much part of Aubelin as his ready smile. The ability to make friends is another major asset of the young reporter. Graduating from the Lycée Pinchinat in Jacmel in 1943 the 19-year-old like most eager young men set his sight on Port-au-Prince and while waiting on customers at Castera's Pharmacie he brushed up on his verbs. After six months as an embryo druggist Aubelin left to reap experience in others fields. Four years later in 1948 Old Man Opportunity gave his biggest rap." He met Marceau Desinor, director ad interim of *Le Nouvelliste,* who said, "You're the fellow I need." Aubelin took to newspapering, the *Sun's* column added, "Like a duck takes to water."

It was the beginning of a career that led to fame and eventually made Jolicoeur into an institution. Aubelin of course became the inspiration for the character Petit Pierre in Graham Greene's Haiti-set novel, *The Comedians.*

Much of the talk in political circles in my early days in Haiti was of the "Revolution of '46." That change in power had not been a bloodbath but a somewhat sophisticated revolution more like an intellectual duel. It was fought with ideas between those who clung to the status quo and young minds that sought to change the country's calcified political system and antiquated, social values.

President Elie Lescot, known as *Tèt Chat* because of his oversized head, was sent into exile with cries of, "*Lescot, ou ale, ou ale, ou ale.*" ("Lescot you go, you go.") A three-member military junta took over on January 7, 1946. Haiti subsequently enjoyed a four-month political "spring" heralded as a time for change. Dumarsais Estimé won the required votes for President in the Electoral College. There was no popular vote; the election was one step removed from the rank-and-file. Representatives of the people made the choice for them. The budding black middle class then sought to be heard. New political parties blossomed. Each had its journal of opinion. There was even a priest among the rising political stars. Father Juste Constant, his Christian faith not withstanding, was both secretary-general of the *Parti Communiste d'Haiti* and the Episcopal Church's parish priest in the town of Arcahaie, until his bishop, Alfred Voegeli, removed him from his parish duties. However, despite the atmosphere of hope, the country's youngest and brightest, who had led the student demonstrations against President Lescot, saw their hopes of real change shrivel in the debilitating summer heat.

HAITI Sun

ÉNARD DIHSEMROI
TOR

GÉRANT RESPONSABLE
ÉDL A.MAINVILLE

ME L.·

SUNDAY JAN 28TH 1951

No. 30

OLONEL ROBERT RUTHERFORD McCORMICK EDITOR PUBLISHER ' THE CHICAGO TRIBUNE IS IMPRESSED BY HAITI

President Paul Magloire in conversation with Col. McCormick on the way at the National Palace.

(Continued on page 8)

Nonetheless those early 1950s were culturally exciting, a heady time for Haitian writers, poets, playwrights and painters. Politics was momentarily placed on the back burner. On the verandah of the little gingerbread hotel, *L'Avenir,* at the bottom of John Brown Avenue, professors from nearby Lycée Alexandre Pétion discussed their pet philosophers. The professors were fluent in Latin and Greek. The hotel owner *Kè Pòpòz,* a large man originally from Jérémie, served a delicious three-course meal for five gourdes, a dollar. President Estimé (and later ousted President) had begun his career as a professor at the old Lycée established by Haiti's first president, Alexandre Pétion, as had Dr. Jean Price Mars, the country's leading intellectual. In the *Aux Palmistes,* section of the capital was the Nedje night club—named after a poem by Roussan Camille. I had a bit part in the play there one night. Haitian primitive artists, not only Hyppolite but others were coming into their own. They had won praise with their exhibitions at *Musée de l'Art Moderne* in Paris.

Doing my own reporting much as on any metropolitan newspaper, I searched out news almost daily. On my beat was the police headquarters Criminal Research Bureau. In a far corner of the old wooden two-story headquarters was the suspect-holding room. Interrogations were aided by the liberal use of a *kokomakak,* a monkey-wood baton. After slavery the use of a whip was forbidden but the fathers of the new Haiti discovered the unbreakable *kokomakak.* Most of the nights catch, accused of burglary and other petty crimes, were lined up facing the wall in the Criminal Research office. (Occasionally there would be an individual who had been accused of a being a *lougawou* by their communities and handed over to police. In most cases they were found to be unjustly accused of being werewolves.)

The prisoners were made to stand for hours facing the blank wall. Whenever one of the arrested foolishly raised or turned his head the *kokomakak* came down swiftly on his skull. The detectives were not without their local cultural appreciations. One day a well-dressed *oungan* (*Vodou* priest) from Bel Air, the populous Port-au-Prince hilltop neighborhood stood before the long desk at which were seated several detectives. They were engaged in convivial small talk with the *oungan* when Capt. Jacques Etienne, head of the Criminal Research Bureau, walked in. "Book him and fingerprint him," Etienne snapped. "I know you all serve him." While they gently pressed the *oungan's* fingers to the inkpad another detective entered announcing that the woman who had brought charges of extortion against the *Vodou* priest had withdrawn them. He straightened his tie and left, but not before the policemen shook his hand enthusiastically.

Before my office one morning people were looking at an object in front of my door. It was the first *wanga* I had encountered and it was obviously meant for me. While I didn't examine its contents in detail the feathers were obviously from a chicken. There were several little bags, one red and the other white, attached to the pile. I knew who was casting this bad spell. A young man who had worked collecting *Haiti Sun* subscription money had pocketed the proceeds and I had fired him. He had been administered the *kokomakak* by the police and allowed to go free. *Wangas* before any office were definitely not good for business. Taking an old broom from the office I broke it in two and added it to the unsavory packet that I put in the back of the Jeep. Before the man's little house in Bel Air and in full daylight and before an audience of curious that soon gathered to watch the *Blan*, (foreigner) I deposited the *wanga*. Not knowing what kind of ceremony if any I should perform I began to mumble and circle around the packet. Then I slowly bowed to three cardinal points, my Catholic religion's Trinity. Even as I drove away my audience remained hushed. The thief never bothered me again. Some said he returned to the provinces.

When Col. Paul Magloire decided to assume the presidency his "election" did strain credulity. An engineer, with the ineffable name of Fénelon J.Alphonse, materialized as the opposition candidate under the banner of an entity called the "Liberal Democratic Party," which some believed was actually funded by Magloire. It was my first election experience in Haiti and I recall that hardly anyone listened to Alphonse's cry of, "Down with Dictatorship." Most people seemed too busy enjoying the charismatic Magloire's endless campaign fetes, which featured *kleren* and *bouyon* (raw rum and hearty soup) for the people. It was Haiti's the first popular vote for president. In the past the legislature had chosen the country's chief executive. Magloire used Daniel Fignolé's *Mouvement Ouvriers et Paysans* (Workers' and Peasants' Movement, or MOP) as his own political party and official vehicle to power. (A year later President Magloire banned both the MOP and the Marxist Popular Socialist Party.)

Nevertheless Magloire's election ritual had its positive aspects. All adults, literate or illiterate, except women were permitted to vote in the October 1950 balloting for president, 37 deputies, 21 senators and 17 members of a constituent assembly. The constituents wrote a new constitution the following month giving women the right to vote. This was indeed progress! Haiti's first president, Alexandre Pétion, in his 1816 constitution had accepted universal suffrage, except for women, criminals, idiots and menials. While idiots and criminals were a relatively insignificant number, women constituted more than half the population and the disallowance of menials ruled out not only the servant class but also peasants who made up the bulk of the new nation. Pétion's so-called universal suffrage thus gave something like three percent of the population the vote, consisting principally of the army and civilian elite.

The official returns of the 1950 election in Port-au-Prince gave candidate Fénelon Alphonse seven votes to Magloire's 25,679. With the ritual over, both Alphonse and his party evaporated like the morning dew.

Imbued with the New Zealand egalitarian spirit (women received the vote there in the 19th century) I knew instinctively that, sooner or later, my sympathies for the underdog would bring me into conflict with the Haitian power structure. In the meantime however I went along with my seasoned journalistic *confrères* and applauded the new regime, which promised to finally bring change. Magloire had the backing of the forces that mattered in Haitian politics: the Army, U.S. embassy, Roman Catholic Church local hierarchy, Haiti's economic elite and even Haiti's neighbor Dictator Generalissimo Rafael Trujillo. However the majority of Haitians remained spectators of their fate.

—

I had long since realized that life is determined by crossroads. Deciding which road to take is always one of life's dramatic moments. I had made my dramatic decision back in England. And now, thrust into the cauldron of politics and contending power in a still-unfamiliar black Caribbean republic, I recognized that the path of adventure I had chosen could be final. It was an acute irony that the term "crossroad", in the Haitian psyche, is extremely important, and the powerful *Vodou* deity *Papa Legba*, whose permission one must request prior to taking a road from the crossroad, guards such critical life intersections.

CHAPTER 2

Where Christ Is Black

The activity, which drew my first visit to the capital's *Centre D'Art* in December 1949, had been the launching of the most ambitious art project to be undertaken in Haiti. No single spectacle offered more insight into the real Haiti as did the paintings of nine Gospel scenes and angels in St. Trinity Episcopal Cathedral. The combined work, by eight self-taught Haitian artists, was unique. Their style—"Haitian primitive" or "naives"—was also referred to as "popular". By whatever name their creative originality was extraordinary. As its symbolism was deeply rooted in the Haitian soul, and took much of its inspiration from *Vodou*, it awakened deep prejudice, disdain, and even loathing among the country's elite. For me however the exhibition proved to be not only good *Haiti Sun* copy but personally educational.

According to Selden Rodman, a New Jersey writer who became one of the driving forces behind the project, the elderly French-born Roman Catholic archbishop of Port-au-Prince, Joseph Le Gouaze, had been horrified by the idea of having murals painted in his Basilica Notre Dame by *Vodouisant* artists. However the resident Episcopal bishop, Charles Alfred Voegeli, also a native of New Jersey, had no such hang-up. The then 37-year-old leader of the Episcopal Church in Haiti quickly approved the project in his cathedral and became its major fund-raiser. An American woman who remained anonymous—it was known however that her fortune came from the manufacture of condoms—contributed $5,000 to help finance the undertaking. The cathedral's leaky roof had first to be repaired to protect the future murals. Painter William Calfee of American University in Washington, D.C., was persuaded to come to Haiti and teach the artists the medium with which they would paint, egg tempura. So ambitious and difficult was the project it was not completed and the paintings unveiled until 1954, the 150th anniversary of the country's birth.*

Not all of Bishop Voegeli's congregates shared his cross-cultural enthusiasm. (Episcopalians have been dubbed "God's frozen people.") Some were shocked and outraged. Artists working at the *Centre d'Art* had been denigrated as *Vodouisants,* the moral equivalent in Haitian bourgeois circles of being called a Communist. (Some of the artists were indeed oungans, *Vodou* priests, while others readily admitted that their inspirations came from *Vodou*.) Faithful Episcopalians visualized their cathedral's taking on the appearance of an *oungfò* (*Vodou* temple) festooned with paintings of *Vodou* Gods. Adding insult to blasphemy for the Episcopalians, was the fact that *Vodou* over the centuries had appropriated Christian saints and installed them in *Vodou's* own pantheon of spirits. This was but one of several reasons why Protestants tended to be intractable enemies of Haiti's folk religion.

However, the great irony in the Episcopal cathedral project was that all but one of the eight artists involved in painting the murals was at least nominally Catholic—the exception being gray-haired Philomé Obin, who himself was of all things a Baptist. Obin, a noted Cap Haïtien artist, had chosen to convert from Roman Catholicism to conservative Protestantism's Baptist church and had even become a member of the Masonic lodge. As a middle-aged man in 1944, Obin had introduced himself to DeWitt Peters by letter accompanied by a painting of angels descending from clouds containing the eye of God and a figure cloaked in the Stars and Stripes. Next to a depiction of the grave of Franklin D. Roosevelt appeared the painting's title: *FDR Interceding in the Great Beyond for the Peace of the Americas*. Peters responded by sending Obin $5 for the painting and $4.50 worth of supplies. Up until then the artist had received a dollar per painting. (In the 1990s before his death at aged 92, Obin's work was fetching more than Hyppolite's at Sotheby's, and one Obin masterpiece was reputedly sold for $75,000.)

Obin's popular realism style was the beginning of what became known as the Cap Haïtien school of painting. These schools particular characteristics were the painting of historic scenes and scenes of Haitians life with their own rules of perspective and without the fantasy that characterized other naïve Haitian painters. Educated and a native of Haiti's second city where he once held a government job, Obin considered himself (not without reason) notches above the other artists at the center. In the Episcopal cathedral, before mounting the scaffold each workday to paint the crucifixion of Christ, the artist would kneel and pray.

He admitted to Rodman, writing in the *Sun*, that he had agonized over what color to paint Christ. He finally chose white—but some, because it was off-white, saw his Christ as a mulatto. What was also striking about this Christ was that Obin had portrayed him as beardless. Obin's Jesus figure looked down from the cross on a typical Cap Haïtien street scene, the people clad in bright-colored attire. Above the city's backdrop of mountains he had painted the all-seeing eye of God.

The other artists involved in the cathedral project had no such qualms about the skin hue of their biblical figures. They were black. Toussaint Auguste's Adam and Eve, for example, are both dark. They are being tempted by a serpent with the head and torso of a woman handing out, instead of an apple, bright oranges.

Artists Rigaud Benoit, Wilson Bigaud, and Castera Bazile painted respectively the Nativity, Marriage of Cana, and Ascension as if they had come to pass in the Haiti of the early 1950s. Bazile's Ascension depicts two boys playing soccer in the street while the crowd looks skyward. Christ is being baptized in a river while nearby Haitian women stripped down to their white brassieres are washing clothes. Wilson Bigaud, still frequented the *oungfò*, and Bigaud's painting of the Marriage of Cana is a wide-ranging Haitian folkloric scene that includes both good and evil—gamblers with fighting cocks, peasants, urban folk, a flamboyant prostitute, a graveyard with *Vodou* symbols, drums, and the Easter *Rara* dances.

The colorful murals turned Haiti into a land of biblical surrealism. They were also an ecumenical achievement, carried out by, Catholics, *Vodouisants*, and a Christian Protestant artist. Nevertheless, jealousies and outrage continued to surround the cathedral murals, and became apparent on the night of Feb. 18, 1950, when vandals splashed pitch all over Wilson Bigaud's nearly completed Marriage of Cana. The young artist was beside himself. He used the Créole word *rayisab* (vengeful) to describe the culprits who he believed were other artists. "They are vengeful and envy anyone who succeeds," Bigaud said. Voicing an unfortunate truth, he added, "Envy is the curse of Haiti."

He cleaned up the mess and painted the mural again. Even writer Rodman helping direct the project assumed envious artists were responsible for trying to sabotage the mural. The police didn't have a clue, which was not unusual. My conclusion was that conservative members of the Episcopal congregation were responsible. To my knowledge the vandals were never publicly identified.

—

The tempera murals painted by Haiti's leading artists in the transepts of the Episcopalian Cathedral St. Trinité were controversial at the time.

Dwitt Peters likened the discovery of Hyppolite to a miracle. It had happened, Peters told me, on a trip back from Cap Haïtien where he had visited Philomé Obin who had become the *Centre d'Art's* star artist. As the bus on which Peters was riding sped through the little coastal village of Mont-Rouis, which sits astride the main road, some thirty miles north of Port-au-Prince, he caught sight, "in a flash," of a colorfully painted door on a little bar. At Peter's request novelist Philippe Thoby-Marcelin later went in search of the painter of the door. Scrutinizing the little bar door, he found it to be painted with jackos—green-and-red parrots—amid intricately drawn foliage and flowers. Prophetically the bar sign read: *"Ici la Renaissance."* ("Here the Renaissance.") The door artist, whom Thoby-Marcelin succeeded in tracking down, turned out to be one Hector Hyppolite, an *oungan*, literally destitute, even though remarkably dignified. Hyppolite used leftover house paint for his occasional decorative jobs, together with chicken feathers for paint brushes.

Leader of the Episcopal Church in Haiti (established in 1861) Bishop C. Alfred Voegeli was a modern thinker and progressive churchman who did much to expand the work of his church in Haiti while helping its citizens.

Dewitt Peters who was responsible for aiding and guiding Haitian artists and established the Centre d' Art.

Excitedly Peters, accompanied by Thoby-Marcelin, caught the train to St. Marc, where the artist resided. Peters recalls the meeting: "We finally found the miserable hut he (Hyppolite) lived in with his young mistress and two adopted little orphan girls. We were told he was not in. The languid, un-fed young woman told us she did not know where he had gone. But at this moment I saw him—unmistakable—far away down the street and coming towards us. As he approached we noticed indeed the nobility of his carriage and the serene and luminous expression of his face. His jet-black hair with its innumerable small waves was parted in the middle and worn long to the shoulder. As he came up to us we rose. Greeting us with a poised and ceremonial courtesy, he told us our visit was no surprise. He had known it long before from a vision he had in a dream. Later on we were to have many other examples of his visionary second sight."

A brother of Philippe Thoby-Marcelin, Milo Marcelin published the book *Mythologie Vodou* in 1950, and Hyppolite did the *veves*. He drew much of his inspirations for his work from perceived visions in his dreams. In the space of three short years, from 1945 until his death in 1948, Hector Hyppolite produced 256 paintings. As his life ended with a heart attack he had hardly begun to reap some small rewards for his extraordinary work.

Haitian artists complemented their mostly illiterate country's oral records by painting its history, and the lives of its people, in vivid colors. As the dance and songs of Haiti had originated in *Vodou* so had painting. Paintings of the *Lwas* (spirits) had first appeared on the inside and outside of the *Vodou* sanctuary. Priests and priestesses were expert at tracing intricate *veves* with flour or corn meal representing the various *lwas,* on the dirt floor of the *oungfò* at the beginning of a ceremony.

The Haitian *haute Bourgeoisie* (élite) turned up its noses at the cathedral murals even as foreign tourists flocked to view them. *Time* Magazine reproduced the murals in color as did other news and art magazines. The murals had been Bishop Voegeli's answer to Ex-President Estimé's plea for a contribution to the Port-au-Prince's 1949-50 bicentennial celebration to help attract world attention. The artists missed their deadline and when completed Estimé was dead. His remains were returned from New York and he was accorded a state funeral in Port-au-Prince.

As in emergent nations everywhere the country's upper class admired only what bore the stamp (real or counterfeit) of "higher" civilization. It was of no interest to them that Haiti's truly indigenous art permeated openly or subtly (like so many things in Haiti) by the spirit of *Vodou* could be creative and even brilliant. The only Haitians to attend the art exhibition at the *centre* were those who were friendly with foreign expatriates residing in Haiti. Only years later, when Haitian indigenous art won recognition and commanded high prices, were the artists accepted by their country's own elite. Some opened successful art shops.

What was even more disconcerting was that members of Haiti's small middle-class often aped the upper class and purported to share its disdain. As Selden Rodman recalled, he and DeWitt Peters had pleaded with President Estimé to allow Haitian artists to participate in the overall work on the "Exposition," as Port-au-Prince's bicentennial was generically known. "Surely we supposed," Rodman recounts in his book, *Where Art is Joy,* about Haitian art, "the first black president since the Occupation would not import white academicians to decorate this prideful "Bicentennial . . . ? Surely such a professed nationalist and Africanist as Dumarsais Estimé would not be turned off by charges that the artists were propagandists for *Vodou!*"

"And yet, unbelievable as it seems in retrospect, Estimé did exactly what we had thought unthinkable. Peters and I had gone to see him twice. Both times we were turned over politely to the Romanian contractor who was giving out the commissions. Close to a million dollars was spent on painting and sculpture, and all of it went to French and Belgian *pompiers* [sycophants] who defaced the walls, to dealers in diminutive cement replicas of third-rate Greco-Roman marbles, or for fountains in the grossest taste. Not one cent went to Haitian artists." A quiet-spoken writer-publicist, Rodman had visited Haiti including King Christophe's fabulous Citadel and ruins of the palace of Sans Souci, but without any intention of writing about Haiti. Inspiration from that trip, however, led him to write a verse play, The *Revolutionists* (New York; Duell, Slwan & Pearce; 1942,) which was based on the conflict among the country's liberators—Toussaint Louverture, Henry Christophe and Jean-Jacques Dessalines. The French-language edition of Rodman's book was translated by Mme. Camille Lhérisson, of Port-au-Prince, and was produced at the capital's Rex Theatre with the financial aid of the government of then President Elie Lescot. For their work in creating the play, Lescot bestowed Haiti's Legion of Honor and Merit, rank of commander, on both Rodman and Mme. Lhérisson.

During 1947-48 Rodman was co-director of the *Centre d'Art* and his 1948 book, *Renaissance In Haiti*, put Haiti's new art movement on the map. Rodman became a regular contributor to the *Haiti Sun*, beginning with articles he wrote on the cathedral murals. In 1953 I had the chance to repay Rodman by helping him with his book, *Haiti: The Black Republic* (the Deven-Adair Company, New York 1954).

(In reissuing this book, *Haiti the Black Republic*" during the Duvalier era Rodman saw fit to remove the following: "Doc Reser of Pont Beudet and Bernard Diederich of the *Haiti Sun* have contributed enough to the Republic to be considered Haitian by adoption." He also found it convenient to omit: from page 159: *Newspapers*. From the point of view of Americans in Haiti, the *Haiti Sun*, a weekly paper in English edited by Bernard Diederich, is a never-ending source of information and amusement. As a matter of fact it is read by most well-informed Haitians, because the Haitian papers, patterned on the French, are primarily vehicles of literature and polemics rather then news. Diederich, a New Zealander, manages to cram into his dozen pages not only most of the local news but a wide variety of columns, gossip, special features and interviews with celebrities. The Sun is also a vociferous crusader against crime, petty injustices and billboards."

As I was exiled and Doc Reser was dead Rodman it was only logical and wise to omit any reference to us. Whatever character flaws Rodman has been accused of, both Haiti and he benefited from the relationship that was to last a lifetime. Rodman died in 2002 at age 93)

Haiti also had its share of indigenous writers. One of the first books to be reviewed in the *Sun* was *The Pencil Of God*, a novel by Milo Thoby-Marcelin's two Haitian brothers, Philippe and Pierre Marcelin* (with a foreword by the American author and critic Edmund Wilson.) Published in 1951 the humorous but grim story of a middle-aged Haitian Lothario suddenly seized in the vise of a strange necessity unfolds with all the precision of a Greek tragedy. The "Pencil of God," according to a Créole proverb, has no eraser, and poor Diogene, the protagonist, finds neither *Vodou* charms nor Catholic prayers can alter his fate. *The Pencil of God* is not a disquisition on why Haitians believe in *Vodou* or why it often "works," but instead the novel explores the subtle, suggestive process by which the demons and spirits are sewn into the fabric of the average Haitian's daily life. *Le Crayon de Dieu* (translated into English as *The Pencil of God*) says God writes hard and fast when he writes; and, again, that "the pencil of god has no eraser."

Their first novel, *Canapé-Vert* (Green Canapé) a candid and subtle study of Haitian peasant life was awarded the John Dos Passos prize for Latin American literature. The book's publication by Farrar and Rinehart in 1943 marked the first time a novel by a Haitian author or authors was translated into English for a U.S. edition. It was also translated into Spanish and published in Argentina. Three years later Rinehart and Company (successor to Farrar and Rinehart) brought out another Marcelin novel, *The Beast of the Haitian Hills* (*La Bête de Musseau*). It was published also in England. *Time* Magazine chose the book for its reading program special edition, publishing 80,000 copies.

As the *Haiti Sun's* Personality of the Week, March 30, 1952, Philippe Thoby-Marcelin one half of Haiti's most successful writing team, was interviewed by the *Sun* before returning to his job at the Pan American Union in Washington after a two-month stay in his homeland. "Phito," as he was known, proved to be a gentle, soft-spoken person. He was still noticeably shy despite the fact that he had for years been thrust into the role of "literary celebrity" in the United States.

A literary background was a familiar one to the Marcelins and Phito's career seems pre-ordained for him. His father, Emile Marcelin, had been a literary critic, novelist, and statesman, serving as Chief of Cabinet and Minister of Finance during the administration of Haitian President Louis Borno (1922-30.) Phito's maternal grandfather, Armand Thoby, was a well-known writer as was an uncle, Perceval Thoby.

So it was little wonder that the three Marcelin brothers, Philo, Milo, and Pierre grew up with ink on their fingers. At the age of ten, Phito was writing poetry. And as he grew into adulthood, Haiti finally became an exciting place for young intellectuals, including participants in a famous student strike, which led to the eventual withdrawal of the U.S. occupation. Their rebellion was against not only the presence of foreign troops on their soil. It was also against the "foreign influence" that had dominated their country's literature. It was time, the young dissidents believed, that Haitians wrote like Haitians and not like imitators of French *haute-literature*.

---

*   It is not unusual for a Haitian to prefix his mother's maiden name to his surname which Philippe did but not his brother and co-author Pierre.

In July 1927 seven young writers, including "Phito" Thoby—Marcelin, founded *La Revue Indigène* to put their ideas into practice. (The review was ridiculed at the time as The Indigestible Review by those of the European school who saw it as a return to Africa.) Their literary magazine managed only to publish six issues but they marked a vital turning point in the history of Haitian letters. Haitian poets and novelists drew on the wealth of folklore, the earthy Créole speech, and the rich spirit of their own countrymen. The result was a virtual literary revolution, one that produced a number of outstanding authors, not the least of who was Philippe Thoby-Marcelin.

He was also a prominent contributor to Port-au-Prince newspapers, writing music and art reviews, humor columns, and vivid appeals for a truly national literature. As a columnist he wrote without pay to ensure that he could say what he pleased. In addition he published three books of verse, including the well-received volume *La Négresse Adolescente*. And he teamed up with his brother Pierre to collaborate in the writing of highly successful novels.

However, precisely because the Marcelins were cultured and members of the mulatto elite, they were denigrated as traitors to their class. As Phito explained, "Our great sin was that we had presented the life of peasants at grips with poverty and religious taboos, instead of idealizing them or vindicating the upper class."

Tous les Hommes Sont Fous, translated as *All Men are Mad*, was the brothers' fourth novel, published by Farrar, Straus & Giroux in 1970. The famous American writer and critic Edmund Wilson wrote in his foreword for the book that it was their best work, a view with which I agreed. The novel was based on a particular egregious chapter in the Catholic Church's efforts to eradicate *Vodou*. The church was usually tolerant of *Vodou*, which had always been technically outlawed, but extremist elements in the church had led periodic antisuperstition campaigns in 1898, 1913 and again in 1941. French Bishop Paul Robert was one of the instigators of the 1941 Operation *Nettoyage* (operation cleanup) better known as the *"rejété"* (rejection) movement designed, according to the Church, to liberate Haitians from their *lwas* and bring them to worship only the "Holy Church. As the campaign was having little results the Church decided to administer an anti-superstition oath.* In order to receive Holy Communion from the priest they made it obligatory for the faithful to have their *rejété* card in their hand. All Haitians

---

*   (The rejection oath stated, "I before God, stand in the Tabernacle, before the priest who represented Him and renew the promises of my baptism. With hand on the Gospel I swear never to give a food-offering *(Manje-lwa)* of whatever kind—never to attend a *Vodou* ceremony of whatever kind, never to take part in a service to *lwa* in any way whatsoever "I promise to destroy or have destroyed as soon as possible all fetishes and objects of superstition, if any—on me, in my house, and in my compound.

    "In short I swear never to sink to any superstitious practice whatsoever. [For married persons] 'I promise moreover to bring up my children without exception in the Catholic and Roman religion, outside all superstition, submitting myself fully to the teaching of this Holy Church.

    "And I promise that with God's help I shall abide by my oath until death.")

were made suspect and, to their horror, even the elite and middle-class were required to take the oath. (Catholicism and *Vodou* were so deeply syncratized that years later several old *Vodou* priests told me they requested that their followers obtain the *rejété* card so as they would not be deprived of the Holy Sacraments, such as baptism.) By the end of 1941 then President Elie Lescot gave his backing to the operation and the army and rural policemen were ordered to join in the anti-*Vodou* campaign. Haiti lost ancient treasures, *Vodou* artifacts handed down for more than a century, in the church sponsored bonfires. It was a shock to learn that the so-called *rejété* (rejection) rites, which had lasted officially only 12 months still, endured. Officially the anti-*Vodou* campaign had failed but many *Oungfò* treasures handed down from generations of priests were destroyed. Ceremonial drums, difficult to hide especially the tall *asotò* almost disappeared.

The campaign officially had come to an abrupt halt in February 1942 when shots were fired during mass in Delmas section of the Capital. The church suspect the Lescot government which quickly called an end to the campaign.

> In his foreword Wilson noted the Marcelin book is based on, though it did not follow literally the real episode in Haitian history. "There was a special effort on the part of the Catholic Church to redeem the *Vodou* worshippers for Christianity. These Catholic priests had long acquiesced in a conveniently stabilized form of what is known theologically as syncretism—that is, the less advanced Haitians practiced a double cult, and for the figures in the Christian hierarchy set up altars which included also a hierarchy of *Vodou* opposite numbers. Thus, reigning with the Virgin Mary, stood the by no means virgin goddess called *Ezili*; the warrior *Ogou Feray*, whose figures in the present novel, was identified with St. James; *Papa Legba*, who presides over journeys, was paired with St. Anthony; and St. Patrick, with his foot on a snake, was paired with *Danmbala* the snake deity.

Wilson also pained put in the foreword that this episode was a "disaster for both the church and *Vodou*." "It is sad," he wrote, "that human beings should be living with such delusions and in such limitations; should be talking such inflated nonsense, suffering helplessly from wretched diseases, be intimidated and dominated by such outlandish superstitions. The *Vodouisants* and the Roman Catholics are equally inept and mistaken. Here again the special plight of the Haitians is made to extend a perspective to the miseries and futility of the whole human race, to our bitter "ideological" conflicts and our apparently pointless ambitions. *All Men Are Mad* is a very entertaining but also troubling book, and it is a most distinguished work of literature." Wilson also noted he was no stranger to Haiti. "I was once in Haiti near Christmas," he added, "and found that the Christmas cards along with Joyeux Noel were sometimes decorated with a snake that represented [the *Vodou* god] *Danmbala*. Wilson's own book on Haiti, *Red, Black, Blond & Olive* was published in 1956 by Oxford Press.

In choosing the *Haiti Sun's* "Personality of the Week", I was determined to feature persons from all walks of life, even illiterate peasants who could only guess what it was that I was writing about them. One particular "Personality" worthy peasant, named Joseph Lifel, or "*Ti Djo*" as he was known agreed to be interviewed if it would help bring rain that he urgently needed to save his crops. I made no guarantees but the request for rain appeared with his story.

"To Many observers the most colorful people in Haiti are the peasants who till the rust-colored soil high in the mountains of Furcy behind the Capital, their individuality is as marked as the ruggedness of their chilly Climate. You'll see them striding along a mountain path in blue denim trousers that end just below the knee, a yoked denim smock and the inevitable tasseled macoute (bag) swinging from their shoulders.

"Or you'll see them gathered together in a group, one man—obviously a born mimic—acting out a tale of some recent neighborhood happening while the others hold their sides or slap their thighs in merriment. It is the time of "odyans", and odyans as the Haitian calls these gossip sessions are an institution and part of the character of all Haitians no matter their social standing. Hours each day are spent on odyans.

"The peasant's sense of humor, larded plentifully with earthy Créole proverbs, is always ready to bubble to the surface. So is their sense of gallantry. Because in a land noted for masculine appreciation of feminine pulchritude, the men of Furcy pride themselves on their outstanding virility.

"If there is one among them who cannot point with pride to his own achievements in providing Haiti with new citizens, he can always point with pride to his friend and neighbor Joseph Lifal or Ti Djo who has made local history by fathering 35 children and even confirmed reports that the 36th is on its way.

"A tall outspoken man of 55 Ti Djo was far more interested in talking about the need for water for his crops on his 50-carreau farm than he was about his prodigious fatherhood. He had agreed to the interview only if I published a request for rain. He explained that rain must come soon if he was to harvest enough food and other necessities for his 15 living children, the others having died in infancy or at an early age. The offspring were the product of alliances with 7 different ladies—each of whom he had provided with a kay (hut) and a piece of land for farming.

"Ti Djo was a true son of the mountains. He was born in their shadow and only ventured away from their ever-changing slopes long enough to try one season of cane cutting in the Dominican Republic. He was sick with malaria practically the whole time.

"He didn't have the advantage of schooling, but he is making sure that his youngsters are. They have all made their first Holy Communion, he added proudly. And he talked wistfully of plans to send one of his boys to be educated in New York.

"The Great Outside World is something that Ti Djo knows nothing about . . . and here again we envied his air of serenity. The clouds of an atomic war did not dim his horizon. His sole concern at the moment is that lack of water and that he had lost pigs from the "fever."

"But he is still far better off than the great majority of Haitian landowners who all too often have no livestock to lose . . ."

"Furcy's Ti Djo fertility was by no means unusual. I was later to meet *Oungans* (*Vodou* priests) who boasted of fifty or more children by numerous women, all swearing they provided for their offspring. Because of the polygamous peasant any census of Haiti is hard work. It is also a cause for alarm as Haiti's population was just over three million then and the land once so productive was already showing signs of being worn out and unable to sustain its population.[Today the population is already 9 million.]"

Ti Djo got his rain. Subscribers to the *Haiti Sun* who had summer homes in Furcy reported that Ti Djo gave credit to the newspaper that featured him in a front-page photograph on horseback.

———

Nothing pleases a true Irishman like the prospect of a big fight. And that went double for a rich-brogue gentleman from County Cork, The Rev. H. Ormonde McConnell. (Cork was also the birthplace of my maternal grandmother, a McCarthy.) From the time he arrived in Haiti in 1934 as part of the Methodist Mission, which had been functioning in Haiti since 1816—McConnell had been pouring every ounce of his Irish pugnacity and energy into the battle against Haitian illiteracy. As the *Sun's* Personality of the Week on January 15, 1952, he had presented me a photo. Although the picture was grainy and shadowy, the sadness on the dignified *Gwo Oungan's* face was apparent. McConnell pointed out the "Big Priest" was burning his drums, *ason*, which was laced on the outside by snake vertebrae, terra-cotta *govis* containing the *lwas* (Spirits) he had so faithfully served and his father and grandfather before him. He had also burned down his peristil (temple) the pre-Colombian stone axes or thunderstones containing part of his deities had disappeared. With the burning the onetime *Gwo Oungan* we were told had rejected the religion of his ancestors and become a member of the Methodist faith.

However McConnell wanted to discuss illiteracy. "It had been a difficult but rewarding fray," I had written of him in the *Sun*, "one that Pastor McConnell guided with unremitting intensity and, luckily, he found an excellent team-mate for carrying on the fight. A missionary by the name of Franck Laubach had worked out a new picture method which gave uneducated masses a short-cut road to literacy . . . in India, in the Philippines and in Africa he had established the validity of his visual-phonetic system. Eager pupils thronged to his classes which were conducted on an 'Each one reaches one' basis. As soon as the pupil learned to read and write his native tongue, he was pledged to teach some one else. Soon the Laubach campaigns were mushrooming and educators who had been making little headway in teaching great masses of adults began bidding for his services.

"It was the Reverend McConnell who succeeded in bringing Dr. Laubach to Haiti and since Créole was essentially a spoken and not a written tongue, there was the problem of standardizing its spelling. (Much later we found that a Créole dictionary had been produced in England as early as 1812.) In 1939 the Rev. McConnell in collaboration with Haitian educator Etienne Bourand, developed a system of writing Créole based on the international phonetics system (and not on English as many accusing Haitian nationalists as well as the Catholic Church had insisted). A year later the Methodist minister initiated his first experiment in teaching illiterates to read and write Créole using the Laubach method. The experiment was carried out under the watchful eye of Mr. Luc Fouché who was Minister of Education at the time.

The government decided that the earnest, round-faced Irish pastor had something—especially after some Haitians began to read in less than three weeks while attending school just a few hours each evening. In 1943, the Haitian Government appointed McConnell to an important post on an official committee, which was spearheading an all-out literacy campaign. With his assistance, three government-supported books in Créole were published on hygiene, history, and agriculture.

Being a man of the cloth, the Methodist pastor was of course greatly interested in spreading the gospel through the medium of Créole. He himself produced books on Christian doctrine, on sections of the Bible, and put the finishing touches on a Créole version of the life of Christ, which was beautifully illustrated with color pictures. The text was written by Dr. Laubach and translated into Créole with the help of the Haitian Methodist minister, Pastor Dépestre.

However the Laubach orthography was not precise, and Créole had to wait another 35 years for the experts to get it right. (Charles Fernand Pressoir and Lélio Fabius had produced the Créole bible in 1950s. Then after seven years of discussion in September 1979 the then Minister of Education, a Haitian specialist on loan to Haiti by UNESCO, Joseph Bernard authorized the spelling and on Jan.31, 1980 it was agreed upon. Meanwhile I continued to use phonetic spelling for the Créole words that we printed in the *Haiti Sun*. Yet we continued to receive complaints. Our readers complained for example that they found the Créole-language column by outstanding Haitian poet Emile Roumer, who had given up writing in French difficult to understand.

For all the challenges translating Créole English-speakers got a valuable assist in communicating in Haiti's native language in the form of McConnell's easy-reading manual entitled, "*You Can Learn Créole.*" Its lessons in mastering Créole were drawn up with the help of Eugene Swan at the suggestion of the local general manager of Shada (Haitian-American Company for Agriculture Development) who was desperately trying to establish communication between his American overseers and the employees of the experimental rubber project the company was engaged in. The controversial wartime U.S. rubber growing project turned out to be a shocking failure with millions of dollars lost and thousands of peasants shoved off their land, their homes destroyed. Not a ton of rubber from an indigenous latex plant, the crytostegia, exported, amounting to an extremely sad chapter in U.S. enterprise that cost Haiti dearly. But McConnell's book on Créole was anything but a failure. It went into scores of printings over the years and is still in print.

A weeklong visit to a UNESCO pilot project in Haiti's Marbial Valley entailed a tough, winding Jeep trip during which we crossed the same river to Jacmel, the lovely coastal town in west, more than twenty times. Marbial produced a lengthy feature in the *Sun*. The Haitian director of the UNESCO project, Emmanuel Gabriel, proved a devoted educator and became a ready candidate for the Personality of the Week column. Poet Félix Morisseau-Leroy and Maurice Dartigue, Haiti's former director of rural education, were also on the trip. I was hoping to meet Alfred Métraux, a French anthropologist who headed a sociological survey of the Marbial Valley. But he had just completed his work in the area. Métraux had told Gabriel that an "anti-superstition campaign" in the Marbial Valley (in 1941-42) had been so successful, and that any *Vodou* research in the area was useless, as the Marbial peasants, while still believers in *Vodou*, were fearful of even mentioning the officially condemned ancestor's faith. An English translation of Meraux's work, *Voodoo in Haiti,* was finally published in 1959, to join such scholarly works as *Life in A Haitian Valley*, by Melville T. Herskovits (Alfred A.Knopf, 1937) and James G. Leyburn's The *Haitian People* (Yale Press, 1941). Harold Courlander, American specialist in African and Afro-American folklore and music, also made Haiti a research project, and his *Haiti Singing* (University North Carolina Press; 1939) was followed in 1960 by *The Drum and the Hoe* (University of California Press, Berkeley; 1960).

Other distinguished foreigners, mostly painters and writers, made the Personality of The Week column but when Anastasio Somoza Garcia, founder of the then-Nicaraguan dictatorship, made an official visit in August 1952 he was relegated to, "Man of the Week". The *Haiti Sun* had its scruples! That year Hector (Negro) Trujillo paid a state visit and was also relegated to "Man of the Week."

Although many outsiders do not realize it, island communities are much like small towns. Secular and ingrown, they share a similar gossip mentality. Just about everyone who is anyone knows everyone else who is anyone. And the local picturesque "characters," including foreign expatriates, are conspicuous by their presence.

Such was the parochial atmosphere of Port-au-Prince. Though the total population of the Haitian capital when I arrived was estimated at 180,000, the number of residents who "mattered" . . . the government establishment, businessmen, artists, the diplomatic community, and other members of the "élite"—numbered perhaps only some few thousand. In effect, they made up a "small town" in which everyone pretty much knew what everyone else was doing as well as every branch of their family trees. If one was seen visiting the "House of Flowers," he could be sure that everyone in town—his social peers—would quickly know about it. Thus Port-au-Prince was a gossip's paradise. Among the non-elite—including inhabitants of the capital's slums and peasants from the countryside trekking into the city to sell produce—there was a marvelously effective gossip mechanism called telemouth.

In Haiti's mainly oral society news was passed by word of mouth at almost literally the speed of sound. Haitians referred to it as the *teledjòl* (telemouth). To compete, I reported what was on the *teledjòl*. Moreover working telephones were as rare as gold nuggets. The U.S. Marines had installed the first dial system, but by the 1950s dialing didn't work; the system had fallen into hopeless disrepair. Especially during the *morte saison* (dead season)—when the coffee crop had been harvested—and the heat had slowed down business—it was a great time for gossip, or *tripotaj* (also referred to as *zin*). "*Koute youn lodyans.*" ("Listen to this audience.") was the traditional opening phrase of such informal gossip sessions, usually called together at work or even conducted on the street and which passerby would gather and listen. The self-appointed narrator often acted out his story, on the sidewalk, in a store or at home with a colorful repertoire of gestures. Every Haitian had a touch of the actor in his or her blood. The *tripotaj* session—or "audience" as it was called in English had to be conducted in Créole. (For one thing, Haiti's richly ironic jokes always sounded better in Créole.)

As for subject matter, even the small expatriate American colony provided good gossip. A celebrated resident American photographer whose lithesome palid wife, a onetime New York model, had flown off for a weekend in the Virgin Islands with a wealthy Port-au-Prince businessman, retaliated by sending him a picture, a blowup of her, naked with dollars over strategic parts of her body. The photographer's houseboy delivered the life-size enlargement unwrapped to the Haitian businessman's office for all to see.

In earlier old days, defamation in a Haitian newspaper could lead to a dual between the editor and the alleged defamed. However by the time I appeared on the publishing scene, usually a published retraction or correction would suffice to satisfy the complainant's honor. (The last editor to have been shot was in 1946.)

There was no quicker way to learn about Haitian culture, politics, and history than by publishing a newspaper. I wrote most of it, set it in pages, proof read it for typos, and sent it to "bed" (press). My Haitian linotypist knew no English, which was actually good, since it meant he followed the copy closely and made few errors. Nevertheless one day under the administration of Col. Paul Magloire, I wondered whether my linotypist had learned some English. The type as it appeared caused some embarrassment. Instead of, "The President and community leaders attended . . ." it came out as, "The President and communist leaders attended . . ." The palace was not pleased.

Up to my elbows in printer's ink I was thoroughly enjoying my new life. One day an employee ran amok in the print shop and chased us all with a ladle of molten lead. We were all good sprinters and he didn't catch us. Certainly we were not Olympic material such as Haitian native son Sylvio Cator, who had represented Haiti in three Olympic Games. In 1928 Cator had broken the world broadjump record with 26 ft. 1/8 inch. A wonderful human being; Cator soon became a good friend. His broad knowledge of sport, even rugby, made me feel at home.

Whenever the going got particularly tough I would recall the words Isaac (Bubbleguts) Sykes, our second mate on the famous four-masted barque *Pamir*, on which I sailed as a boy: "Laddy this life will prepare you . . . You'll be able to do anything after this!"

One of the great obstacles to literacy progress in Haiti was the war against Créole by the elite class and the formal educational establishment. The situation was rooted in historical complexity. As the slaves imported to Haiti from many different tribes and cultures in Africa had no common language, the dialect spoken on the West African Slave Coast became their common tongue: Créole. It contains French lexicon and African as well old European seafaring and Maritime trade figures of speech. Créole eventually became the official language of the Seychelles Islands in the middle of the Indian Ocean, a long way from the West Coast of Africa.

In Haiti however, in homes of the elite, a good matron would scold me with, "Please don't speak Créole to my children . . . ," or, "Please don't speak Créole in front of my children . . . ," It was ironic because the only language the children's nanny spoke was Créole. A mixture of Créole-French was spoken in the city.

It was not only a case of snobbish members of the elite viewing Créole as an uncivilized language compared with French. Even poor Haitians wanted their sons and daughters to learn French not Créole, at school in order to compete with the offspring of the rich. The majority of Haitian students were learning French as a foreign language as they returned to homes where only Créole was spoken.

Félix Morisseau-Leroy, a pro-Créole crusader, began writing a column for the *Haiti Sun* under the heading: *Créole Pale Créole Compran.* (Créole spoken Créole understood.) When Morisseau-Leroy built an outdoor theatre in the Pétionville neighborhood of Morne Hercules and presented his Créole version of the Greek tragedy, *Antigone,* it received rave reviews and was featured in *Time* Magazine. When the director of the local French Institute declined to have the play put on at the Institute's theatre, we prepared placards, in the office of the *Haiti Sun* protesting the French Institute action as unfair to Haiti's national language. When the first protest sign appeared before the Institute official relented and allowed *Antigone* to be produced in their Theatre.

Meanwhile the noted poet Emile Roumer was happy to find an outlet for his Créole column in the *Sun*. He brought his handwritten copy personally to our office on his trips by boat from Jérémie. Years later when Professor Jean-Claude Bajeux, was compiling an anthology on Créole poetry, he asserted that he couldn't include Emile Roumer because the latter's Créole was too "Frenchified." Such were the Créole-French language sensibilities. For our past, to balance things out a bit, the *Sun* published a column in French, *Point de Vue,* written by a professional journalist, Lucien Montas of *Le Nouvelliste.* Also a French column by writer Daniel Arty was extremely interesting.

Ploughing through the labyrinth of Haitian culture the hard way took time. Finally I found a key: a book entitled *Ainsi Parla l'Oncle* (So Spoke the Uncle) (1928). I was in awe of the Haitian author, Dr. Jean Price-Mars, on our first meeting. He quickly put me at ease. Indeed he was almost gentle, with the most unassuming manner and a subtle Old World courtesy. As Haitian poet Jean Brierre had written, Dr. Price-Mars was "carved in basalt".

When I apologized for knowing so little about Haitian culture before reading, *So Spoke the Uncle,* and said that I felt like an interloper, the courtly author smiled and reassured me. I was astounded to learn that his work was not popular with many of the Haitian elite who chose to live in the cool of Pétionville, above the teeming capital and read French novels. At that time many Haitian Catholic schools did not have Dr. Price-Mars on their curricula. In fact the leading French Catholic theologian of the period *Abbe* R.P. Foisset, attacked Dr. Price-Mars' concept that *Vodou* was a religion, an authentic cultural religion, the expression of the rural masses, and not somehow pathological.

In *So Spoke the Uncle*, Dr. Price-Mars had written:

"*Vodou* is a religion because all its adherents believe in the existence of spiritual beings which live anywhere in the universe in close intimacy with humans whose activity they dominate.

"These invisible beings constitute an Olympian pantheon to the gods in which the greatest among them bear the title of papa or grand master and have the right to special homage.

"*Vodou* is a religion because the cult appertaining to its gods requires a hierarchical priestly body, a society of the faithful, temples, altars, ceremonies and finally a whole oral tradition which has certainly not come down to us unaltered, but thanks to which the essential elements of this worship have been transmitted.

"*Vodou* is a religion because, amid the confusion of legends and the corruption of fables, we can discern a theology, a system of representation thanks to which African ancestors have, primitively, accounted for natural phenomena . . ."

" . . . It is thanks to Créole," Dr. Price Mars wrote, "that our oral traditions exist, are perpetuated and transformed, and it is through this medium that we can hope some day to bridge the gulf which makes of us and the people two apparently distinct and frequently antagonistic entities . . ."

Dr. Price-Mars was Haiti's most accomplished intellectual. Fellow intellectuals in the neighboring Dominican Republic liked to say that he was the best Haitian ambassador (1947-49) to their country. His soul-searching concerning Haiti led to the seeking out of a new cultural orientation for his native country. It was Dr. Price-Mars' work, which opened the door to new ideas of justice and respect for human dignity.

"It is remarkable and almost miraculous that The Master, (Dr. Price-Mars) in a milieu in which intellectuals and social evolution is the rule of the day, never yielded to a bourgeois philosophy and that on the very threshold of life he should have had the courage to feel all the riches and heroism hidden in the homes of the masses," Poet Jean Brièrre wrote in the *Sun* in a tribute to Dr. Price-Mars, whom he referred to as *The Uncle*. "And should have put his learning, his pen, his time and his indefatigable energy at the defense of the culture of the people. And he did not do it as a dilettante as many artists and bohemians do. He did it as an expert. This obstinate seeker of truth did not depend only on dusty archives . . . His profession (Medicine) having brought him early into contact with the people of the suburbs and those of the rural sections . . ."

Nor were Price-Mars' lectures ever boring. The last time I saw him and his wife, we had strolled together along a street in Pétionville. Several times I had accompanied him and his wife on their afternoon promenade. He walked with his head slightly bent forward. From both sides of the street came the salutation: "*Bonswa*, Doktè" (Good evening Doctor).

CHAPTER 3

The Laughing Hill &
the Charms of Pauline

In those early days as a publisher seeking to lift my horizons, I found an ideal home. The small, two-room concrete house clung to the hillside at the sparsely populated end of *Cinquième (fifth) avenue,* an old residential section of Port-au-Prince called Bolosse. My new abode was a cut above the neighboring thatched-roof, wattle-and-mud *kay pay* (huts). Placing my bed against the open window gave the feeling of floating above the city. The rent was affordable: fifty *gourdes* ($10.00) a month. (At the time the country's per capita income was less than $40 yearly and the government budget was little more than $20 million.)

In the hills the drums were nearer and louder, while all around me the continuous dog and rooster concert was inescapable. My kind and thoughtful neighbors were concerned with my well being. Repeatedly they warned me to shut my window at night because the *"move lè ap antre."* ("The bad air will enter.") When I didn't take their advice they quietly warned that I was foolishly inviting a visit from the nocturnal *lougawou* (werewolf). Fortunately I was spared any such visitation. However, magic did stream through my window—the most enchanting view and sounds.

"Men bèl chadèk, zoranj, bannann, cheri." The melodious singsong sales pitch was my wake up call. Without electricity or gas, purchasing a fresh grapefruit, orange, and banana from my neighborhood *pratik* (street vendor) was a delightful early morning chore. With dignity and agility the young lady would lower her heavy basket of fruit from her head to the ground. Squatting beside it she would encourage me to have my pick. The young woman introduced me to *kowosòl* (soursop, a tropical fruit) and grenadine and gave precise instructions as to how to make juice from these tropical fruits.

Hers was market capitalism at its purest. Feigning disappointment she would screw up her face when I declined to haggle over her prices. Bargaining was a tradition with the Haitian *pratik*. At *dis kòb* (2 U.S. cents) per fruit, I could hardly argue over her posted prices. Plus she offered credit. Laughing she would chastise me saying, *"Blan,* you are killing me with these prices," pretending that I had bargained her prices down. Her smile etched on a beautiful ebony face was worthy of the refreshing sunrise, and in Haiti the mornings are the glorious part of the day.

My grandiose Fifth Avenue was not to be compared to New York's swanky boulevard. In fact it was then little more than a narrow clay path that had a habit of collapsing into a ravine during the rainy season, making it impassable even for my trusty Jeep. The alternate route was a flashback in time. The dirt road cut across a lush, tropical park only a hundred yards from my home. Towering above this luxuriant botanical garden of native trees and shrubs was a sacred mapou tree. *Vodou* offerings often appeared among the spreading roots of this giant tree.

In the surrounding neighborhood, every little household which lacked running water had a krich (clay water container). Daily I filled mine with crystal-clear water from the park's bubbling spring.

The park, privately owned by Haitian businessman Fernand Crepsac and known as *Chez Pauline*, was identified with history's famous Pauline, sister of Napoléon Bonaparte. The strangest sight was the park's collection of gargoyles and statues bleached to an extraordinary whiteness by the sun. There were the nine muses, a reclining damsel, and a stone statue of Canova's reclining Venus. The Venus was said to be a copy of the one in the Villa Borghese in Rome, for which Pauline posed when she later married Prince Camillo Borghese after her adventures in the onetime French colony that became Haiti. For some, the statues beside the park's swimming pool lend credence to the legend that Pauline had once frolicked in this delightful Garden of Eden among the hibiscuses with her lover, General Humbert, reputedly the handsomest man in the French army. But as the Venus was made many years after Pauline had fled Haiti, the statues appear to have been a romantic gesture of a former owner of the property.

The question was nonetheless intriguing. Had she or had she not slept in this lovely garden? Haitian history has fascinated writers and historians for nearly two centuries. Yet few have assigned any importance to the activities of Napoléon's favorite sister during a disastrous French campaign in Saint Domingue, as Haiti was known by its French Colonizers until 1804.

Forced against her will by Napoléon to accompany her then husband, Gen. Charles Victoire-Emmanuel Leclerc, Pauline had made the most of it. Leclerc, a blond, spit-and-polish military professional, had been assigned command of the largest invasion force ever to cross the Atlantic. His orders: To retake Saint Dominique France's proudest colony, known as the "Queen of the Antilles" (Profits from its sugar, chocolate, indigo, coffee and lumber had built fortunes and even towns in France) from its ex-slaves who were then led by a remarkable ex-slave, François Dominique Toussaint (later to be known as L'Ouverture, the Opening).

The fleet of eighty-six ships was readied in half a dozen French and other European ports. Fourteen of Napoléon's most famous generals were assigned to head the force which included 1,500 officers and 20,000 veteran army troops, 9,000 sailors, and 700 physicians and surgeons. They were accompanied by 3,000 French Créoles (Frenchmen born in Saint

Domingue) who wanted to be on hand to receive back their slave-occupied properties. General Leclerc and his fellow officers reportedly viewed the mission as a pushover.*

Bonaparte was driven not only by the desire to regain France's once richest colony but he was personally infuriated with Toussaint who had appointed himself Governor-General of Saint Domingue for life. What was even more vexing, Toussaint liked to refer to himself as the "Black Napoléon." Toussaint's aim was the emancipation of his people but continued ties with France.

Napoléon ordered Leclerc not only to oust Toussaint but also to reestablish slavery. (Toussaint had not been a leader of the initial slave uprising in Saint Domingue in 1791, but he had joined it and managed to weld the various factions together, and to defeat the French colonials, British invaders, and Spanish garrisons on the East side of the island of Hispaniola in what is now the Dominican Republic. The French revolution had brought with it the principles of liberty, equality, and fraternity, and Toussaint was determined that Saint Domingue's ex-slaves share in those ideals. But to Napoléon such principles did not apply to black slaves.

Miserable about leaving gay Paris and having to accompany her husband, Pauline is credited with at least delaying the departure of the fleet. A headstrong woman she went on a shopping spree for a wardrobe befitting the future Empress of St. Domingue as she saw her role. As Napoléon's European veterans used to sing, *"Pauline s'empare des coeurs/ quand Bonaparte prend les villes."* ("Pauline conquers the hearts /after Bonaparte occupies the towns") Notorious for her sexual appetite the sensuous temptress, like her brother a Corsican, reportedly seduced whom she liked when she liked.

The invasion force finally left Europe and Pauline, with her bold *décolletage* and beauty, was for privileged officers more than a mere distraction.

When Leclerc finally arrived off Cap Français,(the northern city was also called Cap François) capital of the French colony of Saint Domingue, in early February 1802, after what the commanding general described as "a miserable trip," Pauline was enchanted with the view of the city that had once been known as the Paris of the Western Hemisphere. Indeed, New York was then a small town compared with the thriving pre-revolution 18th century sugar port of Cap François, on the island's northern coast, and its tremendous wealth generated by slave labor.

Leclerc's emissary, sent ashore to meet with the town's military commander, Henri Christophe, had reported back in glowing terms the splendor of the place. Pauline was beside herself with joy and anticipation. Her elation, however, soon turned to anger and tears as the fashionable city went up in smoke. Henri Christophe set fire to the town as the French fleet entered the bay. Toussaint had ordered a scorched-earth policy to fight the better-armed European veterans. Christophe and his troops withdrew and left the burning city to the French.

---

*   (Gen. Pamphile de Lacroix states in his account of the expedition that with reinforcements, Napoléon's forces were to reach 55,132. Only 1,200 were destined to return to France. The rest were either killed in battle or died of yellow fever and malaria.)

President Paul E. Magloire and wife, Yole, and family enjoying carnival.

In early April 1802, Leclerc, tired of his wife's complains about living amid the ashes of Cap François, suggested she take their three-year-old son and visit Port Républicain (later to resume it original name, Port-au-Prince) while construction of a more suitable commander's residence in Cap François was underway.

During the French invasion, Generals Bouder and de Lacroix had landed a few miles south of what is now Port-au-Prince on the Mer Frappée beach. They led their grenadiers in tall bearskins along the coast road and took the city before Jean-Jacques Dessalines in command of Port-au-Prince could burn it down. The march took them close to where *Chez Pauline* Park is located, in Martissant, three miles south of the city.

Antoine Métral in his *Histoire de l'Expédition Militaire* (1841; p. 117) states that Pauline Leclerc stayed for two months in Port-au-Prince in a country house on the side of a *"Colline Riante"* (Laughing Hill) which "dominated the sea where she lived in luxury, laziness and pleasure." Georges Corvington in his history of Port-au-Prince (Vol. 1789-1804; p.206) states that while Laughing Hill was somewhere in Martissant the exact location is still not certain. Others without proof, he writes, believe the site was at Fifth Avenue Bolosse, where it meets *Chez Pauline* Park. Possibly Pauline and I had shared the same neighborhood—the French-built Fort Bizoton was nearby and could have afforded protection.

In his two-volume *The History and Conditions of St. Domingo,* published in 1837 Jonathan Brown, a physician from New Hampshire who spent a year in the newly decolonialized Haiti, also writes about Pauline's two-month stay in Port-au-Prince: "She occupied a plantation house situated upon a slope of a hill which overlooked the sea. Here this most beautiful of European women lived in her usual routine of pleasure, while all around her were dying (in the War). Sometimes she was carried in a sort of palanquin to romantic sites on the coast, where she remained for hours gazing upon the bright waters glittering in the hot sun, or in tracing the enchanting outline of the shore as it was broken by inlets or stretched itself into jutting headlands. She forgot the pestilence in a succession of fetes, where in the dance she showed off her grace and beauty; but even here death walked with funereal torches, for those who had danced in the evening was often enshrouded in death on the following day."(From the toll of battle and disease.)

Napoléon's finest troops faced not only fanatical fighters in Saint Domingue but also *mal de Siam* as the deadly Yellow Fever was known. It decimated the legions who had won honor on the battle fields of Europe. In November 1802 General Leclerc contracted the fever and died. Pauline, in a show of mourning, cut off her flaxen tresses and laid them in his coffin. Her detractors noted that her hair grew back more coarsely. She returned to France, after her nine-month sojourn in Haiti, accompanying her husband's coffin.

———

When I first met park owner Fernand Crepsac, he told me he had intended to turn *Chez Pauline* into a model farm, when he purchased the estate more than a decade earlier, but he admitted he also had succumbed to Pauline's charms. He never doubted for a moment that Pauline had made her home there in 1802.

Portly and earnest-eyed, the middle-aged Crepsac, a professional jack-of-all-trades, was then president of the *Cercle Port-au-Princien,* a social club made up mostly of businessmen and located on the Champ de Mars. He was a bundle of energy, which had fueled his elevation to mayor of Port-au-Prince in 1944. He had later managed his brother-in-law's sugar plantation, *Prince de Rouën,* near the village of Cabaret, and his most renowned achievement there had been to act as godfather to nearly 400 children whom he had baptized during his seven years' running the plantation.

Still later, as director of the government *l'Ecole Centrale des Arts et Métiers,* he began a system of naming influential individuals as godfathers and godmothers of the students. Within a short time he had no fewer than 300 elite well-to-do godparents taking an active interest in their needy godchildren. Crepsac likewise allowed children to swim at *Chez Pauline.*

However, he had tired of taking care of the property, and in 1950 sold it to Katherine Dunham, the American dancer and choreographer. Dunham at first turned the estate into a relaxing resort for swimming and dining and later added a "Voodoo floorshow" with dinner. It was there she also trained her dance troupe and settled down to write a book. (In the 1970s *Chez Pauline* became *Habitation Leclerc,* a swanky resort created by a high-living Frenchman, Olivier Coquelin, which attracted the jet set. Greek shipping tycoon Aristotle Onassis and his wife Jacqueline Kennedy Onassis were visitors. Napoléon's sister Pauline would have felt right at home in the erotic atmosphere of *Habitation Leclerc.* In 2006 it had become the headquarters of gangs that were responsible for many killings.)

Driving home across *Chez Pauline* at night I was invariably halted halfway by a man-made barricade. The only way I could proceed was to shout a *Vodou* request; *"Papa Legba louvri baryè pou mwen."* [*"Papa Legba* opens the barrier for me."] For good measure I would roar, *"Ayibobo,* the *Vodou* cry more in exasperation than joy, especially when I was in a hurry." A barrel-chested *blan* in undershirt would appear and survey with pride the barrier of chairs and other obstacles he had placed in the path to force me to stop.

"Banm nouvél-ou, Ti-Blan, kouman ou ye," the white man, an American expatriate named Doc (Stanley) Reser, would shout back in greeting asking me news of myself and how I was in a typical Créole salutation. He had the job of guarding and maintaining *Chez Pauline* during Port-au-Prince's 1949-50 Exposition. Inside a big red shed on a table sat a bottle of one-star (cheapest) Barbancourt rum and two glasses. "I was expecting you," he would say. I soon learned that most *oungans*—Doc was an *oungan*—would say, even when one dropped in unexpectedly, "I was expecting you."

He and I would often talk far into the night. His blue eyes sparkling, Reser would flex his muscular arms and for a moment the red-and-green dragon tattoo on one arm, a souvenir from his days as a U.S. Navy pharmacy mate, first class, would take on the form of a snake. Haitians told stories about the burly Doc feeding eggs to the snake on his arm. Three drops of his first drink were always poured on the ground to salute the *lwas, Vodou* gods. However, Doc was careful not to waste any of his libations in this traditional salutation and he reprimanded me for pouring too much good rum.

Our evening sessions ranged from Haitian riddles and proverbs to *Vodou* practices and Haiti's folkways. (Television hadn't arrived in Haiti; I didn't own a radio; and reading by lantern light, Doc told me, was bad for my eyes. It was better, he said, that we talk, and I had a lot to learn.) He had a limitless repertoire garnered from his years-spent living close to the Haitian people and his involvement with *Vodou.* We would start in the peasant storytelling fashion with Doc saying, *"Krik"* and my reply *"Krak".*

He knew most of the *oungans* and *mambos* in the vicinity of Port-au-Prince, Cul-de-Sac, and Léogane. They accepted him, at least those whom I later met. Reser was generous with his time and had helped many researchers and other visitors understand Haiti's folklore and religion, even escorting them to *Vodou* ceremonies and to meet *oungans* and *mambos*. He assisted Katherine Dunham around the countryside on her first visit in the late 1930s and she later recounted her travels with Doc in her book, *Island Possessed* (Doubleday; 1969). Zora Neale Hurston had devoted a chapter to Stanley Reser in her 1938 book *Tell My Horse*.

Of the many authors and visitors whom Doc had met and helped, the black American writer Hurston, he said, "Was the most sincere and kept her promises." Hurston in turn wrote, "Haitian people, high and low, far and near, love and trust this man." She had asked him why it was that the Haitian peasant loved him so much, and his reply was, "They are infinitely kind and gentle and all that I have ever done to earn their love is to return their unfailing courtesy." A sincere and uncritical supporter of the peasant, Reser was often their spokesman and they returned his affection. (Years later *oungan* Gwo Wòch of Illavois told me that Reser was "More than an *oungan*," What he meant was that Doc had entered into the *Vodou* pantheon.) Doc didn't gossip. Someone asked him in my presence whether it was true that Dunham had been Estimé's mistress before he became president. He fumed and shook his large Nordic head and said, "I've never peeped into bedrooms.")

Doc's and my Créole improved markedly with the one-star Barbancourt, fine Haitian rum even though it was the cheapest. Sometimes Reser would produce a fiery *kleren* from Cap Haïtien where he had once been posted by the U.S. Navy and where he had learned many of the Haitian folktales. It was while serving in Port-de-Paix that his poor Haitian patients began calling him Doc.

As a 27-year-old Navy pharmacist's mate from Utah, Reser was ordered to Haiti in 1927 to join the U.S. Marine occupation. His first tour there was to last 14 years, twelve of which were spent as superintendent of the institution for the Haitian insane at Pont Beudet in the Cul de Sac plain, as well as at the Institute for "*Les désérités du sort*" at Signeau nine miles South of Port-au-Prince. The Marines had first used the pastoral Pont Beudet in this farming area for training and then turned it into the asylum for the mentally ill. "Hitherto the mentally deranged roamed roadways and mountains and forests and were an aberration in a scheme of the gods or were hopelessly possessed by them and paying out some time of penance," wrote Katherine Dunham in *Island Possessed*. "Now they were little better off, but they were in effect cloistered and in some way cared for, and surely enjoyed some measure of pharmaceutical if not psychiatric care. They also enjoyed the ceremonies and dances and *Vodou* drums that seemed never to stop from Friday evening to Sunday night, running over even into Monday on the slightest pretext and these ceremonies may have been their bush psychiatry."

When the Marine occupation finally ended in 1934 the Haitian government asked Reser to remain in charge at Pont Beudet, in a civilian capacity having been given an honorable discharge. He returned to the U.S. in 1941 to reenlist and fight another war against, "the insane fascists," as he liked to say. After the surrender of Japan, Reser returned to Haiti and after two years employed as security at the American embassy, and another year managing a coffee plantation, he retired to a two-room *kay pay* on the main road less than a kilometer from Pont Beudet. There he shared his time between escaping the filial attention of four teenage adopted daughters—with him since they were months old—and studying, playing chess and checkers with local peasants, and assisting at *Vodou* rites. He also enjoyed the good cooking of Cécile, whose *lakou* (compound) it was, and who had followed him from Pont Beudet where she had been his cook and housekeeper.

The tales Doc Reser told would have seemed fantastic but for his sincerity, and encompassed experiences ranging from "zombie care" (nursing back to health a persons believing they had been made into a zombie.) to strange prophesies. He preferred his little Cul de Sac home where he spent the mornings-painting *Vodou* designs or sketching his neighbors in charcoal from his little front porch, which faced the road. Afternoons he would hike for exercise and in the evening he would join his four adopted daughters, whom he put through school, and their friends in telling Créole folk tales. Peasants plodding down the dusty road near his tree-shaded front porch always gave him a hearty hello and gifts including coconuts and, once, an immense hunk of purple-blue obsidian—a dark, rocklike glass—from an old woman who said it came from a sea-goddess with instructions to forward. They reminded him too not to forget their Christmas gifts.

Doc always said he was drawn to *Vodou* through his passion for rhythm and the occult. "In 1909 I was attracted to Igorote drums at the Alaska-Yukon Pacific Exposition in Seattle, and heard the same thing again in Sierra Leone and then again in Haiti." Another case of following the drums.

Stanley (Doc) Reser delivered one of the most remarkable speeches ever given to the weekly meeting of Port-au-Prince's International Club of Commerce. Haiti's leading businessmen sat through the address transfixed by the man whom many in the audience considered an odd ball. They soon changed their minds.

Reser began his speech, covered fully by the *Haiti Sun,* by citing what he called misinformation about *Vodou* spread by such august authorities as the dictionary which defined the practice of Vodou as "to conjure or put a spell . . ." It is not strange, he went on, that people should be so misinformed about *Vodou* when their most trusted source of information is so flagrantly misguided. "*Vodou* is a religion," he declared, defining any religion as a "belief binding the spiritual nature of man to a supernatural being involving a spirit of independence and responsibility together with the practices which flow from such a belief." He claimed that *Vodou* conformed to every point of the above definition.

Drawing on his self-education in such esoterica, the ex-pharmacist's mate recited a passage from Homer's *Odyssey* which described the sacrifice and libations to the dead; in this he found "the prehistoric and universal roots" of the present Voodoo cult, remarking that its ceremonies were almost identical to their 9000 B.C. Roman counterparts. Reser also compared the rites of Siberian Shamanism and East Indian religions to his Haitian protégé *Vodou*.

The contemporary form of the Haitian religion, he told his engrossed audience, sprang from Africa where it still is practiced: the various tribes brought their beliefs with them which have now developed into two main forms, Rada and Petro, with ancillary Congo, Ibo and Mondongue congregations.

Doc's interest in *Vodou* had begun while he was studying religion and paranormal psychology even before he arrived in Haiti: an old woman at his first *Vodou* ceremony had told him what his wife and children were doing in the U.S. and described the house they were living in. Reser had not seen the house but, after checking with his wife, verified the mambo's description in every detail. She also forecast his departure from Port-de-Paix to the "Big Government" (based in Port-au-Prince) for which he was destined to do a great work for humanity for many years. Doc was subsequently transferred from the occupation force to care for hundreds of the mentally ill.

As far as I am concerned no *Lougawou, (werewolve) baka* (mythical creature part animal, part human.) or other nocturnal spirits paid me a visit at Fifth avenue, Bolosse, but Gary Davis, Citizen of the World, did. As a GI at the end of the War in Europe in 1945, Davis, the son of the famous orchestra leader Miles Davis, had publicly ripped up his U.S. passport and declared himself "Citizen of the World." He and his charming young wife arrived for a stay at my abode recommended by Mary Johnson, a fine journalist who was then writing for the *Haiti Sun* and stringing for *Time Magazine*. After a short time I moved out and left the Davises the house, from which Gary sent out his communiqués, with news of the Davises as well as his idealistic policies, to his friends and sympathizers worldwide. He learned to haggle over prices with my *pratik* and in his newsletters to his followers, bragged about the cheapness of living in Haiti with avocados at a few cents apiece.

And there were the predictable contretemps. Even though I realized that my printer, Franck Magloire, would not take lightly to any note in the *Haiti Sun* that was less than praiseworthy of his person, I published an item in a September 1951 issue reporting that honor was still a tradition among Haitian gentlemen. "Thursday morning at eleven," the story read, "Mr. Franck Magloire, director of *Le Matin*, paid a visit to the *La Démocracie* [competing newspaper] office on the Avenue Marie Jeanne in the Exposition. [Three doors from the *Sun*] The director of *Le Matin* confronted Mr. Hubert Carré, *La Démocracie* director, and demanded an explanation of an article that had appeared the previous evening in *La Démocracie*. It was to do with a controversy over tourism.

"Mr. Magloire seemed to be displeased with Mr. Carré's reply, as he sent the contents of a glass into his face . . . The contents of the glass proved to be beer. Air-conditioning was being installed and all present were enjoying a mid-morning beer. What followed was difficult to see from your reporter's position at the window, and the office was rapidly filled with persons from neighboring offices, but Mr. Carré seated at his desk, threw the nearest object at hand, a paper clip. On standing up a gun slipped to the ground via his trousers leg. Both men appeared to have been armed. Both men were prevented from coming to close quarters by those present and it ended with the director of *Le Matin* delivering a fierce speech and striding from the office with a torn shirt. No blood was shed."

In a letter to me dated May 24, 1951, Frank Magloire asserted that "we have, for several months, printed your paper without any benefit on our part; on the contrary, it was in our financial disadvantage." The printing costs were indeed incredibly cheap, but to me that $49.00 for each printing of 14 pages was a lot in those days. (And there was no doubt that Magloire made at least some profit. While I reimbursed *Le Matin* for newsprint (purchased at a grocery store) paper, ink, electric power and leaden type, the linotype operator and other workers were paid directly by me. (I did the makeup of the paper and proof reading.) Magloire stipulated in his correspondence that henceforth the printing costs had to be paid in advance, "in cash each Friday morning at the commencement of the workday." Moreover the hours that I could use the print shop were narrowed. But Magloire's letters always ended in a stated spirit of mutual cooperation and reassurance that the printing of the *Sun* "will be harmoniously accomplished." However, it was a long way from reality. Magloire also owned a radio station, MBC, and a tourist agency. I sometimes helped him out doing a spot on the radio and driving a group of tourists around town. His main interest however was politics and having "his" president in the palace, which paid him dividends in government advertisements and extremely generous handouts. Like the other publishers he was often sent on all-expense paid diplomatic missions. The publisher of *Le Nouvelliste*, Henri Chauvet, was Haiti's ambassador to the United Nations.

Just when I was figuratively bathing in printer's ink and looking forward to a tasty mango season, the Cold War blew into town in the form of two FBI agents. It was the era of Senator Joseph McCarthy and I hoped he was no relation to my maternal grandmother, a McCarthy who had left County Cork in the last century. Lieut. Lucien Scott, chief of Haitian immigration police, came to my office. I had long since obtained my *Permis de Séjour* (residence permit) and the right to work in Haiti and I paid my taxes so I had no fear of being forced again to leave.

Accompanying Lieutenant Scott were two burly men in dark serge suits, sweating and uncomfortable in the torrid heat. They introduced themselves as agents of the U.S. Federal Bureau of Investigation. Haiti was still under the watchful eye of the FBI office in San Juan, Puerto Rico. The CIA hadn't arrived on the scene as yet.

At first I thought I was the object of their visit. Ironically some well-traveled members of the bourgeoisie had suggested that I was a FBI agent.

"We have a list of persons who may be Communists or communist sympathizers," one of the agents said as the other produced a paper containing a list of names. In my family, telling tales on a person was a sin. Moreover, as a newsman I felt I didn't have to do the agent's dirty work. Instinctively I wanted to tell them to go to hell, but at the same time I was curious and wanted to know whether I or any of my friends was on their list.

As the agent read the list of names, mostly expatriate Americans living in Haiti and only one Haitian, who spent most of his time in their midst, it became clear to me who had compiled the list: an author whose poetry I had published. She had made no bones, to me in the past, of being at odds with many of her fellow Americans. Nobody on the list was even slightly ideological. Fortunately my name was not on the list possibly because I had always been kind to the aspiring poetess and her husband's company was an important advertiser.

Satisfied that their list of suspected Reds was nothing but a groundless denunciation, the agents looked at each other and then posed what was obviously a delicate question for these macho G-men. They had the name of a member of the U.S. embassy who had been denounced as a homosexual. I laughed I knew the man was happily married with children. Did I know any members of the U.S. embassy staff that might be homosexual? Answering no, I couldn't believe what I was hearing. They appeared even more embarrassed. As they were leaving, I controlled my anger, and suggested they might remove their jackets and suspenders and put on a flowery shirt and take a seat at the nearby popular Bar Italy that was frequented by the embassy staff and served excellent ice-cream and the best espresso coffee in town . . . "You might be approached, I said, "As the old seaman's term goes, 'It takes one to know one.' They were not amused. Later that day I saw them both seated at the outdoors Bar Italia, facing the sea next to the Foreign Ministry. They were still dressed as FBI agents.

The tourists flocked to Haiti. Mrs. Fritz (Huguette) Mevs serving at her jewelry store part of their tourist center, in the former exclusive Bellevue Club in Turgeau. The Mevs's slogan was, "buy direct from our factory".

Popular French film star Martine Carroll tourist shopping in Port-au-Prince. The beautiful French actress attracted crowds in Port-au-Prince's downtown shopping district.

Famous Hollywood movie producer David O'Selznick visiting Haiti with actress wife Jennifer Jones. Seen here at El Rancho with Albert Silvera, O'Selznick was so taken with the murals by Roland Dorcely at the El Rancho that he invited Dorcely to California to decorate his home.

Frequent tourist, actress Gloria Mosolino, helped the *Sun* advertise Rheingold Beer, by posing with a beer by the Grand Hotel Oloffson's pool. Importer Nadhim Al-Khal was thrilled with the publicity. Gloria later married author James Jones (From here to Eternity) at a ceremony performed at the Oloffson. The beer was later discontinued, but Gloria was known as Miss Rheingold.

Dancer Leon Destiné, next to publicist Gérard DeCatalogne, showing American film actress, Anne Frances, star of the film Lydia Bailey, how to dance the meringue at El Rancho. The film was shot on location at Cap Haitien and the Citadelle.

Sheelagh O'Malley at an evening *vernissage* at the Centre d'Art. Mrs. O'Malley, along with her son John and mother, Mrs. Kennedy, adopted Haiti, and they became patrons of Haitian art. Sheelagh later married Vinton Burns, the Jamaican-born Oxford educated tree expert.

Journalist Aubelin Jolicoeur welcoming writer James Michener at Bowen Field on his first visit to Haiti. Michener author of "*Tales of the South Pacific*", was a young naval officer based on the South Pacific island of Vanuatu. Jolicoeur a frequent dancer at the Oloffson many years later.

Delta Airlines opens service to Haiti in December 1952. The airline's agent in Haiti, Joseph Nadal, at left, informing the media of the service to Ciudad Trujillo, San Juan and Havana and New Orleans. Robert Nadal wearing glasses next to Delta's American manage Robert L. Webb. At the far left is Tourism representative Guy Laraque.

Lieut. Franck Laraque, jumping his horse at the Army's Centre d'Equitation. Along with Lieut. Philippe (Fito) Dominique, Laraque had benefited from training at the famous French cavalry school at Saumur. Horsemanship was a part of the curriculum of the cadets. One of the last buggies in the capital.

Folky U.S. Ambassador Roy Tasco Davis giving a granddaughter a ride on a donkey at the embassy residence. There was no political significance in having the Democratic emblem on the grounds of the U.S. ambassador's residence. There were no elephant available, he explained.

Magloire St.Aude, a remarkable poet with habitual pipe and briefcase on a visit to *Haiti Sun*.

Bernier St. Jean the *Haiti Sun* distributor, circulation, subscription and advertising manager who in later years traded his bicycle for a motorcycle. He was also a trusted friend of the publisher.

The role of godparents carried with it enormous responsibilities at least it did in the 1950's.

Florida contractor Clarence Moody at Cabane Choucounne with friends. Moody is in white suit and on his left is André Théard. Moody whose company also worked in Cuba re-built Cap-Haïtien and sections of the route to the north.

Representative Haitians
Fernand Pierre, painter of the 'Visitation' in the Cathedral, at work on a
box. Milo and Odette Mennesson-Rigaud, authorities on *vaudou*, in their
Pétion-Ville garden. Doc Reser of Pont Beudet and Bernard Diederich of
the *Haiti Sun* have contributed enough to the Republic to be considered
Haitians by adoption.

A page from *Haiti: The Black Republic* published in 1954 by Selden Rodman
and published by Devin-Adair, New York.

CHAPTER 4

A Gun-Packing Abrazo

Carnival 1951 had ended and bleary-eyed celebrants were savoring their *"mal makak,"* the year's worst hangover and facing the Lenten season of denial. Songwriter Irving Berlin was in town (he returned again in January 1955 for two weeks) as was Bill Forbis, *Time* Magazine's Caribbean bureau chief based in Panama. Then an unexpected happening occurred. The director of the government information bureau issued me an invitation that I could hardly refuse. "You are invited on a trip tomorrow morning. Wear a suit and tie. You'll be picked up at 2 a.m." There was no sleep that Sunday night and none of my local journalistic colleagues, who were also invited, knew where we were going or why. It was supposedly a well-kept secret in a country where secrets are rarely well kept. The director of information arrived precisely on time to pick me up at Odette Wiener's Majestic Hotel in Pétion-ville (now the Kinam Hotel) where I had rented a room. It was Monday, February 19th, 1951.

At the National Palace we joined a motorcade led by the President, Col. Paul E. Magloire, then bumped out to the Cul de Sac plain and over the mountains to the Dominican border. By now the purpose of our mysterious trip had been revealed to us newsmen. For the first time in fourteen years, the chiefs of state of the two neighboring republics sharing the island of Hispaniola were to meet. Haitian Minister Luc Fouché informed the press that Generalissimo Rafael Leonidas Trujillo Molina, a man of many titles, President and supreme chief of the Dominican Republic, had extended the invitation, only the day before and Haiti's President Magloire had accepted. For all the supposed secrecy clairvoyant peasants had obviously taken days to construct their roadside arches of branches and flowers, to greet Colonel Magloire as he passed en route to the meeting. Some had hoisted their precious belongings, including an occasional bed sheet, to salute the dusty motorcade. A Port-au-Prince catering service had prepared the official reception in the Haitian border town of Belladère. Crates of champagne had been carefully transported to the meeting site along with the Haitian president's favorite scotch whiskey. Negotiating the protocol of the delicate encounter, which was officially aimed at displaying friendship and brotherhood between the two republics, not two days but at least two months.

As we neared the border I recall feeling increasing excitement, as if I were about to see a rare and dangerous animal. In fact we were to meet the notorious dictator nicknamed "the Jackal of the Caribbean", but much more ferocious than a jackal. Rafael Trujillo Molina, who had ruled the Dominican Republic for nearly two decades, was a cold-blooded tyrant whose long arm reached his enemies both at home and abroad. There was no comparing Colonel Magloire who was only a benevolent strongman.

Trujillo had earned notoriety as author of a 1937 genocide perpetrated against poor Haitians, mostly migrant sugarcane-cutters, caught on the Dominican side of the border. More than 20,000 Haitians had been savagely slaughtered on Trujillo's orders; many hacked to death with machetes. He eventually admitted his Spanish-speaking country's guilt and paid a pittance in restitution, (approximately $30 dollars a head) most of which never reached the wounded survivors of that racist nightmare.

Trujillo was absolute master of his part of the island. Aides and sycophants referred to him as *El Jefe* (The Boss) while he styled himself, on statues and plaques, as *Benefactor of the Fatherland*. In pages of the *Haiti Sun* we often called him simply, "Benny the Factor".

The historic meeting was to be shared by two border towns. Ironically Belladère was the small village that Haiti's ex-President Estimé had rebuilt as a model border town at a cost of 600,000 dollars. Mean-spirited Trujillo hated Estimé and turned Belladère into a model of stagnation by steering what little Dominican border traffic there was to other crossings.

"Please give me your guns," our escort said apologetically. "No guns are permitted at the meeting." Two publishers produced their revolvers and I shook my head. "I don't own a gun."

After a presidential breakfast of bacon, eggs, and wine for Magloire's party at Belladère's Club Hotel our motorcade proceeded to the border gates of the Dominican town of Elias Piña where Trujillo and his delegation were awaiting. The first of a series of 21-gun salutes boomed out. Both sides stood at attention stony-faced as the Dominican palace band played renditions of both national anthems.

Trujillo looked anything but a murderous tyrant. Attired in a well-tailored conservative, dark-blue suit, with polka-dot tie and gray homburg, he appeared more like a highly successful business executive. There *was* the slight expression of a cynic. He stood, starch-stiff and seemingly cool in the morning heat very much in command. I was close enough to see that while he stood ramrod—erect his brown eyes took in everything. He seemed taller than his actual height of five feet, eight inches, and I was later told that his shoes had specially built elevator heels. Magloire in contrast appeared flamboyant in a natty light tropical suit with a colorful floral tie, and flashing a slight grin. Trujillo brought to mind a Haitian Créole proverb that warns: *"Jan chat mache, se pa konsa li kenbe rat."* ("How a cat walks is not the way he catches a rat.")

The formalities began in the small Roman Catholic Church in Elias Piña with the celebration of a Te Deum mass—both countries and their leaders were officially Catholic.

If anyone prayed during the Te Deum it was surely Haiti's foreign minister, Jacques N. Léger, who like many of the Haitian officials present detested Trujillo and needed God's strength to fulfill their duties during the day of high cynicism and hypocrisy.

In a tiny room on the second story of the *Casa Presidencial* in Elias Piña, Magloire and Trujillo sat down at the same heavy mahogany desk and signed their 375-word agreement. Hovering over Trujillo was the bulky uniformed figure of Brig. Gen. Anselmo A. Paulino Alvarez, the dictator's specialist on Haiti and then publisher of Trujillo's *El Caribe* newspaper. A huge and intimidating man with pitch dark glasses, Paulino's presence lent an evil air to the proceedings. Trujillo declined Paulino's pen and borrowed one from his ambassador to Haiti.

Even for an amateur dictator-watcher, it didn't take any great mind to fathom that this was a not a day to try to corral the powerful dictator and pepper him with questions. He had long ago domesticated his own media and considered the foreign press hostile and dangerous as enemies of his fiefdom. The few foreign correspondents and stringers on hand were wedged along the stairway outside the signing room ready to pounce. Quietly I detached myself from the pack before Trujillo descended the stairs and assumed my title of publisher. As he came down the stairs *El Jefe's* bodyguards squeezed the correspondents against the wall. With difficulty they sought to raise their arms to get his attention, but their shouts were lost in the hubbub. As they endeavored to follow in Trujillo's wake, Dominican agents politely but firmly directed them to a side room and out a back door. In a huff most of them departed for Port-au-Prince to file their stories.

The signing was repeated that afternoon in Belladère on the Haitian side. The document was couched in the usual diplomatic language. It stipulated that both countries "would present a single united front in the face of the exceptional situation provoked by the aggressive policies of international communism." As both Trujillo and Magloire classified most if not all their enemies as communists, the document was in effect a blanket defense pact with each side promising not to harbor the other's enemies.

The second article was "to regulate the migratory movements of Haitians and Dominican nationals in the territory of their respective nations." This meant that Trujillo needed Haitian workers for his sugar empire but he also didn't want them to remain and take root in his country after cutting his sugar cane. *El Benefactor* had long since officially declared his country white. (Even though an unmentionable truth was that Trujillo had a black Haitian great-grandmother.)*

---

*   Trujillo's great-grandmother on his maternal side, Diyetta Chevalier, a Haitian woman arrived in the Dominican side during the Haitian occupation (1820-48) and gave birth to an illegitimate daughter with a Haitian army officer. Luisa Ercina Chevalier born of those Haitian parents was Trujillo's grandmother. Luisa was said to be an extremely bright woman who married a not so bright Pedro Molina a relatively poor man from the countryside.

President Paul Magloire in a peace *abrazo* that became famous. Magloire all
smiles as his left hand finds the butt of Generalissmo Rafael Trujillo's revolver.
The peace meeting was held on the border in Feb.1951. The Dominicans later
suggested that Magloire's walking stick was in fact a gun. It was not.

Trujillo was one of the most dangerous men alive, and he fascinated me. German E.
Ornes, editor of *El Caribe* who was present at the border encounter, went into exile four
years later because of a simple typo in the newspaper. The morning daily had printed a
picture of young girls placing flowers at the base of one of the hundreds of busts of Trujillo
festooning his fiefdom. The caption under the photograph read erroneously that the girls
were placing the blossoms on the benefactor's "tomb." Trujillo was extremely sensitive about

his longevity and the typo could have cost German Ornes his life, but he was fortuitously already en route to the U.S with his wife when the "*tumba*" typo was discovered.

Toasts, during the border meeting to the newly discovered friendship made for heavy consummation of champagne.

The day ended in Belladère with Trujillo showing off his macho dancing style to a spirited Dominican merengue played by Haiti's *Jazz Atomic* orchestra. He chose Mrs. Bayard, the Haitian lady who had catered lunch, to dance. I chose one of the daughters of the Elias Piñas army commander with whom I had been talking to dance. It was the first and last time I shared the dance floor with Trujillo. He showed off his knowledge of Créole joking with his Haitian hosts most of who spoke Spanish.

British author Graham Greene has written that the Latin *abrazo* originated not only as ode of greeting but also as a safety measure. The full embrace of the *abrazo* permitted each person to pin down the arms of the other thus keeping him from drawing his pistol or knife. Trujillo and Magloire inadvertently demonstrated this practical rationale behind the abrazo at their peace fest. A photograph of the two embracing showed Magloire with a look of surprise as one of his hands came in contact with the butt of Trujillo's pistol. Trujillo's beautifully embossed holster, sidearm at the ready, was exposed at he stretched forward in the *abrazo*. (The Haitian photographer who had taken the picture worked for the Government and also furnished photos to the *Sun*.) The Magloire government didn't wish to know about this historic photograph which made the pages of *LIFE* Magazine. Learning of the existence of the photo, Jose Enrique Aybar, Trujillo's ambassador to Port-au-Prince on a visit to the *Haiti Sun* to view the photo declared; "See the walking stick in President Magloire's other hand? Well, it's a gun." He sat back with a satisfied smile. So much for the reunion celebrating peace and friendship.

—

Leaving my *kay* to World Citizen Davis and his young wife I had earlier moved along the mountainside to the Grand Hotel Oloffson. The atmosphere there was pure Somerset Maugham. I was welcomed by a hairy spider which—because tarantulas are not protected by *Vodou*—I evicted from my Oloffson bungalow with the help of a clothes hanger. There was a sharp, overriding odor, which I learned, was from gluttonous termites feasting on the ancient structure.

Dinner that first night at the Oloffson was caiman soup. "It tastes like chicken," the old waiter went around repeating to each of the few guests as he labeled out the mysterious liquid from a battered old silver urn. I didn't wait for the main course. Maurice de Young who ran the hotel was Haiti's undisputed White Hunter and had returned that afternoon from Lake Saumatre with a group of tourist-hunters after bagging a single caiman. A member of the alligator family, the caiman shared the lake bordering the Dominican Republic with small fish and migrating ducks. Designed to give full satisfaction, De Young drove his guests in circles around the Cul de Sac plain and made camp among the *bayawonn*. The hunters received their badges of courage, scores of mosquito bites. Eventually the hunters were ferried onto the lake in charcoal boats by peasants who knew the hiding places of the caiman. Nose to tail they usually measure no more than six feet.

Only at the Oloffson during the De Young days was the Haitian cuisine more exotic than eatable. Haiti boasted one of the finest cuisines in the Caribbean. It was then possible to purchase from street vendors excellent pastries prepared by French chef de Vandegeis of Aux Delices.

In his 16 years in Haiti de Young became somewhat of a legend with his off-the-beaten-track exploits as a hunter of caiman, bird watcher, coffee planter, and airline operator and hotel manager. (He finally left Haiti in April 1954 for New York where he was hired as a salesman by International Latex Corp and sent to Dallas, Texas. His pregnant wife left with the hotel, hired a very able manager, Count Victor de Kiserling, who had all the graces of an Old World European hotelier. Mrs. de Young eventually went and joined her husband in Dallas.

In 1887 Demosthenes Simon Sam, son of Haiti's then President Tiresias Simon Sam, had the remarkable gingerbread villa built in Bois Peu de Chose, a suburb of Port-au-Prince. Part of a hillside had to be blasted away to make way for the elegant new mansion with turrets, cornices, and wooden latticwork. From its rooms and long balcony, the villa offered a spectacular view of the capital and its turquoise bay beyond.

The sprawling mansion survived fire and revolutions, but what was more remarkable at the time, it was not torn to pieces by incensed mobs in July 1915. President Vilbrun Guilaume Sam, faced with an uprising, ordered 169 citizens seized and imprisoned as hostages in the National Penitentiary on the Rue du Centre. The prisoners were in the majority members of upper-class Haitian society and mostly mulattos. There is some question as to who gave the order to kill the prisoners, President Sam or his dreaded police Chief Charles-Oscar Etienne. Charles-Oscar whose name lives on in infamy was however present when the jailers began to shoot and hack the political prisoners to death.*

A man who had lost three of his sons in the massacre sought out Charles-Oscar, who had taken refuge in the Dominican legation and shot him dead with three bullets, one for each of his murdered sons. It was no ordinary mob that dragged President Sam out of the French legation. The mob was led by members of the grieving families who invaded the French legation where he had taken refuge and dragged him out from under a bed and into the street. He was already dead when he reached the street.

---

*   Writer Stephen Alexis, a friend, who wrote among other books, *Le Nègre Masqué* (1933), a novel on the occupation and color prejudice told me what he recalled of that bloody July morning in the penitentiary. It was scene not easily erased from the memory. I recalled during my own incarceration the terrible scene he painted of the cell wall covered in blood, entrails and brains of the men and youth of well known families butchered by the jailers. Alexis had miraculously survived through the friendship of a jailer.

It was the era of U.S. gunboat diplomacy, and Haiti's political turmoil was the justification Washington needed to land the Marine and end its fear of German influence in the country. The Sam villa was taken over by the U.S. Marine Corps as a hospital during the occupation [1915-34]. The Marines added a ten-room maternity ward for wives of the Marine. While a lot of children were born there many more were conceived there in the post-occupation period.

When, in 1934, at the conclusion of the occupation, one of the city's largest import firms, Oloffson, Lucas and Company, went bankrupt. Mr. Oloffson's strong-willed Haitian wife rescued the family by going into the hotel business. Leasing the now—vacated stately villa the lady launched the Grand Hotel Oloffson on its path to fame and notoriety.

After a month I surrendered my Grand Hotel Oloffson bungalow to the termites and spiders. One of the most endearing subsequent locales in which I stayed, before settling in a home in Mont Joli, an old city neighborhood, was a third story garret of the Hotel Central on Avenue John Brown. Operated by two elderly spinsters from Jeremie, Lilliane and Lolouse Clérié, Hotel Central was filled with old world charm. The women served delicious Haitian dishes and whenever possible I would return to the hotel for lunch. Many of my fellow boarders were dignified provincial members of the Haitian Legislature. The deputies all wore white starched suits while senators of the Republic wore dark serge suits. (The beautiful old Hotel Central was later destroyed to make way for a vulgar gasoline station.)

Volume 11 Port-au-Prince, Haiti, Sunday July 27th 1952 No.44

Sylvio Cator: The Immortal Torch-Bearer

Haiti lost its greatest hero in the World of Sports last week—and Haitian Youth one of its greatest inspirations. Death came to Sylvio Cator just two days after the symbolic Olympic Torch was borne triumphantly into the arena of the Magloire Stadium, inaugurating a new era in the athletic history of Our Republic.

It was Sylvio Cator who brought this sacred emblem of sportsmanship within reach of the current generation of young Haitians. They grew to manhood proudly aware that just 24 years ago Olympic history was made by one of their fellow countrymen. There hardly is a sporting boy in Haiti who has not heard of that day in Amsterdam when Sylvio Cator set a new world's record in the broad jump before thousands of wildly cheering Olympic fans. The news of his fabulous 7 meter 80 jump (over 25 and one-half feet) spread like wildfire through the Sports World, bringing the name of our Republic to the attention of millions of people who had never before noticed it outside the pages of an Atlas.

Earlier this month, the *Haiti Sun* quoted an article written by Avery Brundage, the head of the U.S. Olympic Association, naming Sylvio Cator as one of the figures in all-time Olympic Hall of Fame—a great tribute coming nearly a quarter of a century after his classic performance.

But Sylvio took such tributes in stride. His triumphs to him were triumphs for Haiti. And he used his fame chiefly in the cultivation of new friends for his homeland. He was the pioneer of Haiti's tourist industry. He opened Haiti's first tourist office as a representative of Thomas Cook and for years served as the Prince of Hospitality to distinguished visitors to Port-au-Prince, gladly paying for entertainment out of his own pocket.

The son of a Haitian General, Sylvio Cator was a patriot from the time he first saw the light of day in the little village of Cavaillon. He spent his boyhood in Aux Cayes and then traveled to Jamaica to receive an English education that thoroughly intermingled classics and sports.

He lived for the hours he spent on the football field and in athletic arena where he pitted his Herculean strength against the leading track stars of the West Indies. It was soon evident that the little Nation of Haiti had produced a phenomenon in the field of sport. But even Sylvio hardly dreamed of climaxing his career by the Haitian flag on the mast of Olympic champions.

When he returned to his homeland after his 1928 triumph it was to serve as a guide and inspiration to a new generation of young sportsmen. What he had done, perhaps one of them could also do. Sylvio's popularity and friendliness, however, extended through the ranks of the young and old alike, as well as the rich and the poor.

In 1950, he was elected Deputy to the Haitian Legislature from Aquin and as in everything else, served his government with loyalty and devotion. He kept up his role as host to foreign visitors, planning to provide a hospitable welcome to the U.S. contractors that are to arrive in Haiti next week to carry out the construction of the new Worker's City.

But the Prince of Hospitality was forced to give up the role that he enjoyed so much. Death intervened, striking with a suddenness that left the entire country stunned with surprise and sorrow. Monday morning Sylvio was paying his habitual visit to the Petit Four Barber Shop when he became ill, complained about a swelling in his throat. Dr. Manes Liautaud had him taken to the General Hospital where he was given oxygen, but to no avail. In a few minutes time, the star of Haiti's Athletic World bid farewell to his homeland. His grief-stricken country, in gratitude for Sylvio's achievements and devotion, repaid him with one final honor—a State Funeral.

Tuesday afternoon at 2 p.m. the body of the lawmaker and Olympic Hero was laid in State in the *Palais Legislatif* on a catafalque guarded by six officers of the Haitian Army with sabers drawn. A Battalion of soldiers with drums and bugles formed before the building.

At 3:30 p.m., the body was taken from its resting place and the solemn march to the Notre Dame Cathedral began to the dirge played by the Palace Band. The President of the Republic was among the distinguished column of mourners as well as members of his Cabinet, with top hats in hand. The coffin was carried by Officers of the Haitian Army with members of the Senate and Chamber of Deputies holding the *cordons du poele*. From the Cathedral the body of the Haitian Hero made its last trip through the streets of Port-au-Prince as thousands of sorrowful onlookers stood by the roadside with bowed heads and tearful eyes. The bright jerseys of the football teams made vivid splashes of color in the long column of mourners . . . but jerseys were the type of youth costumes that Sylvio loved the best. Among the sports delegation was the visiting Jamaican team and a number of old friends from the neighboring isle that Sylvio had known since his days as St. George's College. Most of the Haitian Capital's leading merchants also accompanied the caravan on its long trip to the Cemetery. Even the street vagabonds that Sylvio had befriended put on clean shirts and walked with unaccustomed dignity through the streets as the Canons of the Fort National boomed their five minute salutes.

Sylvio's aged father—General Milien Cator, his brother George and his sister Madame Roche gathered at the graveside as the noted hero was laid to rest. Short Eulogies were made by Minister of the Interior Paracelse Pélissier, Deputy H. Bright, Senator W. Sansaricq, M. André Chevallier, Raoul Coicou and Aquin Commissioner J. Emmanuel Théart.

But no words could do more than echo the pang in the hearts of the people of Haiti who has lost not only a hero but also a friend. This editor was among those who mourned the passing of a great friend and teacher.

CHAPTER 5

The Golden Age

"It seemed almost a pity to turn a legend into a fact with documentary pictures. But in this case the *Haiti Sun* finds the fact almost as fantastic as the legend. A monster did exist in the Bois de Chêne and we offer the skeptics photos to prove it. Haiti's peaceful "golden age" was not without its monsters.

On the *Sun's* front page the report read: "Caiman's career in Bois de Chêne ended with Police bullet." Appearing in the June 15, 1952 edition, it recorded a historic chapter in the life of the Capital city.

"The alligator was forcibly evicted from his home in the culvert under Boulevard Harry S. Truman by a well aimed bullet through the eye, a bullet fired by Lieut. Jean-René Boucicaut of the Port-au-Prince police department. The crack shot ended the career of the Caiman but it did not solve the mystery of its presence under one of the most traveled thoroughfares of Port-au-Prince.

"*Le Nouvelliste* suggests the possibility that the reptile was thrown into the canal by an American. It is true American children sometimes have baby alligators as pets, when they are about the size of the green lizards and larger mabouyas. But it is hard to see how an alligator could grow to the robust size of the Bois de Chêne specimen in a canal that normally has only a trickle of water that empties into the sea. And during the rainy season flash flood takes all before it into the ocean, mainly valuable top soil.

"Webster's dictionary describes the caiman as a member of the crocodile family that lives in fresh water. But evidently this alligator was determined to acclimate itself to its strange surroundings. At any rate it served as a good source of amusement and amazement during its tenure.

"Shortly after the close of the Port-au-Prince Bicentennial World's Fair reports began to circulate of a monster sighting. Almost every Port-au-Princien, at one time or other, joined afternoon crowds on the bank of the canal to catch a glimpse of the monster.

"The shout of "*Caïman! Caïman!*" was enough to send people running back and forth across the busy boulevard for a sighting. Sometimes its ugly snout was visible at the opening of a culvert. When a ten-year old boy drowned while playing in the canal after a heavy rain, rumors spread that he had been eaten by the monster. When his body was found the caiman was exonerated.

"Late Tuesday Colonel Marcaisse Prosper decided it was time to get rid of the highly unpleasant creature who made itself comfortably at home in one of the loveliest sections of the city. The Chief of Police (1946-56) accompanied by two lieutenants dropped down at 1 p.m. to pay a call on the caiman who seemed to enjoy the noon day sun. As Lieutenant Jean-René Boucicaut's bullet struck the alligator in the right eye the giant reptile did a back flip dive into the water, thrashing its powerful tail. Lieut. John Beauvoir sprayed the area for good measure with his Thompson submachine gun. But the alligator's days were over. Its limp body was hauled from the water under the gaze of hundreds of eager onlookers and taken to be placed on ice at Brasserie de la Couronne (Coca Cola bottler) to await taxidermist High Whiteman.

"Is it the end of the legend of Bois de Chêne? No. But the sport of monster-watching refused to die. This week the canal bank habitués are peering into the murky waters again. This time they claim they have spotted an even bigger caiman". (The yellowing pages of the Haiti Sun today reveal proof of the monster's size, a paltry five foot from tail to snout.)

The caiman led the *Sun* to discover the city had a taxidermist. Hugh Whiteman was a natural for the "Personality of the Week". "The taxidermist who was to prepare the caiman of Bois de Chêne for posterity we found to be a quiet 47 year old specialist in preserving all kinds of birds and *bêtes*. He lived with his robust wife Lucie "in a small two-room *Kay*, a little house behind a house and yet another house facing the Holy Trinity Cathedral. When we finally found the taxidermist his son Luc was putting durable insides into a dead turtle and stuffing a little green, red breasted humming bird. Whiteman described how he had launched his little business in 1936 after an 18 month correspondence course with the Northwest School of Taxidermy in Omaha, Nebraska. He complained that customers were often far apart, and he stuffed a bird or fish for $5, and the work took at least two weeks. His dream was to move out of the family backyard "cour" squashed behind houses and move into a house facing the street not the rear of another house.

———

The 16-pages of the *Sun,* that June, 1952 Sunday, were filled with high drama. Minister of the Presidency, Mauclair Zéphirin, had actually touched on Communism during a rare press conference. The touch of Red, however, did not taint the golden glow of tourism. It was towards the end of his conference that the suave Capois declared that he had received a number of reports that Haitian students studying in France on scholarships had been 'inoculated with Communist ideology during their stay abroad.'"

(The *Sun* covered Mr. Zéphirin's conference, but was careful not to enquire about the medical term on infusing students with Communism.) The *Sun's* report: "*Le Nouvelliste* recently published reports from its Paris correspondent on the subject and the paper's representative at the press conference asked the Minister what measures the Government was planning to meet the problem.

"Minister Zéphirin told members of the press that the government is "*au courant*" on Red activities and finds strong indication that there is an organized movement aimed at launching Communist action in our country."

"He cited the case of René Dépestre, a student who was detained in Cuba on his way home to Haiti. It seems that the youth, he said, had received special training as a Red "shock trooper" and was coming to Haiti to organize Communist cells.

"The Minister declared that Haiti must guard against an influx of Reds now that they no longer feel safe in Cuba under the regime of President Batista. He warned that they might pick Haiti as their rallying point. He cited the case of a bookseller at Cap Haïtien who had recently been spreading Communist propaganda in books and pamphlets. The books had been seized.

"The Minister reported that the Government has also been *au courant* of the fact that the bookseller of foreign nationality established, "*sur la place*" also has been spreading Red literature.

"As to the students studying in France, Zéphirin said, he believed those who became imbued with Red teachings did not realize the danger of Communist ideology on the political level and were approaching the matter on a purely intellectual plane. He expressed the opinion that the Communist menace might be thwarted by limiting the number of scholarships to France to study. He pointed out that those who attended American universities and colleges were not faced with this problem.

At the bottom of Zéphirin's charges were 28 book titles that had been declared banned as Communist literature. Those cited by the government were books by Karl Marx, Lenin, Stalin and Jacques Duclos. These books, the government charged, had been seized at the Minerve bookstore. The government also claimed to have seized pornographic books and post cards in its raids on the establishments. Lawyer Martial Coulanges later (June 27) declared in a letter to *Le Nouvelliste* that there was not a single piece of Communist literature among the books withdrawn from the public showcase by government action.

Haitian painter Max Pinchinat studying in Paris had written to *Le Matin* protesting an article in *Le Nouvelliste*. Reproduced in the *Sun* Pinchinat stated: "I was dumbfounded to read in *Le Nouvelliste*," he wrote, "that Haitian students and scholarship holders in the French capital have allowed themselves to be tainted with certain subversive ideology." The artist charged that *Le Nouvelliste* correspondent cited three cases of students with Red leanings to back up his story . . . and remarked that judging a thousand persons on the action of three can only be "an absurdity."

"Upon his own investigation, Pinchinat said he learned that only one Haitian— Franck Lizaire—was on the list of foreigners who had been expelled by the French police for their membership in the Communist Party. The cases of René Dépestre and Roger Gaillard are still pending. Artist Pinchinat asked the correspondent of *Le Nouvelliste* if he believed himself a better investigator than the French police by attempting to put a red label on the Haitian colony in Paris.

It was a custom for a publisher to shake hands with the president.

Deputy Daniel Fignolé of the MOP who was too populist for president Magloire. The president was angered at *Haiti Sun* for making Fignolé their Personality of the Week.

(Collection Maud Wadestrand)

"Pinchinat points out further that the majority of the Haitian students in the French capital are members of the privileged class, with cultural rather than revolutionary interests. He said they are far too busy with their serious studies to sit at the tables of sidewalk café where subversive ideologies are bruited about."

The Haitian government then expelled the proprietors of the Minerve bookshops; identified as Joseph Zanasco of Italian nationality and Robert Pierrette and Georges Zanasco, French citizens. Case closed.

As a footnote in the *Sun's Beachcomber* column noted that a "typical Russian dinner at the Grand Hotel Oloffson featured 17 different types of "zakuskach" (sic) hors d'oeuvres and the finest home-made Vodka. Fourteen persons dined and Vodka-ed to the wee hours of Sunday morning and the numerous toasts went to the old Czarists and none of the numerous dishes were tainted with Communism."

The United States Embassy had other things to be worried about than "inoculated Reds." The *Sun* reported: "American Ambassador's wine cellar on fire. Champagne corks are a sound often heard at the diplomatic functions held in the beautiful residence of the American ambassador", the *Haiti Sun* noted in its June 22, 1952 edition. "Rarely does the "pop" turn into a virtual bombardment. When the sound of exploding corks greeted Larry Sutton on his return to the residence at 12.30 Sunday morning he wasted no time in heading for the wine cellar to be greeted by a wall of smoke.

"It seemed that internal combustion set off a blaze in the bottle-filled room, a fire that was quickly fed by the straw in which some of the wines were encased. By the time Larry got to the scene, the flames had already buckled the steel mesh that served as partitioning wall and had become too intense for the fire extinguishers to control.

"Larry telephoned an embassy guard (on the Champ de Mars) to notify the Fire station (On the Grand' Rue) and then concentrated on rescuing, Victor the ambassador's three-legged dog, who was locked in another section of the cellar. Once that was accomplished, he climbed into his car and headed for the Petionville road to direct the fire engines to the right driveway. Unfortunately Larry backed his car too far and got stuck in a ditch. However, the fire engines—all four of them—arrived in record time and the *pompiers* formed a bucket brigade that had the flames under control in record time. Thanks to the efficiency of (Fire chief) Captain Georges Elie and his son, Lieut. *Ti Pouce* (Little Thumb) Elie a good part of the wine and liquor stock was saved—relieving the threat of a severe drought at the forthcoming Fourth of July celebration.

"However some 500 dollars worth of champagne and other 'throat tonics' went up in smoke and blistered woodwork caused another estimated 300 dollars in damages. Needless to say, there was plenty of scrubbing and refurbishing in the ambassador's residence . . . but everything will be in order for the big Independence Day *fête*.

"Larry, who is the dispersing officer at the embassy, has been staying in the residence during the absence of Ambassador Howard Travers, now in the States receiving medical treatment."

When the *Sun* was launched in 1950 the U.S. ambassador was William Earl DeCoury (born 1894 in Tenn.) who was then in the U.S. for medical treatment. He served from

1948 to1950. For unknown reasons President Harry Truman left Haiti for most of 1951 without an ambassador. The envoy's duties fell to First secretary John Burns whose title was *chargé d'affaires*. Finally in November of 1951 Ambassador Howard Karl Travers arrived and presented his credentials to President Magloire. Then he fell ill and was hospitalized in Washington D.C. Haiti appeared to be the last post for elderly career U.S. diplomats.

There were also sad tidings to report and the *Sun's* obituaries were not relegated to the back pages but were important enough for the front page. Such was the case of the passing of Dr. Wilhelm Lemke in August of that year. The German physician had come to Haiti 28 years earlier to join his brother Ernest. He loved the mountains that reminded him of his home near the Elbe in East Germany and he had realized a dream of opening a mountain hotel in Furcy called, The Obléon and planted on its spacious grounds 20,000 pine trees. He had hoped some day that his hotel would serve as a convalescent center—with its natural beauty and its wonderful mountain climate but the road leading to the hotel could only be negotiated by jeep and Dr Lemke finally closed its doors.

———

President Paul Eugène Magloire was gaining popularity as a "Bon Papa." A true son of the North the robust officer was born in 1907 in Quartier-Morin in the shadow of King Henri Christophe's famed Citadel. The town on the once rich Plaine du Nord was between Cap Haïtien and Christophe's royal palace at Milot. His father, a farmer, had become a general in the old army that had a surplus of generals, only to be killed in a shooting accident in 1908. Brought up by two older brothers in Cap Haïtien, Paul Eugène Magloire, went on to gain a degree in arts and letters at the Normal school in Port-au-Prince after graduating from Cap Haïtien's Christian Brother's school. Making a career move, he left teaching and entered the gendarmerie established by, and controlled by the U.S. Marine Corps. He graduated as a member of the class of 1931. Handsome and charismatic, he moved upwards, and in 1946, when the military seized power upon the forced departure of President Elie Lescot he was named a member of the three-man Junta. When Estimé was ousted, the Military Junta took control again and this time Magloire made another career move and became president.

In the first edition of the *Sun* 1950 candidate Magloire received four lines and only because he had been received at the compound on the Hasco sugar land by Monestime André, a personal friend of the editor. He was elected to a six year term of office and the constitution barred him from succeeding himself. He was energetic and physically fit.

It was not until Magloire's inauguration December, 1950, that the *Sun* gave the new Papa full coverage. President Magloire was a jovial *Bon Vivant* who liked to party but, at the same time he was a tireless workers who was determined to elevate his country to equal status with other nations on the world stage. He also sought foremost to accelerate the sluggish pace of his country's development.

To gain respect he treated all visiting dignitaries like royalty, offering state banquets, and ball in the palace which was lit up with blue lights making the evening as impressive as any white house.

At one such state banquet his guest, Gen. Hector B. Trujillo Molina, *El Jefe's* brother (April 1952) appeared at a state banquet attired in the most elaborate general's gold crusted formal uniform that hadn't been seen in Haiti since the 19th century. President Magloire, a colonel, wore white tie and tails. Soon after, Magloire had the legislature elevate his rank to general, and he ordered a well tailored formal uniform with gold braid and epaulets. During ceremonies he added to his six foot frame with a plumed hat. Of course neighbor, Generalissimo Rafael Trujillo, had the most elaborate generalissimo's uniform and an abundance of medals and no one but he was permitted to wear a plumed hat in his fiefdom. However Magloire's formal uniform was to place him on equal footing with his guest. In the town and country, women wore dresses made of flour sacks (Pillsbury flour shirts and dresses became popular with tourists) while men wore tough denim shirt and pants.

On Army Day August 1, 1952 (the date was later changed to Nov.18) the commander-in-chief ordered an open air party for his soldiers of the Casernes Dessalines barrack. It was held across from the palace on the lawn before the Kalmar Café operated by Georges Héreaux and wife Gerty. When suddenly a cloud burst, pouring rain down on the officers and soldiers their commander-in-chief, a good soldier, remained at his post and finished his dinner. Nor did he indulge his son and three daughters. Discipline extended to them and their school grades. Politically he was accused of being too kind to mulattos but he insisted that neither blacks nor mulattoes should have the monopoly of power over the other. In fact he continued Estimé policy of bringing blacks into government. Once in the presidency, he had launched an ambitious 40 million dollar five year development plan mainly to boost agricultural production and become self-sufficient in food production.

The keystone of the plan was the building of the Péligre Dam which would control the Artibonite River and turn 80,000 barren acres into fertile farming land, and make the Artibonite the country's bread basket.

—

During a typical day, hundreds of tourists streamed ashore at Columbus Pier from the Ocean Monarch of the Furness line, or the Massdam and the Nieuw Amsterdam— among others cruise ships to be welcomed by a kneeling Christophe Columbus, Haiti's first tourist, a gift from Italy. Tourism had a genuine trickle down effect to the poor and middle-class. It soon appeared to be gaining on coffee as Haiti's major foreign exchange earner, (A promising tourist industry had doubled since 1951) was immediate, as taxi driver and young guides self-educated in the ways of visitors and English-language offered their services. There were also City and mountains tours, with lunch at a hotel and free port shopping with visits to mahogany factories and sisal handicraft makers.

Tourists filled the streets of the Capital and discovered the friendly Iron Market, the closest thing to a Middle-Eastern bazaar. Primitive paintings had yet to blossom onto the streets but a fabulous selection was available at the Centre d'Art. The city was also a liberty port for American sailors. Unlike Cuba and Jamaica, Hotels in Haiti were owned by Haitians, not by foreign enterprises, and the food they served the tourists was locally grown food, lobster and fish—even the chickens were home grown. Orange juice was not imported from Miami. The tourist dollar was shared by many. Enterprising Guy Douyon had taken over the tourism department from poet Jean Brierre and promised to make tourism Haiti's major dollar earner. Douyon stressed Haiti's assets: great weather, fabulous history and unparallel scenery with a peaceful friendly people.

But not all arrivals were tourists. The motorboat Express periodically arrived from Santiago de Cuba with scores of repatriated Haitian cane cutters. Some had lived in Cuba for years cutting cane, and were being shipped back by the Batista government.

—

The Yale Glee Club performed in the National Palace and Xavier Cugat and his band were at the Hotel Roosevelt (later the Hotel Riviera.) But the fiesta to end all popular public shows drew ten thousand to the Magloire Stadium. It included Cuba's Sonora Matancera, two middle weight boxing matches and women wrestling

Thrills and Spills at Stade.

Haiti Sun: Sunday July 26, 1953: "The Sonora Matancera orchestra played in the boxing ring and gave a full measure program of mambos and guarachas and rumbos. The band played with the usual combination of needle-sharp technique and happy exuberance, brought the stadium down with renditions of *Zu zu ba bae, Ma Brune, La Reine* rumba 'when I am with you, you are as sweet as a mango'—the audience loved that one and *Coco mai mai.*

Into the ring clambered torch-singer Celia Cruz, dressed in a tight gold ensemble with matching laced high heels. She couldn't really dance much in those shoes on the canvas, and all of Port-au-Prince's house flies were buzzing under the lights above the mike, but that hardly held her back. She wowed the audience, as per her torrid song styling.

A white clad enthusiast in the north stand stole the show as the rhythm took him and he rocked and shook to the pulsating beat. If this was the band's first appearance in the ring, then they have made a sensational beginning and Celia (see photo with gloves on) was a knockout.

Next in the ring were middle weights Dempsily Kid of the Dominican Republic and the champ of Cap Haïtien who rejoiced in the name of Phébus Cherenfant.

Phéb was the favorite and could have won. He had a punch and was agile at ducking, but his fight education ended there. He signaled his blows before delivering them, did not follow up until the crowd told him to, and learned the hard way from Dempsily how to counter-punch. Dempsily Kid kept his guard high, clinched when tired and threw a whirling bolo punch which did not land too often. But he was the smarter boxer, and at the end of the 8th round was leading on points.

One judge scored the match even; the referee and the other judge gave it to Dempsily. It was a good but not a popular decision to a fair but not wonderful match.

The *grande finale* was the revanche match between Mexico's Yoli Perez and Cuba's Silvia Hernandez, the women wrestlers who met last week. Yoli entered the ring, in her green bathing suit and black boots; Silvia the red-haired Amazon appeared in black with orange boots.

Yoli the aggressor began by giving Silvia a twist on her bad knee, then a throat lock and a full nelson which Silvia slipped out of. Yoli landed on Silvia's face . . . a series of somersaults . . . grasped Silvia by the hair and flattened her for round one.

A romantic half-moon a cloudless sky waited on the second round. Silvia attacked, put her opponent on the mat with an arm-lock, and then jumped on her arm. Yoli got up and threw Silvia across the mat for a two-point landing. Then a series of derriere—bumps from a body scissors. Yoli launched Silvia into a flying somersault. Silvia fighting mad held her in the air with terrific strength by feet and forehead, won round two.

In the third round rough stuff, they fell out of the ring, bashed each other with their knees, rolled into the spectators and fought on. Finally referee Pantera Negra brought them back into the ring. Red sent Yoli out of the ring head first, amorous fan let his hand linger too long in assistance, Yoli turned on him and Montezuma her second bares his teeth. Fight ended with Silvia being flattened.

Yoli the glamorous was victorious and she left the ring to the cheers of her admirers—all the men in the stadium."

It was only a brief $25 dollar round trip flight on Cubana from Port-au-Prince to Santiago de Cuba. It was carnival time and no place in Cuba was carnival celebrated like in Santiago. We had planned to see it for ourselves but had decided against 1953 putting the trip off until 1954. Just as well. At dawn on the 26 of July, 1953, a young Fidel Castro and his followers in an abortive attempt to launch the revolution against Dictator Fulgencio Batista Zaldivar had attacked the Moncada military barracks in Santiago.

———

It seemed that everyone was employed or self-employed in the city. Hand-me-down clothing *(Pèpè)* had yet to arrive and put an end to streets filled with tailors and cobblers. No country had such talented craftsmen and artists. Schools were being built and scholars were disserting about the future. A worker's city was being constructed by the Government at St. Martin. It was not perfect, but for many, even *habitants* (I hate the title peasant), there was still land, and only nature and corrupt lawyers were the enemy. The middle-class was stirring and women had finally been given the vote through the Constitution of Nov.1950.

The great events in the city were the arrival of five traffic lights that made pedestrian crossings extremely dangerous, especially for a horse and buggy. Two officers of the police traffic department Capt. Fritz Brierre and Lt René Léon had returned with the lights after training in Illinois. The lights presented amusement on the capital's main street as donkeys and market women were often color blind. When one light blew a bulb a taxi crashed into another car.

At the beginning of 1951, Col. Robert Rutherford McCormick, 70, editor-publisher of the Chicago Tribune, flew into town and added the Haitian flag to 62 others he had painted on his plane. He was accompanied by Jules Dubois, chief of the newspaper's Latin American coverage. So interested in the drumming of Ti Roro was publisher McCormick that he joined the drummer on stage at the Cabane Choucoune nightclub. The Colonel suggested building a paper mill in Haiti and creating forest farms to provide the raw material! He already owned paper mills in Canada. We need the forests but not the paper.

There was no lack of news and features. We had a love for odd-ball stories and sometimes found them in the column of our French colleagues which we translated, giving them full credit.

A typical front page in June 1951 contained the following headlines: "Winner of free, all-expense, paid week in Haiti arrives from California 3 years late;" "Flying Saucer comes to Haiti"; "Ten million dollar road program signed with French company". "President inspects new military academy." "Vagabond Jailed for Impersonating Detective".

The Sun three years later, in 1953, featured Yvan Michel, the young director of the International telephone service who had picked up a cloudy image from abroad on an old TV set. Happily it was a while before television arrived in Haiti.

A 75-ton Carrier air-conditioning unit was installed at the Casernes Dessalines theatre by distributor Walter Braun. Soldiers could enjoy three movies a week in cool splendor. Arnold Braun the father of Walter and Fritz was the Sun's *Personality of the week*. Arnold had come to Haiti from Jamaica where he slipped over the fence of an internment camp during the First World War (1914-18) donned woman's clothing and sauntered down Kingston town in search of an owner of a sailing boat. He arrived in Haiti and didn't have to climb any more fences.

———

On July 20, 1953 Haiti received the sad news of the death in New York ex-President Dumarsais Estimé at the Columbia-Presbyterian Medical center at aged 53. He had been suffering from uremia poisoning. He had expected one day to return to Haiti, as ex-President Stenio Vincent had to be followed by Elie Lescot to live out their days at peace in Haiti. But Estimé was destined to return in a coffin.

President Magloire did not hesitate in ordering a state funeral for the man he had ousted from power. First Mrs. Estimé returned from New York and the *Sun* noted: "when Mrs. Estimé arrived Thursday afternoon, two large groups were at Bowen field to meet her. Close by the plane steps were high government officials, while in the waiting room stood partisans and relatives of the late ex-president. Descending from the plane was a trim, heavily veiled figure in black; Madame Estimé paid scant attention to the first group. Accompanied by Mr. and Mrs. Maurice Carrié and Madame Luc Dominique, she departed in the car of friends. Next day a large mourning crowd waited the arrival of the Pan-American plane bearing the remains of exPresident Estimé . . . the exPresident lay in state of the Palais Législatif on the exposition ground—which he had built.

On Monday August 3, 1953, his funeral was sung at the Cathedral, and the large official cortège, included an Army officer carrying the ex-president decorations on a red cushion following the hearse. At the Port-au-Prince cemetery, the military rendered the last honors. Years later, Mrs. Lucienne Heurtelou Estimé who campaigned for Dr. François Duvalier was rewarded with her appointment as Ambassador of Haiti in Belgium, the first woman to hold such a high diplomatic post. There was also speculation at the time that Duvalier wanted to rid himself of Estimé shadow in order to assert himself. On May 19, 2006 Mrs. Estime, age 89 was shot to death by bandits during a hold-up at the Maison Dacarett Jewelry shop in residential Bois Verna.

Page 12	Haiti Sun	Aug.31, 1952

Some Jottings for a Travel Book "Haiti"
By **Bertram Collins**
Pride and the People:

A passionate faith in his Haiti and in things Haitian is the mark of the citizen here. The traveler never hears a cynical comment on home affairs from any Haitian. There is either a feeling of satisfaction with things as they are, or of anticipation of better things which will come inevitably and soon. No Caribbean country has had such a memorable history, nor possesses as many monuments as reminders that great things have been done in the island. The tourist industry is booming and agriculture is now almost being encumbered by Government assistance. And if, as you drive along the winding road to Petionville, lined with flamboyant and poinsettias covered with masses of scarlet blooms, you observe to your Haitian friend that Haiti is "belle, très belle", he will nod solemnly in accord: "Oui, très belle, très belle".

Haitian hospitality makes that of Jamaica seem crude by comparison—is the opinion of Jamaicans on holiday here. Haitian hospitality is more than the offer of food and drink—tourists after all, *always* have the wherewithal for that. It is a manifestation of warmness of heart, genuine interest and a willingness to take reasonable, or if need be, unreasonable pains to provide comfort and entertainment for the visitor.

One visitor had tears in his eyes when the little grand-daughter of the owner of the hotel where he had booked a reservation, met his wife at their arrival at the airport, and presented her with a bouquet of roses. "It is these little things", he said, "these little things that make such a big difference." The simple but gracious courtesy of every peasant astonishes the stranger, who did not expect to find such manifestations of a truly old-world civilization in every level of Haitian society.

Pomp and Circumstance

Military display is a conspicuous feature in Haiti. The Police is but a section of the Army wearing an additional badge (the incidence of crime is low, almost as low as in Tahiti) other sections of the unified armed force are the Navy (chiefly Coast Guard vessels) and the Air Force, whose Transport planes find gainful occupation as the country's internal air service.

Army officers are trained in the modernistic Military Academy, in the French military system, wear American styled uniforms, and complain that promotion is as slow as in the Regular British Army.

The people are proud of the army, and one often detects the tone of voice of so many South American Republics, jealous, pugnacious, and self-consciously national. But here the Army is the shield against, not the instrument of tyranny.

As much as in any other country in the world, a mark of distinction is compulsory. Sardonic observer's remark that the first badge of success is the Dynaflow; (Buick) the next is the smart suburban villa, like the scores nestling amid the high-walled gardens on the main road out of the city. Along the suburban road you pass houses with swimming pools. You also pass old-looking black women in coloured print dresses, some with hoop earrings, nearly all in poverty no less painful, because it is picturesque.

Town and Country

The foreigner quickly remarks the strong lateral cleavage between the elite and the uneducated mass of the populace. There is an inherent weakness in a society which lacks a wide, stable middle-class, but sociologists claim to see a growth in the post-war years of a new Haitian middle-class, from which will spring a body of leaders with strength and vision enough to unite the force of a whole country in a common wheel. Later, the foreigner remarks the other cleavage—a vertical one between town and country. Where the paved roads ends begins another Haiti, not sufficiently changed from the Haiti of 1805, when freedmen gathered to the tunes of the combite to till the land at last truly their very own.

You cross the same sparkling river a hundred times en route to picturesque Jacmel—the tourist booklet says. Actually bridges are rare in Haiti, and your vehicle, like a turtle, must wade through mud and river for hours on end, while native women bathing unconcerned in the streams, turn to watch you pass.

At Jacmel you are struck by the old-fashioned houses, the ancient edifices which characterized the architecture of the colonial epoch. Shade conscious visitors remark the general lighter complexion of the inhabitants. They are told that Polish soldiers sent by Napoleon to crush the rebellion preferred to settle happily and peaceably along the southern shores, and their descendants play a prominent part in social life. At La Fond, just about five miles away you hear the music of the *combite* as weary villagers return home blowing on bamboo pipes, singing Créole chants, and stirring to the music of the tambour.

Foreigners are planted comfortably in the fertile soil of Haiti. They are planted firmly too because their businesses are considered as being of Haitian nationality, and are subject to the same documental requirements as all Haitian businesses. With self-respecting commonsense the Government accords or denies the rights to aliens in measure as such rights are accorded or denied to Haitians by the alien's Governments. At the swank elegant Casino you hear voices in every tongue, from German to Jewish. Haiti is not only a Tourist paradise, fashioned by Nature and by History. It is also a land where enterprise is never vain.

(Guyanese-born Bertram Collins, a student at the University of the West Indies, Mona, Jamaica campus on holiday in Haiti wrote several articles on his experiences traveling around Haiti for the *Sun* during the summer of 1952.)

—

The *Port-au-Prince Times*, I had helped established, finally closed down in May 1952. Its last editor was a fine old professor, Dr. Paul Périgord who later wrote an occasional column for the *Sun*. Allan Benson had vanished much earlier.

—

After waiting three years, the *Sun* finally was blessed with a working telephone: 2061.

CHAPTER 6

Personality of the Week

Looking back at the yellowed pages of my newspaper it told the story of a very different Haiti from today. Haitians literally burst out of the *Sun's* pages with pride and love of country, where the talents of Haitians shone across the world, and attracted not only visitors, but new residents, men and women who could afford to choose their Island home. And we are not talking about Frenchmen who managed to escape Devil's Island and take up residence in Haiti. Some were featured in the *Sun*.

The long list of "Personalities of the week" was a varied lot. From **Charles Collingswood**, who made his name as a broadcaster during World War 11 with CBS and wife **Louise** Albritton, the stage and TV actress, to Jacques a blind man who walked up and down the Petionville road daily aided by a white stick which he told us "It (the stick) knows every rock on the path."

The staid and distinguished **Supreme Court Justice Christian Laporte** was an early choice for the weekly column. Judge Laporte was an outstanding personality as the top authorities on the country's laws. His father, Ernest Laporte had been Minister of Justice, a deputy and first president of the court of appeals. Judge Laporte himself made his début on the legal scene in 1913 in his hometown of Gonaïves. He later married Inez Smith an African-American writer whose mother, Southern belle Mamie Lee Smith, joined her daughter in Haiti in 1935. Mrs. Laporte was in the mid-1950's to join the *Haiti Sun* as office manager.

The Personality of the Week was chosen in recognition of persons, big and small who had made a contribution to the Republic or made news that week. Some were foreign residents but most were Haitians who had made their mark and we were proud to write about them. This is how they appeared in the *Sun* with typos and all, but that was how it was, rustic and as American Columnist Westbrook Pegler wrote after a visit to Haiti that the *Sun* was shades of Mark Twain in the Caribbean . . .

The personalities say a lot about the period of Haiti golden age, here are some:

Gustav della Valle: "A man responsible for developing a whole new branch of tourism could have been called Haiti's King Neptune. His trident is kept sharpened and is a symbol of terror for the undersea creatures of Port-au-Prince Bay. The minute Gustav Della Valle got his first look at the coral reef waters lapping at Haiti's front door he knew he'd found his happy hunting ground. The Italian-born sportsman is one of the world's best spear-fishermen. And the clearness of the Haitian waters, the brightness of the coral floor of the Bay as well as the year-round good weather made Haiti an ideal spot for Gustav to establish his school, the only spear fishing school of the western hemisphere.

"But the undersea Tarzan found on serious obstacle to his teaching career. When his school opened for business back in 1948, he couldn't find a single student. Residents of Haiti refuse to put their foot in the water . . . too many sharks and barracuda. Gustav's first educational chore was the business of destroying popular legends. He insisted that neither fish is dangerous under ordinary conditions. The barracuda, he explained, will only become vicious when there is blood in the water, and there must be a fair amount of it at that. The same goes for sharks. Gustav said the only time one of these bad boys of the sea ever caused him any trouble was when he speared him and the shark doubled back. The harpoon jutting out from the wounded fish shattered his goggle mask.

"Soon Gustav's reassurances and enthusiasm took effect. Port-au-Prince found itself with a new and thrilling sport as well as a major tourist attraction. In addition Gustav conducts marine sight seeing tours. The handsome blonde spear fisherman counted among his students such illustrious visitors as Actress Jennifer Jones, her husband, David O. Selznick and Prince Napoleon. Alberti, manager of the Splendid Hotel, donned rubber fins, grabbed his spear and contorted with Gustav on the floor of the Bay. They felt such fun should be shared so they formed a "Goggle Club" which now has 15 members.

"Gustav emphasizes that you don't have to be a good swimmer to enjoy the hand-to-hand encounter with fishing catch. He also says you don't need brawn, but he glanced down at his own 190 pounds in fighting trim and added, "It helps." However, when there's a will there's a way. He recalled the 75-year-old Ohio lady that came to Haiti for spear fishing lessons. She had to be lifted from the boat into the water, but after her fifth lesson, she'd gotten herself a fish!

"Gustav's one spirit of adventure caused him to fall in love with his undersea sport the first time he laid eyes on it in the Mediterranean 18 years ago. And even a few close brushes with death have failed to put a slack on his enthusiasm. There was the time, for instance, that he dove to 82 feet and suffered a lung hemorrhage. But he got his worst fright off the coast of Naples. On an ordinary spear fishing dive he stayed under water until his oxygen was exhausted. Then he placed his foot on the bottom to catapult himself to the surface for a deep breath. But he found he couldn't move. He was stuck. An octopus had wrapped itself around his left leg. Fortunately, a companion who had been watching him from a boat came to his rescue. But Gustav was unconscious by the time he reached the surface. He added laughingly, "That was my record for an underwater stay."

"The marine sportsman has had plenty of adventures "top-side" as well as under the sea. During the war [World War II] he served as a photographer with the Italian army . . . and was in Rome when word got around that the allies were about to launch their invasion of Sicily. But Gustav's army boss seemed to be more of a newsman than he was a patriot. He just rubbed his hands gleefully at the thought of the marvelous newsreel shots the enemy would provide him. But after the Sicily invasion was recorded and it was time to return to the mainland, Gustav, along with the Hermann Goering panzer division, found that allied bombers were making chop suey of the narrow straits separating Sicily and Italy. So Gustav took time out from the war. He went spear fishing off Messina . . . with the water exploding not far away.

"When the Germans took Rome after Italy's surrender Gustav hid out in the city's catacombs and got asylum as a photographer in the Vatican. Later, he worked for the British as a camera man. After the war, Gustav headed for Paris . . . to paint. But he said, "I hate mediocrity." And after a year I decided to see what was happening in the new world.

"In 1948 he arrived in Haiti . . . and decided to make it his winter home. He lives in Laboule with his attractive wife Renée Roosevelt, the granddaughter of the manager of Ibo Lele and the daughter of Denis Roosevelt, well-known motion picture producer. Gustav's diverse talents came in mighty handy in establishing his ménage. He taught his wife to cook (and from the sample we had of her Thanksgiving feast, he did an excellent job.) The sportsman used his artistic flair to make his home one of the most beautiful in Haiti, with its Swiss atmosphere and back drop of Pines.

"At the end of the month, we will also celebrate the completion of another masterpiece of construction . . . the new pier he is building for the Casino's yacht and marine basin.

"For additional interest, Gustav enjoys good music and good books (he has a fine collection of both) and takes great pride in growing his own vegetables for the dinner table.

"He speaks many languages . . . in a fashion that can be termed unique . . . and has the kind of personality that makes him a natural for newspaper and magazine writers not only here but in the United States as well."

Two well known young Haitians, Gaston Baussan and Jean Coicou, both students of Gustav began a daily cruise to Sand Cay where tourists could relax on a glass bottom boat and enjoy observing coral reefs teeming with sea life. Graham Greene enjoyed being towed around the reefs on an inflated tube.

André (Cheu) Chevalier: "Born in Haiti, he is old like the country. His great grand-father signed the act of Independence and since that day this family has belonged to Haitian history. Chevalier sprouts from old French stock, Louis Chevalier of Puilboreau. He is related to the Benefactor of the Dominican Republic and his god-father was President Salomon, who he says was one of Haiti's greatest Presidents because he made him a full general the day he was christened. Descendant of Victorin and Fontanges, André Chevalier has been: Secretary of the Ministry of Interior, Aide and Chief of Staff to President Simon, Director of the Central School of Port-au-Prince; Secretary and High Commissaire of the International Exposition of Port-au-Prince; President of the National Sports Association and of the Haitian Olympic Committee for many years. A well-known writer and humorist, he edited the illustrated review "*Aya-Bombe*".

He wrote in collaboration with Ernest Chauvet and Leon Laleau a review called *Cine-Pretention*.

He also contributed many fine little sketches and a drama entitled, *Admiral Killick* with Charles Moravia. Then Black Aphrodite and last year L. Grimard and Chevalier produced a book *Bakoulou* which he says kicks Voodoo in the pants. His latest novel *Ciné Nouvelle* will be published at the end of this year, his preface is written by Simon Lando, the director of the *Institut Français*, and in the forwards of the book is a letter written by Yvonne Bernader, a French book agent. Chevalier says, he does not speak English but American slang he adds and "I don't write French but Haitian."

From The New-Yorker No. of 28 October 1933 Shouts and Murmurs

André Chevalier, Secretary of the Gendarmerie was a light mulatto, big, handsome with an irresistible chuckle and the complexion of strong coffee, with plenty of rich cream. His teeth were bigger and whiter than those of Montana wolf; he was a gargantuan fellow who could eat more, drink more, work harder, and talk louder and longer than any other person in Port-au-Prince. My first meeting with Chevalier had opened with a surprise. We had been introduced and had shaken hands. "Oh, but certainly," he had chuckled, "I know the captain. I have just finished reading of his adventures in a Profile in the New-Yorker." *Captain John Graige* U.S.M.C.

"Always smiling", used to say the late President Franklin Roosevelt. "Chevalier is the friend of everybody and shakes hand with everyone," wrote Paul Morand in his book "Hiver Caraibes." Chevalier's home is like a comfortable treasure house, it contains old paintings, china, a snuff box belonging to Adline, Emperor Soulouque's wife, among many others souvenirs of days gone by.

"I don't want to say too much" . . . he said standing at the gate of his home in Avenue du Sacré-Coeur bidding *bonsoir* to all who passed specially the ladies whom he addresses as his daughters. But . . . all my life is a smile," he said in ending the interview.

> **Attilio Briani**: 70-year old Attilio Briani, the Italian born inventor who built planes in the days when they jumped instead of flying. We found him living quietly on the outskirts of Bowen Field—still tinkering with his beloved engines. And, fittingly, he makes his house in a converted air terminal—the first one that was built at the airport site.

The small dynamic technician arrived in Haiti 17 years ago to help PAA set up it seas plane base where the international casino now stands. He became a citizen in 1941 . . . just 48 years after he left his native village near Milan to go to Switzerland to study mechanical engineering. He began his studies at the precocious age of 11 . . . and by the time he reached the advanced age of 16 he was already a working engineer . . . employed at the Astor Auto plant in Paris . . . and a budding inventor. Before he was able to shave he perfected a special wheel for gun carriers of the French Artiltery, enabling them to trundle over rough terrain before breaking. Young Attilio really turned out a forerunner to the modern shock absorber by making his wheel with pump-like spokes that worked on an oil and air compression system. He received six thousand francs for his invention from the Michelin factory in Paris.

Shortly thereafter he was helping build the tiny 60-horsepower monoplane that the French pilot Bleriot used to make the first flight across the English Channel. He also had a hand in constructing the <<Demoiselle>>—the monoplane that had all Paris on its toes when the Brazilian pilot, Santos Dumont, daringly circles the Eiffel Tower. In the first decade of the 20th century any flight was a hazardous undertaking . . . as the young inventor soon found out. Serving as his own <<test pilot>> for his home-constructed jobs, Attilio found himself meeting the ground much faster than usual one day in 1907. And when he picked his way through the wreckage he considered himself lucky to get off with a broken arm and injured leg.

Nevertheless he recalls bisembryo air babies with great tenderness . . . and brought out treasured photos of weird looking "flying machines" to show this reporter. This plane below pictured on this page he constructed in 1907 . . . forged together with gas pipes, a bit of fabric and a 16 horsepower engine. The pilot's compartment consisted of a hammock slung between the structures. When asked whether the contraption flew Mr. Briani replied, "No, it jumped . . . each jump averaging three to four meters", He said he built it for experimental purposes to calculate suspension of the wings. By 1909 Italy officially awarded the pioneer flier with a pilot's license, one of the first ever issued. It was the same year he invented the Heart Steering System . . . a big step in the advancement of aviation. It was displayed in Paris along with another Briani brainchild . . . a model of a plane driven by wind turbines. I was really the granddaddy of the jet propelled fighters of today, but Briani found too many "bugs" in the construction and wrote it off as a failure.

The army trapped the busy engineer for a three-year stint in the anxious days preceding World War 1. During his time in uniform he managed to stick close to his beloved engines by driving a Fiat in the famous car races from Paris to Madrid and Paris to Bordeaux. Asked whether he won, he replied, "Ah, no, but that didn't matter. It was fun anyway." He didn't say how much fun it was crossing the Alps in a small car powered by a belt driven coke engine that had to be stoked every few miles but at least it was adventure.

Briani's exploits won him the nickname of "The Eagle" . . . and it was under this glamorous title that he was welcomed in Cuba when he arrived in the Caribbeans after doffing his military uniform. The Cuban papers made much of this colorful young man with the handlebar mustache and made even more of his homebuilt car that he constructed around a fiat engine. Briani worked for two years for the Cuban telephone company and then opened up one of the first auto repair shops in this part of the world.

Launched in a solid business career, Briani found himself a pretty Spanish bride and settled down for 15 years of family life in Havana. Next he moved to Santiago to construct a brewery for the Bacardi rum company, and it was there that he was discovered by an infant flying organization known as Pan American . . . a discovery that turned out to be a mighty good thing for all concerned. Briano opened the PAA airport at Camaguey, helped extend the huge air network of Para in Brazil and then eventually came to Port-au-Prince where his inventive genius was put to a real test in forging a sea plane base on the Haitian waterfront. Among other things he built a special windmill to suck the salt water away from the gas storage tanks on the sea shore.

Gustave della Valle who in 1950 opened a whole new tourist venue on the Gulf of Gônave that included spear fishing. He, Gustav, shows how to spear a shark.

American agricultural expert, Atherton Lee who made Kenscoff bloom with flowers became a *Personality of the Week* and a contributor to the *Sun*. Lee also ran a popular auberge, Châtelet des Fleurs.

Jimmy Plinton an important figure in the 1950's, seen here besides his aircraft at Bowen Field. Plinton had been a member of the all-black 99th Pursuit Squadron raised at the Tuskegee Institute in Alabama. He pioneered the laundry and dry-cleaning business in Port-au-Prince, and was a contributor to the *Haiti Sun*.

President Magloire with Father Rémy Augustin and the Papal Nuncio. It was a historical moment when Father Augustin became the first Haitian born Bishop in the Catholic Church.

Another Personality of the Week was:

55-year-old Ti Dio's 36th child is expected

The man of the mountains.

Historian Edmond Mangones at work in his home office. Mr. Mangones had compiled an enormous library and archives on Haiti, and was an excellent historical source.

Gendolyn Grant Mellon, wife of William Larimer Mellon at the Hospital Albert Schweitzer they built in the Artibonite valley. The author took this photo in September 1956 when the hospital opened.

Incidentally windmills are one of Briani's favorite gadgets. He formed a company just before the war to construct windmills of his own design but two of his American partners were killed in the conflict and his plans never materialized. Altogether he has invented 15 different types of windmills . . . including the one pictured in this issue built to provide the power for a home made welding plant. Briani called this model a failure because the 2,000-dollar piece of machinery was too expensive to make and too complicated for commercial use.

Asked about his future plans, the energetic septuagenarian said he might take time off from his workshop to make a trip to Italy next year . . . but he is going to make sure that it is during the Italian heat wave . . . he doesn't want to risk a European winter with his tropics-thinned blood.

Since his wife died eight months ago, Briani has been living alone in his small house listening to the familiar roar of the planes overhead and keeping a careful eye on his two Cuban papaya trees in his back yard. For company he has a little brown dog "beauty" that seems to understand Briani language which is a thorough mixture of Italian, Portuguese, French, Créole, English and Spanish.

Each day he is up with the sun . . . ready for hours of careful labor over his engines. Automatically one feels that such a life is not a deserving reward for one of the founders of modern aviation. But on second thought one feels a man of Briani's caliber would never be happy just sitting back contemplating royalties from his inventions. The pride and joy of such a man includes . . . grease on his hands.

Placide David: He is a historian and diplomat and his great grandfather had been in charge of finances for King Henri Christophe (1807-1818). David has been awarded the *Grand Prix de littérature des Antilles* for his *Sur les Rives du Passé* . . .

Auguste Désert: When Auguste appeared in the Personality column a photograph showed how he was dwarfed by his giant rum barrel—perhaps the world's largest. He was typical of the people who run *Clairin Avenue* (*Rue Macajoux* near *Croix des Bossales* market). His barrel was reputed to hold 4,000 gallons of fiery *rhum*.

Professor Ulrick Duvivier: (Nov 18, 1951) "Last week a tall, dignified quiet-spoken man became *Officier de l'Ordre National Honneur et Mérite*" in an impressive ceremony at the Seminaire St. Martial. It was a fitting reward for Professor Ulrick Duvivier whose life has been consecrated to upholding the torch of learning for Haitian youth. His achievements in the educational field have been so outstanding that they brought him recognition not only in his homeland but also abroad.

"Back in 1933, the French Government awarded Professor Duvivier the title of *Officier d'Académie*. And last month the 52 year-old educator was chosen by the organization of American States to be a permanent member of the Cultural Committee of the Pan American Union . . . a high honor since it gives Haiti the privilege of being one of the five nations represented in the group of experts chosen to work out a program for increasing cultural relations between the 21 American States.

The professor expects to leave shortly for Mexico City to take on the duties of this new post, placing the name of Ulrick Duvivier once more on the list of distinguished diplomats of the Americas.

The Professor's father served as Minister to Washington as well as Haitian Foreign Minister and Secretary of State for Education.

Duvivier fils began his studies at the *Séminaire St. Martial* and at the age of 14 sailed for France to continue his education. He spent five years at *Janson-de-Sailly* and a year at the *Sorbonne* while the guns of World War I wrote another bloody page of world history. Then he returned to Port-au-Prince and took his degree at the Faculty of Law.

But while he was studying the complicated legal records he took time out to launch his 30-year teaching career. The budding educator lawyer drilled French, Latin and Greek into the heads of youngster at the Lycée Pétion and gave embryo school ma'ams and masters at the two teacher's training schools lectures on the job that lay ahead of them.

In this reporter's opinion Professor Duvivier himself made an important stride in the history of the Haitian school system when he became director of the *Lycée Pétion* in 1942. During the three years he held the post he gave his pupils a chance to learn a trade in a special class which offered practical training in carpentry, electrical repair, book binding and other skilled occupations. It turned out to be a highly controversial move. Those in favor of it pointed out that many of the 700 students at the free government school would benefit greatly by such a practical course since their parents could not afford to give them a lengthy professional education. And it was also pointed out that Haiti would benefit as well since "skilled labor" has always been a rarity.

But the opposition also had its argument. It insisted that the daughters and sons of small wage-earners should be offered the same education as the more fortunate pupils from wealthier homes . . . pupils who would eventually take their place in the professional world. The trades' class was discontinued when Mr. Duvivier retired in 1946.

At the present moment, however, there are two government trade schools in Haiti with an attendance of some 400 pupils . . . they are *J.B. Damier* and *Ecole des Arts and Métiers* of the *Frères Salésiens*.

The next phase of Professor Duvivier's educational career came about by accident. One of his four daughters failed to find a suitable secondary school (college) to continue her studies, so the professor began to tutor her. Soon her friends became interested in the classes and asked if they might join.

Today the school has 80 pupils.

Professor Duvivier and his wife, the former Mademoiselle Claire Rouzier, have two sons as well as their quartet of *jeunes filles* and three-year-old François is the darling of the family.

The grey-haired educator has little time for hobbies but nothing can keep him from his favorite exercise . . . a promenade. Every evening the Professor takes a long walk, finding it an excellent time for meditation.

Though he has never mingled in politics he has represented Haiti on two previous occasions. In 1943, he toured United States War Plants with two fellow Haitians under the auspices of the Office of the Coordinator of Inter-America Affairs. Recently he was a delegate to the Fifth General Assembly of the Pan American Institute of Geography and History, held in Santiago Chili.

As a historian, the Professor had a crowning moment last July when he received a precious packet of documents from Mr. H. Miller of Ottawa, Canada, whose wife is a descendant of the British tutor of Prince Victor Henri Christophe. The packet contained a lengthy essay on Haiti and letters written during Mr. William Wilson's stay at *Sans Souci*. It also contained a bible that once belonged to the Prince Royal, a Liturgy or form of common prayer for the use of the Haitian Royal College and a French-Créole dictionary printed in England 1806. Letters of King Christophe with a specimen of his signature were also included in the treasured packet . . .

Dr. Rulx Léon. One of the most interesting lectures of the current "Mardi" series was given at the French Institute last Tuesday night by Dr. Rulx Léon who is certainly one of the men most qualified to speak on His subject—the History of Medicine in Haiti.

The 63-year-old Paris-trained physician has already published three major works on the subject and a new book is now on the presses called *Histoire des Maladies dans Haïti*.

But Dr. Leon is not satisfied with the research role only. He is still actively a part of Haiti's medical corps and is now in the Artibonite where he has taken charge of the Brown and Root Dispensary at Borelle.

He began his long and arduous career in his birthplace of Aux Cayes as Port Doctor after obtaining his degree from the Port au Prince Medical School. In 1925 he joined Haiti's budding Public Health Department serving at Cap Haïtien and Port de Paix. In recognition of his work, the Rockefeller Foundaton awarded him a fellowship in study obstetrics in Paris. Upon his return, he was chief of the maternity ward at the Port au Prince General Hospital and taught obstetrics at the faculty of Medicine.

In 1931 Dr. Léon became Director of Public Health, a position he held for 10 years before going to New York to serve as Consul General of Haiti.

Since his return to his homeland he has not only won an enviable reputation as an author and lecturer but has also given considerable time to treating the underprivileged that need medical care.

Dr. Leon's son Gerard is following in his father's footsteps and is at present resident orthopedist at the public hospital. Another son, Maxime, is an engineer with the Brown and Root Company. Daughter Josette married Engineer Daniel Godefoy and Adeline is now Madame Gérard Alexis.

A man with widespread interests . . . literature, folk tales, biology, etc . . . . Dr. Léon is always in demand for his witty and erudite lectures.

The Highlights of his highly interesting talk last Tuesday were taken down for us by Max Wilson and we are passing them along to our readers.

During Colonial times Haitian Medicine was based primarily on the flora of the island with the dreaded yellow fever, malaria and skin diseases playing the most havoc among whites and blacks alike. During the 10 years of fighting most Surgeons operated without benefit of training or diploma. But the island of St. Domingue had 200 full-fledged Doctors and medicine was at par with medical progress in other countries.

The First Medical School of the New Republic was the Academy of Haiti, established in 1823 with the famous Dr. Cevest as the first Professor. With the help of the Scottish Dr. Stewart brought to this country by King Henri Christophe and French Dr. J. B. Mirambeau who located in the western part of the Island, many Haitians were trained in medical aid.

In 1864 the Medical School was re-opened and re-organized by President Geffrard with the help of some colored nurse imported from the United States and the newly acquired knowledge of the first batch of *boursiers* who graduated from the University of Paris. Among them can be found the names of Drs. Louis Audain, J. B. Dehoux, Jobert, etc.

It was Dr. Audain who launched the *Poly-Clinique Péan,* Haiti's first attempt at using modern therapy, scientific research and laboratory techniques. When the Rockefeller foundation built the present Medical School and annexed the General Hospital as a place for young Doctors to get additional training, Haiti's progress in the Medical field took a great leap.

According to Dr. Léon, Haitian medicine was preventative in the 18th century; the progress of our Public Health Campaign will be such that patients can largely be protected from diseases before they acquire it.

> **Parnel Marc:** Sunday July 1953: "He spends the school year dashing from the Medical College to the *Ecole Polytechnique* to *Lycée Pétion* where he pours out knowledge of physics, statistics and cosmography into the minds of Haitian youth. Then he goes home and relaxes with a good book? Oh, no, dear reader. He tutors private students in physics, maths and chemistry. Such a schedule gives Professor Marc about six hours to himself. And he spends that sleeping. But if he finds himself awake and no students are on hand, he turns into a student himself.

"When we arrived in his unpretentious but comfortable home on Avenue Boyer, we caught him hard at work studying Hebrew grammar. It's the sixth language he tackled in his lifetime. He already speaks fluent, English, Spanish and German . . ."

"Our interview with Professor Marc touched on Einstein and he said, "He wouldn't be surprised if Haiti produced a scientist of that caliber someday. He feels that such a genius will never have the opportunity to blossom however until our Republic gives it the necessary grounds to flourish—laboratories for specialized scientific research. And the books and teachers to instill the proper pioneer spirit."

Préfète Dufaut (Jan.6, 1952) somewhere between the city of Jacmel and its palm-fringed beaches stands a little white *Kay*, its ornate gate posts covered with religious figures and its walls with colorful Haitian designs. A tiny sign proclaims it the *Centre d'Art de Jacmel.*

"If you stop your car and step inside for a visit, you will be greeted by a shy, soft-voiced young man with a beard who introduced himself as N. Préfète Dufaut. It's a name now being recognized in art capitals on both sides of the Atlantic. His primitives have hung in the plush art galleries of New York, Paris and Mexico City. Yet the 29-year-old painter stays on his tiny strip of land, raising vegetables, chickens, goats and pigs to eke out a living for himself and his growing family. Dufaut, like many an illustrious artists before him, finds it wiser to have a secondary means of income than to depend entirely upon sales of his "masterpieces."

His deep attachment to the land comes naturally. His mother raised produce for the market while his father worked as a carpenter in and around Jacmel. But like most parents of humble origin they hoped to give their son a good start in life. They sent young Préfète to the Catholic Brothers School in Jacmel for five years. He was anxious to continue his education but family finances prevented it. At the age of 12, he set out for the town of Bainet to learn the ship building trade. In between long stints of labor on fishing vessels, young Préfète used to love to take a pencil and draw designs for more elaborate boats on rocks along the shore. The yen to be an artist stayed with the growing lad as he continued his apprenticeship at Léogane and Port-au-Prince. But it wasn't until he paid a visit to La Gonâve that he got the chance to put his yen into practice. He painted a tabernacle at the church of Notre Dame de Lourdes.

After he returned to Jacmel to settle on his mother's land. Préfète spent many long hours with cans of Sapolin painting on walls, cardboard or anything that presented a smooth surface. One day in 1946, a strange white man spotted the intricate star on the wall of the young man's *kay* and knocked on the door. He introduced himself as William Cast, asked to see Préfète's other paintings and then suggested that he take them to the Art Center in Port-au-Prince. Préfète trudged into the studio of Dewitt Peters with the fruit of his budding art efforts under his arm. Peters took a careful look and then offered the young Jacmel painter materials and the encouragement he needed to continue his career. He soon made his first sale . . . a primitive that was bought by an American for 30 dollars. It was as much money as he could get in months of hard labor on the land, and Préfète decided that painting was something worth sticking to. He brought more pictures to the *Centre d'Art.* Some of them were sold. Then he began his most famous project . . . painting the huge mural of the Last Judgment at the Episcopal Cathedral. It is an impressive interpretation derivative of the Haitian culture. A procession of the dead are winding up a curving mountain road which could be found anywhere in our Republic. Religious themes are favorites of Dufaut along with patriotic motifs. Like most primitives his work is literal with a lack of perspective. But the colors he uses are clean and pure, his designs expressing the accumulated richness of centuries of religious ceremonial and folklore. Dufaut used his beloved hometown for inspiration for a number of his works. On the wall of his *kay* is a framed certificate showing that the art judges at the Exposition have awarded him a bronze medal for the painting entitled, "View of Jacmel". Also on the wall of his small living quarters are many of his earlier works, ranging from a meticulous pen and ink sketch of a large sailing ship to an oil of a white Venus lying on a couch, the beauty of her curves outlined by the glare of an unshaded electric bulb. Nearby was a pin-up print of Grant Wood, the rolling Iowa countryside contrasting strangely with the primitive landscapes of the young Haitian artist.

Even though the influence of the outside world has now reached Dufaut, he is still content with this simple life, his few carreaux of land and most of all his growing family. He has been married four years to the girl he fell in love with when a child in Jacmel. And now he is the proud father of three sons, the youngest only a few weeks old.

As your reporter sipped a demi-tasse of the young painter's delicious coffee and observed his courtesy, dignity and pride of his host he was somehow glad that Dufaut had chosen to remain a part of the people from which he had sprung. Simplicity has often been called the keynote to greatness.

> **Robert St. Brice:** In the old days it was the men of great wealth who served as patrons of the arts, often providing struggling painters and writers with the means to live as a mere matter of vanity. The hole made in their coffers by such charity was negligible . . . the recognition in the elaborate dedication of their protégés, great.

In Haiti, where many traditional patterns have been broken, this one was broken also . . . by a poor man who had little to give and nothing to gain. Robert St. Brice expected no reward when he opened the doors of his small wooden home to shelter—at various times—a penniless poet, an out-of-work actor and a young painter. But the hand of destiny saw to it that he received his reward in a particularly fitting manner. While Robert St. Brice befriended those who sought to perfect their talents, he learned he had an untapped treasury of talent himself. The middle-aged baker who could neither read nor write became one of the most promising of the Haitian primitive artists. His works are now bringing in a tidy sum, fulfilling the old adage, "Cast your bread upon the waters and it shall come back cake."

An art career was something undreamed of for Robert St. Brice who was born in Pétionville 56 years ago, the son of a farm hand. He learned a useful trade and at the age of 29 married his sweetheart, Anna. She is now a gentle old lady who keeps the small boutique in front of the St. Brices house, a boutique that features her husband's excellent baked goods.

During most of his married life Robert St. Brice worked as cook and baker for a Kentuckian named Jessie Craddock, who died in 1949.

Ten years ago the St. Brices savings went into the purchase of a home. A quaint wooden two-storey house in Bizoton that they could afford only because it was reported to be haunted.

Robert St. Brice found it haunted all right . . . with good luck. Maybe the luck had something to do with the welcome on the mat. An American poet Wilmer Lucas turned out many a verse while living under its roof.

Actor William Major was broke and homeless until St. Brice took him in as member of the family. But his luckiest day came when an American Negro merchant seaman came to his door in 1948 and asked if there was a room for rent. Alex John was no ordinary man of the sea. He was a good pianist, an avid reader and an earnest painter. Since his parents had originally come from St. Lucia, he remembered Créole from his childhood days and soon there were no barriers of communication between the American and his landlord.

One day while Alex John was working on a canvas, he noticed his landlord standing in the doorway. "Here", he said, "you might as well keep yourself busy." And he thrust a wax crayon into St. Brice's hand. In no time the landlord was busier than his tenant creating pictures with enamel on prepared cardboard. Alex John turned from teacher to pupil and now insists that his landlord is the greatest living painter in Haiti. Dewitt Peters also was enthusiastic over the St. Brice efforts which feature a lavish use of color stippled on with fast strokes—some from the point of the paint brush, somewhat reminiscent of the French painter Seurat.

When Anna hears the sharp rhymic dabs of the paint brush, she laughs and says, "The machine is running again." At the beginning she used to sign her husband's paintings for him, but today he carefully draws his own name. Like so many of his countrymen, St. Brice's lack of formal education is more than made up for his wealth of vision and simple wisdom. It is because of that wisdom he is seeing to it that his children have the chance to go to school. Sixteen-year-old François and 15-year-old Edouard walk to classes at Toussaint Louverture each day . . . a remarkable distance. Thirteen-year-old Marie and 9-year-old Iassette complete the family quartet.

St. Brice says he owes a debt of gratitude to Dewitt Peters who through the *Centre d'Art*, marketed many of his paintings and gave him much needed encouragement as well.

But he has a special spot in his heart for the young man who first uncovered his treasury of talent . . . the man who spent eight years sailing the seven seas and finally chose Haiti as his favorite home.

Alex John has made three return trips to our Republic after his first trip in 1948. He says he fell under the spell of the voodoo drums as he listened to them echoing form hill to hill and that the fascination for the rhythm of the tambours has never left him. He is also fascinated by the study of Haiti, its culture and its people with which he feels a deep kinship.

Right now Alex is living at Carrefour, brushing up on his painting, music and his French. But as far as his art work goes, Alex says he will take a back seat to his landlord any day.

André Dimanche (Sept 14, 1952) in the city of poets—Jérémie—there is a man who used wood instead of words to express the beauty that lies in the world around him. His name is André Dimanche.

The quiet, earnest agricultural agent lives on a rubber plantation at Chambellan, some kilometers from Jérémie. During the day he is constantly busy with his trees, collecting the sticky milk called latex that trickles from their slashed trunks. After his day's work is done, André walks alone through the tropical countryside—where some of Haiti's most exotic plants are found. Nature seems to be using Jérémie landscape to put on a permanent exhibit of its most lavish generosity. And André's attitude toward nature can only be described as reverent.

When he sees a large almond tree with a branch broken by the wind, he has the wood carried back to his home. Some months later the branch has been transformed into two pieces of sculpture—a dreamlike mermaid and an officer in dress uniform.

André often draws on Haitian folklore for inspiration and subject matter. This summer he brought to Port au Prince one of his latest creations—a statue of Baron Samedi responding maliciously to the call of Voodoo Priestess. Another piece in his current exhibit is called The "Belle Créole" . . . a bust of a mother feeding her child at the breast.

Foreign visitors especially have found it hard to believe that such remarkably finished pieces of sculpture have been turned out by a man who works with nothing but a simple pen knife, a Gillette razor blade, a small hammer and some glaze. They do not have the stylized simplicity of the primitive Haitian sculptor Valentin, for instance, whose mask-like heads hark back directly to the African motif. André's figures have a sensitivity of expression-a reflection of inner spirit that seems incredible to find in the works of a man whose "studio" is a humble *kay* in the provinces.

CHAPTER 7

Populist Politics

In my early months of publishing the *Haiti Sun* I reassured our readers repeatedly that the *Sun* was a nonpolitical journal that I would not be as presumptuous as to write editorials telling Haitians what they should or should not do. The goal of my newspaper was to help bridge the yawning gulf between the many strata of Haitian society and to do everything possible to facilitate the country's struggle to progress. My newspaper's dedication to reporting the facts as faithfully and objectively as possible would, I believe, ultimately assist in making Haiti a much more healthy and balanced society. But, the island republic's small-town environment being what it is, politics were unavoidable in the publishing business in Haiti. The *Sun* eventually had to get involved.

Our leap into the fray occurred in the late summer of 1953. It was spurred by what I perceived as an act of foul play. However, it nearly got me shot and expelled from the country. The chronology was as follows:

President Paul Magloire had launched his own newspaper, *Le National*,* whose office was located just a few doors away from the *Sun* on *Rond Point de la Liberté*. In a front-page series *Le National* had targeted Port-au-Prince's populist leader and National Deputy, Pierre Eustache Daniel Fignolé. The demeaning attacks on Fignolé backfired by making the charismatic hero of the capital's poor the talk of

---

* *Shortly before Le National began publishing, in late 1952, Roland Lataillade, a powerful member of President Magloire's informal "kitchen cabinet", and assistant secretary of State for Interior and National Defence, told me that the president liked my newspaper and wanted me to run his new daily. Shocked I protested that such a thing would be impossible. "I appreciate the president's confidence but I could never get involved in a government project." Lataillade laughed. "This is an order, not a request. You have carte blanche to make it work. The tall mulatto, known as being well informed then recited my leisure activities. To save the honor of a lady, I had no recourse other than agree. After three months I happily relinquished my editorship of Le National with the excuse that I had to fly to the U.S. However by that time the president's men were relieved*

the country—and, as far as I was concerned, a candidate for the *Sun's* "Personality of the Week" column.

However, allowing Fignolé a tribune to answer his critics was dangerous policy especially when the strongman president of the country was clearly behind the attacks.

"We generally prefer to leave politics alone, strictly," began our "Personality of the Week" column. "But our attention has been brought forcibly to a prominent local political figure . . ."

"We decided to see Daniel [Fignolé] in his den on Rue du Peuple. His house was plain, unlovely, but by far the best dwelling in the working class area of north Port-au-Prince. We sat in his office-study, near his busy-looking desk. Around were stacks of neatly arranged books on all topics, but especially mathematics, history and economics. Two shelves contained books and pamphlets he had written. On a blackboard were geometric figures. "Just for relaxation" professor Fignolé said as he entered, pointing to the blackboard, and greeting us. 'I used to be a teacher of mathematics at my old school, Lycée Pétion, before I was dismissed by the [former President] Lescot government, for publishing the revue *Chantiers*. I stopped teaching, except privately, and continued publishing the magazine . . ."

"He talked on, replying incisively to all questions, with no hesitation, no saving clauses. As he spoke, a little of his Chamber (legislative) experience mannerisms displayed themselves. He half-closed his eyes expressively, tightening his strong, not unhandsome features, revealed a flair for gesture, and a touch of the flamboyant.

He was born, he related, in 1913 of poor parents in the village of Pestel. His father, a farm worker and part-time teacher, died in 1927. Daniel and one other boy survived from six children. Their illiterate mother brought them to Port-au-Prince, and there slaved to bring them up. "She was devoted to the point of sacrifice," says Daniel. Others helped their education. Daniel went through secondary school, had begun to attend law school, returned to the Lycée Pétion to teach his favorite subject, mathematics. When he lost his job in 1942 for dabbling in politics, he was quite unshaken. A month later he married, and soon founded the political party called the *MOP, Mouvement des Ouvriers et Paysans—Workers and Peasant Movement*. He took an active part in the revolution of 1946, which replaced the Lescot regime. For 75 days he was Minister of Education. Two secondary schools, one the Lycée Toussaint L'Ouverture, in town, were set up in that period, before he broke with Estimé.

Back in the political wilderness, he actively interested himself in trade unionism. He organized among others the union at Hasco (Haitian-American Sugar Company) which demanded and got a daily wage increase from 1 *gourde* 50 to 5 *gourdes* a day. (Five *gourdes* equaled the U.S. dollar.) In 1950 he was elected Deputy for Port-au-

---

*   *that I was bailing out, as some of the reporting under my watch was not always favorable to the regime. My conscience was further eased by the fact that I had declined any salary or recompense, and that I had simultaneously been able to continue publishing my Haiti Sun.)*

Prince, Pétionville and Kenscoff, a constituency of over 200,000 voters, and then as tribune of the people, had a powerful following, especially among the working class. He had no political party, as such then; that had been stopped, by order. But he had not renounced his party . . . The Party newspaper *Construction* had also been stopped, by order. So he personally published *Haiti Démocratique*. He had been called a communist. He denied this hotly, as a lie, a pretext. He had never been anything other than a true democrat, had never been, in contact with any foreign countries, never traveled. Where did he stand politically? "As an independent, and a democrat, he can commend the government when he agrees with its actions, can castigate it fearlessly when he is not in agreement, without fear." The taxation of coffee, for example, he considered excessive and unjust, inasmuch as it weighed especially on the small producer, discouraging the peasant, raising the cost of living. His social views? "The social revolution must consist in a change of viewpoint among the elite; or rather the old traditional aristocracy should give way to an aristocracy of merit, of which all should have equal access." The present government? He was disappointed. "The ideals of the 1946 Revolution have lost ground." He was disappointed in the country's failure to attract more foreign investment, to raise higher the general standard of life. In liberty and democracy he saw the way to a better Haiti . . . and he didn't think there is now sufficient of either.

The Deputy continued to answer questions, alert, cooperative, and precise. Awake at 5 in the morning, to read the newspapers [including *Le National*], and to appraise the day-to-day situation. A frugal breakfast (he was a light eater, lived on his own nervous energy), then worked in his office planning for the day's sitting (in the legislative Chambers he was a redoubtable speaker); he returned home to work on his newspaper, the tri-weekly *Haiti Démocratique*—the paper carries no advertising.

In the afternoon, from 4 to 5, he relaxed with wife Carmen and their six children, drove out in the controversial shocking scarlet Ford—"there is nothing to the color, it does not matter to me; and the car is a gift from my wife, from a little inheritance." In the evening he often conducted classes at the little private school owned by Mrs. Fignolé, or sat up late under the huge painting of his idol and model, President Salomon [1879-88] "one of Haiti's most progressive leaders," laboring to create by dint of fearless effort, the free, democratic, progressive Haiti as he, the Deputy Fignolé, envisaged.

Le National called him an "eminent confusionist . . . a professor who writes like a schoolboy." "How?" howled *Le National*, "can you deal with a man who thinks he is the center of the world?"

We asked other people about this phenomenon, Fignolé. Some called him a Red, mentioning the color of his scarlet Ford. Others hailed him as a fearless dedicated patriot, who would face any opposition in the interest of his liberal principles, which he upheld. Some considered him a good, parliamentary obstructionist, an oppose-for-opposition sake type, a professional underdog with a persecution mania.

———

As expected the interview increased the *Haiti Sun's* circulation, caused a loss of advertising from businessmen who detested Fignolé, and raised considerable comment. The *Sun* received a front-page bouquet from the dean of Haiti's dailies the French-Language dailies, *Le Nouvelliste*: "The *Haiti Sun* has, consistent with the rules of a modern and objective journalism, examined as its personality of the week, the figure of the Deputy Fignolé."

President Magloire's paper, *Le National,* hurled a sizeable (two-column) brickbat. It carried the gibe: "We have no doubt that the article of August 23 will make all readers think that, like the immortal hero of Cervantes, Mr. Dietrich (sic) has simply mistaken windmills for giants."

In my personal front-page reply to *Le National* I stated: "After warming up for a week our young confrère [*Le National*] proceeded to show off the deplorable and undignified habit of being personal in its comments. We will ignore this. This journal accuses us of naivete in not conducting an investigation into the controversial Deputy and in publishing his interview straight without verifying his statements. But our column, Personality of the Week, is always his or her side of the story. Finally as to insinuation that in our innocence we are being impelled by interests—which is ironic, coming from this estimable newspaper—we assure our confrere that we have NEVER had affiliation with anybody. When we choose journalists or industrialists, dancers or sportsmen, for Personality of the Week we only do so through the human or general interest of his or her story . . . or because as in the case of last week, the figure was brought back into the public eye through headlines in a leading journal."

I concluded: "We are most pained however that despite its prominent display every week, *Le National* spelled our name wrongly."

President Magloire was not the only one angry. The editor of *Le National,* Max Pinchinat, pulled his gun from his desk and threatened to blow my head off, and was only restrained by members of his staff. The elite saw Fignolé as a dangerous man and a political threat. Equal-opportunity critics that they were, they condemned him as both a communist and a fascist. Claiming he was mentally unbalanced, they said he had suffered numerous mental breakdowns. They were worried by his electrifying hold on the people. He could call his fanatical followers into the streets where they formed the *rouleau compresseur* (steamroller) that rolled over the streets as an unstoppable mob. In his file to *Time* Magazine from Port-au-Prince while covering the 1946 choosing of a president by Haiti's new congress, Canadian-born correspondent William Krehm wrote: "Inflation and wartime speculation have ground the people down into issue-less despair and left them receptive to the advent of a messiah. He came in the person of Daniel Fignolé, a twenty-eight-year-old former mathematics teacher, a black son of peasants. Slight, bashful, with embers for eyes and a rare magnetic timbre to his voice, Fignolé preaches a racist war of the blacks against the mulatto elite. The Faubourgs of Port-au-Prince were soon ablaze. Too young himself to run for president, Fignolé advanced the candidacy of Demosthènes Pétrus Calixte, a humdrum black soldier risen from the ranks and named first Haitian commander of the *Garde Nationale* by the Americans in 1934. Fignolé was reported promising the blacks the houses, cars, and mistresses of the elite as soon as Calixte came to power. Poor blacks took to insulting mulatto women and boasting that they would bed them once Calixte was elected." Krehm reproduced this *Time* file in his book *Democracies and Tryannies of the Caribbean* (published in 1959 in Spanish in Mexico City.) Calixte lost and Estimé won the presidency.

As for my profile of Fignolé, Haitians, unused to a free and independent press, found it difficult to fathom that someone could write about a political figure without being either a backer or enemy of that person. They didn't believe anyone could be neutral. Neutrality was unknown in Haitian politics and politics was all-pervasive. Nor for that matter was the U.S. embassy happy with the *Sun* profile. Magloire was their *Man*, and they preferred to leave Fignolé tarred as a Red.

Shortly after the Fignolé piece appeared, President Magloire returned from inaugurating a renovation project in his beloved city of Cap Haïtien. The night after he returned I happened to be having dinner at Nobbe & Bondel's restaurant on the *Rond Point de la Liberté* when the presidential motorcade passed. A Haitian friend with whom I was dining in the open air noted, peering after the black limousines, that "the president has stopped before your office." I thought I should hurry over and see what he wanted. My friend, more attuned to his country's politics, said, "No. It is a good thing you are not in your office," adding, *"Rat la toujou soufle avan li mòde."* ("The rat blows on his victim before it bites.")

The next day, the president's lady friend walked into the *Sun* from her women's wear shop next door. "Paul," she said, "is hopping mad with you. He wanted to kick you out of the country. But he won't." laughingly she added, "I told him you'd be good boy in the future." The lovely lady had need of my telephone, as it was one of the few that worked in our business neighborhood. She talked to the president on my phone frequently. I thanked her for her intervention on my behalf.

Not long after that exchange, Bernier St. Jean, who was in charge of distribution of the *Sun,* chose the next-door lady and me as godparents for the baptism of his daughter. Keeping with protocol I paid a visit to the lady with a gift. Then I received a visit from an Army officer from the palace who told me that the President was not happy about my visiting the lady. In the spirit of this verbal jousting, the following week the *Sun* appeared with a full-page story on the protocol and duties of godparents as required by Haitian tradition, with a photograph of the lovely godmother and myself with her holding the baby before the parents' little hut.

Clarence Moody, a fine figure of a man in tropical white suits, was said to have built Hollywood, Florida. His *Compania de Industrias Maritimas,* based in Cuba, benefited from a $7 million Haitian government contract for the renovation of Cap Haïtien, which included a sewage system, and paving of streets. He was close to President Magloire and upon completion of the work Moody was decorated with Haiti's *Honneur et Mérite* medal.

Whether out of a sense of good business or other motivations, Moody astonished me by saying he would like to invest some money in my newspaper and suggested the figure of $10,000. When I refused his generous offer, he assured me that if I would accept he would not exercise any editorial control over the *Sun,* something I doubted. Over drinks, I explained to Mr. Moody that, even though it was tough and often unrewarding work, I loved publishing the *Sun,* at time single handily. If he or anyone else invested in my paper it just wouldn't be the same. And I warned him that the Haitian governments, as well as the U.S. embassy, were often unhappy with what the *Sun* published. He said he found my response reasonable and we parted friends.

———

That same issue with the famous Fignolé, *Personality of the Week,* the Sun carried a long informative article on Haiti's Black Gold—coffee. "Agriculture under-secretary Claude Préval, had journeyed to Marmelade to focus public attention on the importance of coffee to Haiti's economy, to herald the bumper crop expected that year, to demonstrate the success of the first year of the government's five year plan to develop agriculture.

"Public attention was drawn more forcibly to coffee last year when a failure in production revealed how vitally important is this one crop to Haiti's economy and how uncertain is the source from which 65 per cent of the nation's income is drawn. Taxes on the product of the peasants and small farmers who reap the berries in little holdings all over the country are the main source of government revenue. Value of the coffee exported in 1951-52 was 32,700,682 dollars, though after systematic taxation the original producer got a small part of this amount. When a bad harvest diminished revenue last year the present government came near to its most serious crisis since 1950. One of its first measures was the drastic reorganization of agriculture extension services; another was the implementing of plans to plant 10 million trees in 5 years. Such steps would benefit Haiti immensely, if they went further. For many difficulties are to be surmounted if Haiti is to increase or even maintain its coffee production. Prevailing conditions hamper as well as favor coffee cultivation.

Heavy seasonal rain falls on the steep mountain slopes cause severe erosion, washing the best soil down the hillside. The best coffee grows on young wood, so that only the second and third year is there an optimum production. Careless planting allows trees to grow unpruned; bushes become too thick or too tall and berries fall on the ground. Coffee must grow under the shade (except over four thousand feet) and improvident deforestation has ruined many suitable areas. Finally the price of Haiti's coffee is helplessly subject to world economic cycles (controlled in Brazil or in the New York purchasing market), and when the cycle adversely coincides with the bottom of the Republic's own production cycle, disaster could threaten the country.

The near disaster of last year, like an ill wind, helped to point out the potential good, if a thorough-going program is accepted. Haiti is rich in manpower, while coffee cultivation more so than in Brazil can be controlled, and can also be properly directed by agricultural extension services. The planting of productive shade trees, like castor oil, or bigger fruit trees, and increased terracing could increase production by 30 per cent in two or three years. If such a sustained program had been started by Haiti in 1934, right after the end of the American Occupation, Haiti's coffee production this prosperous year would have been twice its present production. And a great amount of priceless top soil would have been saved too. Today the soil washed away annually from the exposed, deforested mountain area in the Artibonite is equivalent to the loss of a farm of 2,800 acres with soil 12 inches thick.

Haiti cannot afford this loss. Coffee and other crops will continue to bring increasing wealth to the country *when* and *if* present program of soil conservation, composting, and afforestation are carried out in full measure and enlarged.

It was this greater prosperity to *pays* and *paysan* that the Minister wisely stressed when he talked to coffee farmers in his home town of Marmelade in the department of the North. For the fate of coffee seems always to bear a close parallel with the economic condition of the country. In 1739 the Jesuits introduced coffee here from North Africa, planting it first a Plaisance, a few miles from Marmelade. In 1791 the beginning of the revolution St. Domingue's prosperity, coffee production on 800 estates totaled 60,151,180 lbs., a figure not equaled for over one hundred years. After Independence when sugar production declined coffee production remained large enough to provide the state with considerable income. By 1839 the figure had reached 43,854,666 lbs. In 1935-36 a century later, the Vincent government reported the export of 79,400,000 lbs of coffee compared with 76,600,000 lbs of sugar. The war, shipping difficulties and loss of the European market, hit Haiti's coffee hard. Haiti was able to sell 11,162,390 dollars worth of coffee to Belgium in 1951-52, and 15,024,331 dollars to the U.S. Big news now is not only that the coffee crop will be good: It is the promise that the coffee price will be excellent. Brazil which produces just half the world's supply did not over produce this year. Rather a frost which nipped this year's coffee buds has considerably reduced world potential supply. After sparing a little sympathy for their Brazilian counterparts, the Haitian peasants, the Haitian government, the Haitian people in general have the feeling that they are beginning to ride on a boom, as the price of their Black Gold begins to rise on the world market." (By 2006 much of the Haitian coffee crop was sold across the border to the Dominican Republic by the peasant growers who received a higher price than from the Haitian coffee speculators.)

———

Sunday May 24th, 1953: Haiti is mourning the death of the man who not only brought the joys of music to the youth of our Republic but also enabled the world to share in our great musical heritage. Professor Werner A. Jaegerhuber, pioneer arranger of Haitian folksongs, passed away at the age of 53 Tuesday afternoon at his home in

Pétionville. He was a semi paralytic who had kept on with his arduous labors despite his weakened physical condition. Just several weeks ago his talented pupils provided Port-au-Princians with an excellent evening of music at the American *Pavillion*. And the Professor was hard at work on plans for the musical program of the coming 150th Independence celebration at the time of his death.

During his busy life, he produced an Opera Naissa based on Jacques Roumain's dramatic tale of the Haitian peasant's struggle for water *Gouverneur de la Rosée*. He also provided a three-act cantata based on voodoo airs, a Symphony *L'Ile Enchantée*, a *symphonietta* and a book of folklore songs for the schools.

In fact, Professor Jaegerhuber was the first to tap the rich lode of Haitian folklore music by going out in the mountains and recording the ancient songs of the peasants— preserving the freshness of the melodies while transcribing on paper what had only been handed down from mouth to mouth.

Werner Jaegerhuber's love for music was noticed short years after his birth in Turgeau on March 17, 1900. His father, Anton, was an American of German ancestry. His mother was Marie Tippenhauer. When he was still very young he was sent to Germany to become the pupil of Dr. C.A. Bieber, later studying at the world famous Voigt Conservatory at Hamburg.

In 1921 he returned to his homeland and began the study of Haitian Folklore. The rich musical heritage of his maternal ancestry dominated his production. That same year he returned to Germany to teach. He was Professor of Contrepoint at Von Bernuth Conservatory and became Director of the Musical Faculty at Spetzgart and later Salem. In addition he directed several noted Philharmonic Orchestras and offered piano and organ concerts in leading European Capitals. In 1928 he wooed and won Anne Burkhart and went on to even greater successes before returning to Haiti in 1937 . . ."

A familiar scene in the country side.

A *chef de section* (rural policeman) with his fighting cock.

The national sport in the countryside, cockfighting draws a record crowd.

Everyone worked in Port-au-Prince. It was a city of tradesman.

Even Old Glory was for sale.

The Iron Market

A group of Port-au-Prince businessmen of the 50's: Elias Noustas, Fritz Mevs, Raymond Roy, Clémard Joseph Charles and Henri Merceron.

Members of the Haitian Press at lunch on the left Max Chauvet, director of *Le Nouvelliste*, and, across from him, writer Jolibois.

Active newsmen Lucien Montas of *Le Nouvelliste*, *Haiti Sun* editor, photographer Charles of the Tourist Department and writer Prof. Ernst Trouillot.

Editor C. Sealy of the *Daily Gleaner* of Kingston, Jamaica (standing) at a luncheon with Haitian journalists.

Visitors from Port-au-Prince admiring the new engineer marvel, the Péligre Dam, one of the largest engineering project since King Christophe built the Citadelle.

During Magloire's presidency the capital city got a new National Bank as well as a new Post office.

Artist Gesner Armand from Croix des Bouquet visits the *Haiti Sun* to show off his early paintings. André Dimanche with a statue he fashioned from Haitian hardwood.

Christmas cover by artist Wilson Bigaud, one of Haiti's great artists.

CHAPTER 8

Bon Papa

[Gustav's Sunset Cruises departing the Casino pier on a 100-foot luxury yacht and watch the Golden sun go down on Port-au-Prince bay to the guitar of Ronnie Hollyman.

Good drinks and congenial company. $2.50.]—advertising in *Haiti Sun*.

To a relative newcomer Haiti gave me the impression of having slipped back into the 18th century. Indeed, the country all too frequently appeared mired in the past, in both deeds and not only rhetoric. The dawning of the 150th birthday anniversary, for example, appeared to have awakened Haiti's historical devils in President Magloire.

In January 1954, opposition Deputy Daniel Fignolé, despite his official immunity as a member of the legislature, was arrested and his small print shop was smashed. Government agents carted off even his precious handset type. It was the end of *Fignolé's* newspaper *Haiti Démocratique*. Deputy Rossini Pierre-Louis, along with, editor Georges Petit of the *Independence* and scores of others deemed troublemakers, were also ordered arrested. Senator Marcel Hérard managed to escape the police, having been delivered in a carpet to the safety of political asylum in the Mexican embassy.

Two months earlier anti-Magloire posters and mimeographed appeals to students and workers to strike, and the military to oust the *backward* regime had begun to circulate. When a policeman reportedly shot and killed two men putting up subversive posters, Magloire took time out to explain that while he was against abuses, the police had done their duty. He congratulated them.

Those arrested were all accused of plotting against external and internal security. However, many saw the action as a preemptive strike, rounding up the usual suspects who might make trouble during the sesquicentennial celebrations.

Standing on the Palace steps that January day in 1954, beside a larger-than-life oil painting of himself in army general's uniform; Magloire thanked a government-organized rally of state employees for their putative support. During a series of equally choreographed Palace lawn rallies the president declared that it was time to get tough, to take control. He emphasized the point by announcing that he was pulling on his *kanson fè* to "repress some vagabonds." For foreigners "*kanson fè*" was a mystifying Haitian Créole term that came to be widely translated as "iron pants." In reality *kanson* refers to a man who has gotten his act together, who is strong-willed and capable of running things—in short, organized, firm, and efficient. Magloire added *fè* to signify that his resolve was set in iron.

For his part Fignolé entered the National Penitentiary with great dignity, his dark suit somewhat frayed and dust-covered. It was not difficult to feel a pang of sympathy for the *Deputy of the people* as some referred to Fignolé. Former President Estimé had also feared Fignolé and his magnetic populist hold on the capital's poor and found it necessary to outlaw Fignolé's party. Now it was Magloire's turn to fear the charismatic Daniel. However, Fignolé had instructed his followers to, "*chita sou blòk glas*" ("sit on a block of ice"), meaning not to react to his being jailed.

—

Meanwhile, publishing the *Sun* continued to be what could be termed tough fun. In its fourth year the paper was prospering in advertising and even overseas subscriptions. Haiti remained an inspiration to nonwhite nations in Africa, the Caribbean and elsewhere still under colonial rule. In Haiti itself, tourism had now equaled coffee as a moneymaker.

No international news made its way into the *Sun* unless it had a Haitian angle, even if the angle had to be rather contrived. (Example: "Joe Stalin of Moscow died last week. He had never visited Haiti.") News-wise for my readers, there were more important local wars to be fought than that taking place in far-off Korea. One typical battle: The U.S. Department of Health had banned the importation of the then-popular Haitian-made "Voodoo-doll swizzle sticks." At the time they were being manufactured by the millions in Haiti. The stated reason for the banning was that the cashew-nut head of the doll contained a chemical similar to the one that produced ivy itch. Further, the little red grain that made up the eyes of the doll was said by the U.S. health experts to be toxic.

The *Sun* went to bat for the swizzle sticks and several American bartenders, in letters to the *Sun,* protested, that the "Voodoo rash is so much wishwash." The ban remained but the *Sun* at least helped Haiti make its case.

Following the "Voodoo doll" epic, there was the great flap over Old Glory. A Port-au-Prince Syrian rag merchant importing by the ton, bales of misprinted—minus a star—U.S. flags, which he sold to poor Haitians for bedspreads and dresses. This eye-catching material was cheap and soon American tourists were shocked to see their Stars and Stripes doubling as fashionable wear for economically challenged Haitian women. My story on this innovative use of Old Glory, complete with a photograph of a *machann* (female vendor) sitting in the Croix des Bossales market decked out in American flags, was published in *Time* Magazine. The Syrian merchant found it necessary to defend himself in the *Sun*—and revealed that he had had a similar offer from Great Britain but that the Union Jack was too expensive.

And there was no lack of good local feature topics as well as news stories and challenging issues. Also, a steady flow of distinguished visitors to Haiti provided entertaining interview material. The celebrities included Sir Hugh Foot, the British Governor-General of Jamaica, who with his wife made an official visit. The renowned French theatrical troupe *Comédie de Paris* opened its annual season in town with Moliere's *L'Avare* (The Miser), at the *Rex Théâtre*.

No longer content to publish a newspaper devoted only to news, I ran hard-hitting editorials assessing what those happenings meant. I decided the *Sun* had earned its editorial spurs when we began coming under attack for our positions by our French colleagues. The *Sun* was no longer an outsider. Operating a newspaper you either fought for what you believed in or printed obituaries and comics. That was my philosophy. Thus promoting Haitian tourism, defending Haiti against unfair and/or inaccurate criticism, and closing the communications gap between classes the country's social were our overriding objectives. Editorials dealt also with such nagging domestic problems as soil erosion, the need for better farming methods, creating jobs for 6,000 college graduates who eschewed returning to the family's primitive little farm or trade in the towns. There were few jobs for university graduates in those days as owners of the few established businesses and industries traditionally held the best jobs for members of their families whether they were qualified or not. (Today more than one hundred thousand sit for their baccalaureate exam)

The *Sun* pleaded to save "our historical monuments and other treasures" and to get rid of the nightmarishly unsightly billboards that marred the beautiful scenic route to the mountains behind the capital. Only once did I take the law into my own hands. Gently jogging my Jeep (it had suddenly become mightier than the pen) at the thin legs of several tall, roadside billboards, I dropped them expertly like pinball's until one fell forward onto the Jeep, smashing its canvas top and bruising the editorialist.

Haiti's population in the early 1950s was manageable with a little more three million inhabitants most of them peasants living in the countryside where it was still possible to farm on non-eroded plots and feed their families. In the *Sun* the elite class could read about common people, their working trades, their misfortunes, their glories. The *Sun's* interviews let members of the rank-and-file speak in their own way; we presented their biographies and published their pictures. A special topic, *Down Every Rue*, depicted more than 40 diverse trades, such as the stone seller, the bottle merchant, the coconut vendor, the suitcase maker (out of beer cans), the water carrier, the 4-cent shower bath, the street cleaner, the mystery of the *lamayòt*, the *bouretye*, the shoe maker, stone breaker and tailor. The *Sun* ran photo after photo of firemen standing before a blazing house with limp hoses. Annually there was a fire in the old *Croix des Bossales* market place that destroyed merchandise and homes. The wooden gingerbread homes were not the only victims of fires. *SHASA (Société Haïtienne d'Automobiles SA.)* was hit by fire as it was refurbishing its offices and showroom on *Rue Pavée*. As one of the first Haitian owned company its directors, Marcel Gentil and Fortuné Bogat, were undeterred and their business hardly missed a beat. The *Sun* noted that SHASA had been established in 1932 when the American owned *West Indies Trading Company* close down. Two employees Fortuné Bogat and Marcel Gentil who had been with the American company for 13 years as sales manager and general stock manager took over and established their exclusive agency for General Motors, RCA and Goodyear tire with $15,000 working capital (Daniel Brun, Armand Malebranche and Philippe Charlier were also members of the company). The Madsen Company put their losses from a fire that gutted their cotton mill near *Portail St Joseph* at $200,000.

Fire was a terrible hazard in most Haitian towns. In the capital the ancient wooden gingerbread structures often caught fire and the firemen—the most active unit in the Haitian army at the time—was hindered by a lack of water.

President Magloire on Feb. 22, 1954 was featured on the cover of *Time* Magazine in a long highly complimentary article which noted his efforts to modernize the country, including building roads and bridges and workers' cities. Reporting the story along with the newsmagazine's Caribbean bureau chief Bill Forbis was a veteran *Time* correspondent, Jack Dowling, who was later to lose his life in a plane crash flying from Paraguay to Buenos Aires. When I asked Dowling how he was going to treat the still—imprisoned Fignolé, Pierre-Louis, and other politicians, he replied, "Not at all. This is going to be a positive article".

The article in *Time's* Hemisphere edition set the stage with: "Cinnamon-*skinned* girls in Dior dresses, starchy diplomats and officers sparkling with gold braid gathered one night last week in the majestic, tile-floored great hall of the Presidential Palace in Port-au-Prince. The occasion: a ball in honor of Jamaica's visiting Governor Sir Hugh Foot and Lady Foot. Just at 10, the orchestra blared out a march, and Lady Foot entered the room on the arm of a huge, kingly-looking black man resplendent in white tie, tails and full decorations. His Excellency Paul Eugene Magloire (pronounced mah-glwar), President of the Republic of Haiti and host of the evening, stayed on until 2, ceremoniously dancing with each guest in the order of her husband's rank, gravely bowing to Lady Foot's parting curtsy".

"The ceremonial public appearances of Paul Magloire are always kingly . . . . Magloire carries off his formal appearances with unerring dignity. When on parade he is being what he knows many lowly Haitians want in a President: a father-king, a national Bon Papa of regal mien. Loving it, they sing:

> He gives us jobs and money—oh! oh! oh!
> He can stay in the palace as long as he wants!"

"In the palace, between ceremonies, Magloire puts aside fancy dress and operates as the kind of detail-cracking, eleven-hour-a-day executive that any topflight Detroit industrialist could understand. He rises in the dawn cacophony of his capital's unbelievably numerous roosters, and hops on an exercise machine. After a rubdown, he breakfasts in bath robed comfort on fruit and *café au lait.* Then, in a suite filled with alabaster busts, stuffed pink cranes, Empire clocks and pictures of himself and other Haitian heroes, the President reads reports and mail, takes a thoughtful second look at work saved over from the night before. At 7:30 he showers and dresses, usually in grey gabardine or white linen, a silk tie with a gold clasp, grey suede shoes. Soon he is sitting at a cluttered desk in a smallish office conspicuously free of ornament."

"He speeds through his work, reading documents and penning "O.K. PM" on them. When his ministers call, he half turns in his chair, folds his hands in his lap, watches sidelong from penetrating brown eyes, and rumbles out courteous, unruffled answers. He usually lunches with his family of one son and four daughters (although Mme. Magloire is currently in a Baltimore hospital for a checkup and the two elder daughters are attending a Brookline, Mass, convent school). After a siesta, he goes back to work until dinner at 7. He sometimes takes an evening off for poker or bridge, and occasionally drops in at the City's biggest nightclub, where he sits with a few young aides, cradling a highball in his big hand, beaming at the dance-floor merriment but taking no part in it. More often he works through until 10 or 11 p.m., especially if the next day's schedule calls for another public appearance. Pageantry takes time—but Magloire recognizes that it is part of his job of ruling tiny Haiti."

"Magloire passionately argues said *Time* that "Haiti has shown by its struggle for liberty and progress that the black race and small nations can . . . achieve a status equal to that of any other human group. Haiti has given the lie to those who pretend that certain races are unfit for liberty, equality and self-government."

Not everyone was happy with the *Time* cover as it revealed, " . . . The hungry outsiders naturally begin to grumble, agitate, fire bitter charges of inefficiency and graft. Magloire's good friend, Chief of Police Marcaisse Prosper, has provided an unfortunate focus for criticism. The juiciest current gossip of Haiti concerns Prosper's new hilltop home in fashionable Pétionville, (Bourdon) big as a U.S. small-city high school, lavishly furnished by Manhattan's W. & J. Sloane. The prosperous Prosper's salary is $350 a month."

As for my own foreign correspondent chores for The Associated Press there was little spot news of importance until Hurricane Hazel struck Haiti's Southern peninsula in

October 1954. Much of my ongoing reporting involved covering Haiti's favorite sport, soccer, whenever an international game was played at the new Magloire Stadium. (Unlike in the neighboring Dominican Republic baseball was not played in Haiti.) The heads of the newly formed Haitian Football Federation, Pan American Airways (PAA) Haitian employee William (Tison) MacIntosh and Army Lieut. Alix Pasquet had convinced Magloire to spend money on building a Port-au-Prince soccer stadium rather than send the national team to play in Argentina. The construction of *Stade Magloire* cost $125,000, a significant sum at the time. Under the glare of electric lights important games were played at night. Jamaica and Haiti always had close ties and in the 1950s with daily plane service between the two countries provided by PAA, football benefited with games against their best teams. Jamaican Jocelyn McCalla became a leading promoter of the sport in Haiti and wrote for the *Sun*. McCalla's by-line began appearing in early 1953. He covered Peru beating Haiti's national team at *Stade Magloire* and later losing to both *Violette* and *Aigle Noir* clubs.

As indicated by the *Time* Magazine cover story the President's popularity had blossomed beyond Haiti's borders and he basked in the international approval like a proud soldier. In preparation for a three-week summer "goodwill" trip to Latin America he heeded a plea from parliament in April and released Fignolé and the others jailed politicians, declaring a general amnesty. Secure at home, the handsome, debonair chief of state with his broad open smile looked abroad for further support. He departed to a tumultuous send off on June 21 accompanied by 37 members of his government including military, along with their wives.

In neighboring Cuba, his first stop, Magloire exchanged decorations with Dictator Fulgencia Batista y Zaldivar and during a press conference in Havana denounced Communist aggression, while asserting, "My country is not threatened by communism." Batista for his part also noted that he too was cracking down on Communists. Anti-Communism made good political sense vis-à-vis Washington as the new Eisenhower administration was completing its final, not-so-secret plan, carried out by the CIA, to overthrow that very week the leftist Guatemala government of Col. Jacobo Arbenz Guzman. No mention was made at the Magloire-Batista toast fest of Fidel Castro who, having survived a disastrous July 26, 1953 attack on the Ft. Moncada barracks in Santiago de Cuba was in prison on Cuba's Isle of Pines (He was later to be pardoned.) However one of Magloire's aides confided to me on his return that Castro's speech at his trial, "History will absolve me," was just beginning to circulate clandestinely in Havana. In prison Castro's popularity had soared.

In Nicaragua Magloire and his entourage were feted by Dictator Anastasio Somoza Garcia who decorated the Haitian strongman with the National Order of Ruben Dario, Rank of Grand Master. Dario was Nicaragua's most famous poet. Somoza was assassinated two years later, on Sept.21, 1956 by another Nicaraguan poet, Rigoberto Lopez Perez.

In Venezuela Magloire was embraced and feted by yet another dictator, Col. Marcos Perez Jimenez, who had succeeded Venezuela's noted novelist and President Romulo Gallegos. Perez Jimenez was overthrown in 1958. (The Haitian army's C-47 carrying the president's luggage, his civilian suits and uniforms, was missing for nine hours and believed lost. The pilot explained when he finally showed up in Venezuela that he had been forced to land in Panama for mechanical reasons and to refuel.)

Next stop was Panama. Magloire was the first Haitian chief of state to visit Panama. The isthmus country bore a special significance for Haiti because it was in Panama City in 1825 that Haiti was excluded from the first meeting called to promote Inter-American solidarity. By no manner or form was the U.S delegation about to sit at the same table with representatives of the black Pariah State of ex-slaves.

Nor did the Latin Americans recall their debt to the former Haitian President Alexandre Pétion who had assisted Simón Bolívar with arms and men on his last attempt to oust the Spanish from South America and create Gran Colombia. At the time Haiti was rejected from participation in the 1825 hemisphere conference, President Jean-Pierre Boyer, a mulatto, labeled the meeting's behavior as an "outrage" . . . reflecting "absurd prejudice resulting from the difference of color." Not until Abraham Lincoln freed the slaves in the United States in 1862 did Washington officially recognize Haiti.

In Panama President Col. José (Chichi) Antonio Remon Cantera greeted his Haitian colleague effusively. At the time Chichi Remon was sparring with the Eisenhower administration in Washington over negotiating a new Panama Canal treaty. U.S. President Gen. Dwight Eisenhower, who had served in Panama for three years as a young officer reportedly, felt fondly of that small but strategic nation. But John Foster Dulles, Eisenhower's secretary of state, was far too concerned about communist penetration in the region to make any concessions to the Panamanians. Six months after Magloire's visit, on Jan. 2, 1955, Remon was machine-gunned to death while attending the horse races at the Panama City track by two men wielding submachineguns. It was never proved but the common theory in Panama at the time was the gunmen were working for Lucky Luciano the Mafia mobster.

In Colombia strongman Gen.Gustavo Rojas Pinilla was just beginning his four-year dictatorship having overthrown a previous dictator, Laureano Gómez, the year before. As elsewhere docile citizens, following the local strongman's suggestion lined the streets for the visiting Haitian president, waving the blue and red flag of Haiti. As elsewhere Magloire's delegation was wined and dined. Magloire placed wreaths to the heroes of the host country's Independence, made laudatory speeches, and exchanged decorations.

In Venezuela and Colombia the speeches by the hosts as well as the visitors did contains special mention of the historical fact that President Alexandre Pétion had furnished Simón Bolivar with arms and men, plus a printing press, to free South America from Spanish rule. Pétion had asked in return that Bolivar free the slaves. However rather than face a much superior Spanish force after his 1816 landing on the coast of Venezuela Bolivar sailed back to Haiti to prepare for his last and successful attempt the following year. Prior to returning to Haiti, Bolívar kept the promise he had made to Pétion by decreeing freedom to all slaves, even though he didn't have the power to enforce the decree.

Magloire returned home to be greeted by a wildly jubilant crowd and a 21-gun salute from Fort National, in time to celebrate his birthday on July 19. Four impressive Arches of Triumph had been erected over the road from Bowen Field airport. Medical dispensaries and other public works were to be inaugurated to coincide with the president's birthday. In his birthday address he spoke of strengthening the bonds of friendship with sister republics. Here was a president who was genuinely loved by the Haitian rank-and-file. Or so it seemed. Carnival-loving Haitians adore a party and Papa Magloire was a gregarious fun-loving partying man. He enjoyed dancing and had no inhibitions about taking to the dance floor.

On the serious side he announced in his speech a six-year plan for Haiti that encompassed a new international airport and other public works to the tune of 25 million dollars. A newspaper analysis of the plan appeared in *The Washington Star*. The article deemed Haiti outstanding in Latin America—with "free elections, majority rule, free speech, free assembly, religious freedom, property rights, [and] private enterprise."

———

Tourism was booming when the late author/playwright Truman Capote came bouncing into the El Rancho Hotel accompanied by the more sedate British stage director, Peter Brook. They were in town to put together a Broadway musical based on a short story Capote had written after a 1947 visit to Haiti entitled, *House of Flowers*.

Haitian officials, highly protective of their new tourist industry, were somewhat troubled by the play. It was Brook who had to convince them that the musical, set in the red-light cafes along the Carrefour Road, would not hurt the country's image or damage the nascent tourism industry. Nevertheless the officials were not convinced and remained hypersensitive about the musical.

———

While at work on the musical director Peter Brook invited his friend British author Graham Greene, to drop over from Jamaica (where he was vacationing) and join the fun in Port-au-Prince. The tall lanky Englishman Greene had his legs entwined around a tall stool at El Rancho's circular bar when I first met him. As the *Sun* had greeted the famous writer's arrival with a front-page story stating that Graham Greene was a "winner of the Nobel Prize for literature"—a mistake—I feared may have hexed his ever receiving the award. At El Rancho I was somewhat hesitant about approaching Greene for an interview as a cloud of gloom appeared to have settled on him. It acted like a reverse magnetic field, keeping strangers at bay. Even when he did dispense a few words through his pursed lips my first impression was, "another pissy pommy!" He was not. I was mistaken.

However he was somewhat shy and clearly treasured his privacy above all. Reluctantly he said he had recently returned from Indo-China, that he had found Haiti not unlike that region, and that he felt much more at home in Haiti than in Jamaica. He was working on his novel *The Quiet American*. It was obvious that Greene, though a celebrity in his own right thoroughly enjoyed being shielded by the hullabaloo surrounding the "House of Flowers" musical. Truman Capote primping about, in his Bermuda shorts, drew all the attention anyway.

I had seen Greene off at Bowen Field Airport on Monday, August 27. The next day when I passed by to pick up the daily newspapers from Puerto Rico and the Dominican Republic that arrived on the Delta daily flight, there was Greene again. He had suddenly become a non-literary newsmaker. Because as a student at Oxford University Graham Greene had for a very brief time been a paid-up member of Britain's Communist Party, he was automatically barred from entry into the United States or its territories, without special permission from the U.S. attorney general. The 1952 U.S. McCarran-Walters Act prohibited foreigners who had ever been members of the Communist Party from setting foot on American soil. As reported by the Puerto Rican newspapers the following day Greene had been denied entry upon arrival in San Juan.

He had been en route to England from Haiti and thought he just might be allowed to pass through the U.S. in transit. The U.S. Immigration & Naturalization Service (INS) thought otherwise. INS agents had given him a pleasant evening in San Juan and the following day put Greene on the Delta flight back to Port-au-Prince. I arrived in time to witness a heated exchange between Greene and the American manager for Delta in Haiti at the in transit bar of the little Bowen Field airport. The Delta manager said the author could not proceed on "his" plane since he had arranged with Haitian immigration officials permission for Greene to remain in Haiti and, " . . . we can ship you on to Jamaica tomorrow." The irate writer went ballistic. "I'm no parcel, I'm not going to be shipped anywhere. I am going on this plane to Havana." Blue in the face the Delta man declared firmly: "You are not going on my plane." It was then that the captain—pilot of the Delta airliner came forward and ended the uproar-, which delighted the fellow passengers—stating that, "This gentleman is going on my plane." Off went Greene to Havana, the flight's next stop, which he eventually used as the setting for his novel spoofing the British Secret Service, *Our Man in Havana*. It was the Port-au-Prince airport bout that endeared me to Greene.

In December 1956 he returned to Haiti accompanied by a lady. It was the end of the affair with the lady and for me the beginning of a long friendship.

Perhaps by association with Truman Capote and his coterie some of my Haitian colleagues wondered whether Greene was gay. At *Le Nouvelliste*, during an afternoon *odyans* (gossip session), one newspaper colleague asked, "Do you think Graham Greene is a *masisi*, (the Créole word for gay)? I said, "I didn't know for sure but I very much doubt it. Read his books, you'll find the answer."

Homosexuality carried a serious stigma in Haiti and a popular song of the day was suggestively entitled "*Mon Kapitenn*" ("My Captain"). Capt. Vic Blanchet, commander of the Pétionville police, had recently broken up a closet gay party whose revelers included respected fathers and husbands. They pleaded their innocence, telling the captain all kinds of lame excuses. The story of the raid produced "*Mon Kapitenn*" which was sung in a seductive voice and is made up of all the excuses, e.g. "My Captain, I am not from here, I'm from Jacmel . . . My Captain I was on the way to the cinema . . ."

CHAPTER 9

Revisiting History

"To write this act of independence we need the skin of a blanc (white man) for parchment, his skull for an inkwell, his blood for ink and a bayonet for a pen."

Such were the unforgettable lines of Boisrond Tonnerre's brutal preamble to Haiti's act of independence on January 1, 1804. It was revolutionary rhetoric but for the new nation's victorious ex-slaves it was no more barbaric than what they had suffered under their French colonial masters, who had treated them as a labor commodity and subhuman *chattel*.

Nevertheless, the uttering of this phrase in Haiti in 1954 caused the wife of the French ambassador to press her handkerchief to her face. As I watched I could see she was stifling tears. It was a touch of realism not foreseen in the historic day's protocol. The distinguished guests and officials were seated before the new modernistic Roman Catholic cathedral in the town of Gonaïves listening to the country's dapper army commander, Brig. Gen. Antoine Levelt, much lighter in color than the mulatto declaration of independence author Boisrond Tonnerre. In the front row Gen. Paul Magloire, presidential sash over his general's uniform and his riding boots polished to a high sheen, appeared more pensive than exhilarated. One wondered whether he was wearing his famous *Iron Pants,* which he had unveiled in a get-tough speech to his opposition two months earlier.

It was January 1, 1954, Haiti's 150th birthday. Army Commander Levelt read on. The words of the Caribbean republic's act of independence had committed the rebel slaves' victorious generals to renounce all allegiance to France forever, and to declare they would rather perish than submit anew to French control. As Levelt droned away, the French ambassador's wife still had her face buried in her handkerchief. The British ambassador seated adjacent was trying to comfort her.

In the writing of Haiti's act of independence, Tonnere's fiery words directed at the French *blancs* had been whole-heartedly endorsed by Haiti's revolutionary leader Gen. Jean -Jacques Dessaline, and were a rhetorical climax to a brutal war and its horrific cruelties.

The French had lost their jewel in the Caribbean. Slavery had made Saint-Domingue (as Haiti was known under the French) France's richest colony. It was said at the time that one Frenchman in five lived from the prosperity of Saint-Domingue. In the wake of the slave uprising and victory, the towns, prosperous plantations, aqueducts and machinery lay in ruin from the *dechoukaj* (Créole for uprooting) of the colonial power.

Le Tricinquantenaire (150th anniversary) festivities on New Year's Day, 1954, had begun with prayers in the new cathedral which the Magloire government had built. Outside the church, roaring skyward was a bronze bas-relief memorial obelisk depicting Haitian forces defeating the French, the work of a Cuban sculptor. While the celebration was a stiff and staid affair on that glorious, cool morning in a town, which by midday normally becomes oven-hot. It was easy to drift back to 1804 and visualize the excitement and exuberance, which must have reigned among the victorious generals and their troops. They were led by the short and muscular ex-slave, General Dessalines, whom the revolutionary commanders nominated, to rule as governor-general along the lines of a constitution, which had been drawn up by Toussaint L'Ouverture in 1801.

In Haiti, history is alive. It is a passionate subject that must be approached with caution. In 1954 after a century and a half, there were families who still argued about and ardently defended their ancestors' role in the birth of the nation. Among the guests at the sesquicentennial ceremonies in Gonaïves were the country's most distinguished historians, writers, and poets who, each in his own way, could describe in detail the events of that day of national glory in Gonaïves 150 years earlier. On the hallowed *Place de l'Armée* the triumphant Dessalines and his generals had declared the first day of the independence of Haiti. To rid the country of all vestiges of France's once-thriving slave colony the victorious generals changed its name from Saint-Domingue to the original aboriginal name, *Ayti*, meaning, *land of mountains*. Until the rule of Jean-Pierre Boyer (1821-44) it was spelled Hayti. (Under Boyer an "i" was substituted for the "y". *Cap Français* became *Cap Haïtien*. *Port Républicain* had already been changed back to *Port-au-Prince* when the British captured the town in June 1794.

Dessalines had ridden on horseback into the coastal town of Gonaïves, on the eve of the great day, to discover that his secretaries charged with writing the act of independence had spent too many words in justifying this momentous action. He was furious. Boisrond Tonnerre, a mulatto secretary, understood Dessalines' chagrin and uttered his famous phrase on how they should write the act. The blunt and brutal phrase captured the mood of the moment and Dessalines quickly charged Tonnerre with writing the act of independence, expressing the ex-slaves' and freemen's feelings toward the white Frenchmen. Moreover Dessalines' constitution, which was to follow the declaration of independence, stated that all Haitians were to be known as *noir*, (black). Tonnerre spent the evening of December 31 writing and the next morning had to be shaken awake. History states that his candle was still burning on the table next to the completed act of independence.

A century and a half later, President Paul Magloire was among the few Haitians who believed that discrimination based on shades of skin had prevented all Haitians from obtaining the full fruits of independence, that color had been a great obstacle to the country's progress to working together. Even so, Magloire himself was the darling of the mulatto elite. With a reputation as a *bon vivant,* he had been admitted to the elitist Bellevue Club in Port-au-Prince which at the time was exclusively mulatto. Thus ironically, the president of the country was credited with breaking the club's color bar.

Magloire knew that he was accused of *doublure,* a pejorative descriptive given black presidents who favored the mulatto elite. Nevertheless in an interview Magloire said he believed firmly in the country's motto, "*L'Union Fait la Force*" ("Unity forges strength") as the only avenue of progress. During his 1950 campaign for the presidency he was billed as the *apostle of national unity.* He attacked politicians who exploited Haiti's intrinsic societal divisions by setting one group against another, accusing them of using that old sword of internal color prejudice, black against mulatto. Meanwhile the politicians in black middle-class accused the mulattoes of being the real racists.

Thomas Madiou, the Haitian mulatto historian, stated in his *Histoire d'Haiti,* Vol.3, that Dessalines "conceived the generous and salutary idea, after the deportation of Toussaint Louverture, of reuniting a single body, to face our oppressors; this was the constant and persistent idea of his whole life." Madiou, who was born in Port-au-Prince in 1814 and educated in France, noted that Toussaint was "the symbol of black supremacy, while Dessalines symbolized an alliance between black and mulatto."

As Madiou explained, knowledge of the past is vital in order "to direct a society in the ways of progress." Unfortunately, throughout its violent history Haiti's leaders have not always learned the lessons of the past or have incorrectly interpreted those lessons. Too often their own ingrown racial prejudices and blind ambitions for power have shaded their decisions, leading to bloodshed and political disaster for their people.

Three years of publishing the *Haiti Sun* had made me addicted to Haitian history, as were most Haitians, including the peasants. This was also very important to a journalist because it didn't take a visionary to know that in Haiti, perhaps more so than in many

---

*   Two of my wife's ancestors, Gen. Laurent Bazelais on her mother's side and Raphael Mallet on her father's side, had signed the Act of Independence. Historian Edmond Mangones, a relative, one day informed my father-in-law that his wife's ancestor had killed his ancestor. Gen. Laurent Bazelais, a mulatto who rose to be Dessalines's chief of staff, had initially given refuge to Raphael Mallet, a *bon blanc* (active in the non-white cause). But when Dessalines ordered the liquidation of all Frenchmen left in Haiti, Bazelais had complied and killed Mallet, the *bon blanc* signer of the Act of Independence.]

other countries, one had to look backward to discern the future. Moreover, I quickly learned that Haitian writers differed more than they agreed in their eulogies to the heroes of independence. It was understood that these intellectuals'essays, and we published many of them, were pure, untouchable *hagiography*; they were not to be edited, not a word was to be changed. Many were published in the hopes of enhancing the authors' political careers.

As for foreign authors' books on the Haitian revolution, it was likewise remarkable how many of them also differed in their interpretations of that historic event. Toussaint, the *Black Napoléon,* appeared to fascinate Haitian and non-Haitian writers most. More books were published on Toussaint than on any other hero of Haiti's revolution. Authors seemed evenly divided in their bias about the man's decision to remain allied to France and not declare independence.

Henri Christophe, born on the British island of Grenada and the man who pronounced himself king of Haiti's North, was the subject of books and plays, principally by English writers, and largely because he had sought alliances with anti-slavery English abolitionists of the day. And much was written about the mulatto Alexandre Pétion, who became Haiti's first president and assisted Simón Bolívar in his liberation of Latin American people from Spanish colonialism.

One reason that Toussaint was a favorite with biographers was that he was literate and had left thousands of letters, while Dessalines was illiterate. Nonetheless the latter was a true revolutionary who wore the scars of slavery on his back and once in power ruled, as only he knew how, with an iron fist. In December 1804 when news arrived of Napoléon Bonaparte's intention of being crowned Emperor of France, Dessalines beat him to the title. The coronation of "Emperor Jean-Jacques (Dessalines) the First" of Haiti took place in Port-au-Prince, on the 8th of October, 1804.

The Empire lasted only two years. On Oct. 10, 1806, rebellious military, while entering Port-au-Prince, killed Dessalines in an ambush at Pont Rouge. Their shouts of *Down with the tyrant!* would become a familiar cry as one Haitian leader after another was overthrown through the years. Paradoxically, almost fanatical loyalty to the ideals of the French revolution kept them in a state of constant rebellion against the very authoritarian rule to which they were periodically driven by their uncompromising individualism. Hating dictatorship, Haitians found themselves continually setting up dictatorships, only to knock them down again. This historical contradiction of character has been a hallmark of the country's history during most of Haiti's nearly two centuries of independence.

On Dessalines' death, Christophe was chosen to be President for a four-year term but objected to Alexandre Pétion's being named to head the National Assembly where most power would reside. Christophe denounced Pétion and his followers as rebels and went to war. All Haiti needed was another war! Haiti was divided between Christophe in the North and Pétion in the South and the war was to last until both were dead.

Influenced by Britain rather than France, Christophe on March 28, 1811, declared his part of Haiti a kingdom and in June was crowned as King Henri I. Pétion died in March of 1818 at age 47 and King Henri followed him to the grave on Oct. 8, 1820. Both old lions were gone. Pétion, who had been president-for-life with the right to choose his successor, had appointed General Jean-Pierre Boyer, his aide and close friend. Six years Pétion's junior and also a mulatto, Boyer ended the war and unified the island. His rule lasted an astonishing 25 years, from 1818 to 1843, until he too was overthrown.

The 1804 independence celebration was hardly the occasion to honor a Frenchmen but there were those Haitians who privately commended the role played by one controversial figure of the French Revolution, Léger Félicité Sonthonax. It was on Aug. 29, 1803 that the then 30-year-old *commissaire civil* after nearly a year in Saint-Domingue, proclaimed the abolition of slavery in the colony. His proclamations were published in French and Créole.

As the dominant member of the second governing commission sent to Saint-Domingue by the National Assembly in Paris, the young lawyer had enthusiastically embraced the French Revolution become known for his articles on the revolution. In one polemic published in September 1790, he had quoted Jean-Jacques Rousseau; "When one wishes to link the peace of despotism to the sweetness of liberty, I am afraid one wants contradictory things. Rest and liberty seem incompatible to me; one must decide," Sonthonax continued: "Citizens! You will surely not waver in the choice. A tempestuous liberty will seem preferable to a despotic but tranquil government, whose calm is that of annihilation and death."

However, it was Sonthonax's essays on slavery, at the time the Western world's most important economic commodity, that brought him to the attention of the French National Assembly. They sent him off as a member of the second commission to Saint-Domingue. In one article he had accurately predicted that the days of the slave trade were numbered and that the principles of universal liberty were germinating and spreading among nations.

———

During the afternoon of the commemorative day of January 1954, Mrs. Paul Magloire, wife of Haiti's President led the lady guests on a visit to the cemetery in Gonaïves, to pay homage to Dessalines' widow, Empress Marie Claire Heureuse. She is said to have hidden white colonists in the days following independence when Dessalines decided to eliminate all Frenchmen left in the nation to prevent them from taking up arms in the event that the French should try to return. Ending the day's festivities was a reception for the presidential party at the residence of a wealthy mulatto coffee exporter, where Magloire was praised for honoring the forefathers with a new cathedral and repairing Gonaïves dusty streets. Early the next morning a long line of buses and automobiles headed north over the recently tar-sealed road to Cap Haïtien. Guests were to witness a replay of the last battle against the French.

Poet Jean Brièrre, director of Tourism, introducing Marian Anderson the famous
African-American singer during a special events to mark the 150th anniversary
of Haiti's birth. The scene was a reception at the Milot palace of King Henri
Christophe. Marian Anderson's singing and the setting made it a memorable
event.

That final battle took place at Vertière, a short distance from Cap Haïtien. Unlike
the battle of Waterloo there were no newsmen present to cover this French loss on Nov.
17-18, 1803. The reenactment on the other hand was well covered by the foreign media,
including reporters and photographers for *Look* and *Life* magazines.

On the field the reenactment was reaching a climax when above the sound of mock
battle there was heard an angry howl in plain English: "Shit, he shot the horse." *The
March of Time* newsreel cameraman who uttered the expletive took a second look through
his camera lens and confirmed that a horse was indeed dead. "We are screwed," he said.
"No American audience will accept the sacrifice of a horse in any reenactment." During
the actual battle the great moment had come when Haitian General François Capois,
known as Capois la Mort, valiantly led his troops forward against the French only to have
his steed shot from under him. General Donatien Marie Joseph de Vimeur, Vicomte de
Rochambeau commanding the French troops ordered his drummers to sound a pause in
the battle, and sent an officer to congratulate Capois for his bravery. During the 1954
reenactment Lieut. Frederic Arty of the Port-au-Prince police department, playing Capois

La Mort, shot his horse with his service revolver as he rode forward, causing a hushed outcry from the foreign visitors. The horse crumpled to the ground its legs thrashing in the air and died. When a Haitian mulatto officer, dressed in French uniform, carrying Rochambeau's congratulation faced him, Arty let fly a string of choice Créole expletives. In fact extending congratulations was an uncustomary act by Rochambeau, a man whose brutality and cruelty had made him the most hated man in the Caribbean, at least by the blacks and some whites. At 47 when he took charge of the remnants of Napoléon's great army in Saint-Domingue on the death of Leclerc, Rochambeau was driven by hatred so deep that he sought to annihilate all the blacks. He took great pleasure in devising methods of torture and disposing of his captive. His importing of man-killing dogs from Cuba, as a sport to kill captive blacks, made Haitians fear large dogs even to this day.

Rochambeau's professional career had suffered in the Caribbean and he blamed the blacks. After serving with his famous father, General (and Count) Rochambeau (a friend of George Washington), who led the French expeditionary force in the American revolutionary war and is credited with the decisive victory over the British at Yorktown, the younger Rochambeau was promoted and given command of France's possessions in the Windward Islands. In 1794 however he was besieged in Martinique and surrendered to the British. Shipped to America as a captive he was later exchanged for a British general and returned to France. He was ordered to Saint-Domingue where, although he embraced the Republican cause, he was arrested and sent back to France by the French Directory commissioner Sonthonax. Unemployed, Rochambeau wallowed in self-pity until Napoléon gave him command of troops in the Italian campaign and then appointed him second in command to Leclerc. With Rochambeau now involved, no rebellion or war, during that period of history, was fought with such ferocity and brutality as the French onslaught against the army of ex-slaves.

———

During the reenactment President Magloire had edged away from the guests who were watching the progress of the "battle" from a newly erected grandstand. He stood alone, deep in thought. It was then that I noticed his right arm. He had slipped it into his tunic. Whether he did it consciously or not—or had needed to rest his hand after so much handshaking—he struck a pose so reminiscent of Bonaparte it was a shock.

The finale of the battle took an unexpected turn. Although Maj. Paul Corvington, the tall and handsome commander of the Haitian Military Academy, had carefully scripted the reenactment, he had not foreseen the fact that the battle was an emotional issue for even the local peasants. Thousands of farmers had gathered on the hillside, returning from tending their crops with machetes in hand. Through generations, oral accounts of the war, and the participation of their ancestors as foot soldiers, had made them knowledgeable about and sensitive to the battle. As the clouds of cordite rose from the rough grassy field and Capois's troops kept failing to dislodge the French occupying Butte Charrier Fort, recently reconstructed with plaster for the reenactment, the peasant onlookers became restless.

Suddenly, overcome with the spirit of their ancestors, they charged down the hill to join the battle as Capois's men cried: "*A l'assaut grenadiers! Sa ki mouri zafè pa yo. Nanpwen manman nanpwen papa.*" ("Charge grenadiers! Whoever gets killed doesn't matter. You have no mother; you have no father".) The cadets from the Military Academy playing the part of the French troops, were soon routed and the French tricolor torn down. By this time the French ambassador's wife was nowhere to be seen.

It was difficult to replicate the heavy tropical rainstorm that had helped Rochambeau extract his remaining troops from Vertière and escape to Cap Français. The actual storm lasted three days. Retreating to the port city Rochambeau,the general whom generations of French teachers had told their Haitians students was "cruel but brave.", capitulated to Dessalines, agreeing to hand over Cap Français' fortifications intact within ten days. At the same time Rochambeau sent an officer to open negotiations for his troops to surrender to the British (France and Britain had been at war since May 1803) who were blockading the bay.* They finally surrendered and 8,000 troops, the survivors of Napoleon's ill-fated Saint-Domingue army, were taken to Jamaica.

Rear Admiral Sir John Thomas Duckworth, the British commander of the Jamaica station, refused to meet Rochambeau because of the atrocities he had committed against the blacks of Saint-Domingue which were well known throughout the Caribbean. In fact Admiral Duckworth was so concerned that the notorious Frenchman's presence on the island of Jamaica might incite its blacks to take matters into their own hands that he shipped Rochambeau as a prisoner to England. Repatriated to France seven years later in a prisoner exchange, Rochambeau finally returned to the battlefield and was mortally wounded in the battle of Leipzig in 1813. As for Napoleon's famous sister, Pauline Bonaparte Leclerc went on to marry again, continuing her life of seduction, and died in Florence, Italy, in 1825. Bonaparte himself was defeated at Waterloo in 1815 and exiled by the British to the lonely island of St. Helena a thousand miles off the west coast of Africa, where he died in 1821. His war in Haiti had cost him more lives than at the battle of Waterloo—over 55,000—and many of his best generals. Haiti had lost half its population of 400,000 and the country lay in ruin. Napoléon has been quoted as saying of Saint-Domingue "Damn sugar and coffee!" (It is strange that in the Marine museum in Paris there is no mention of Leclerc's armada crossing the Atlantic. The French prefer to mention only their victories.)

---

*   It was when the British commander of the Squadron saw the red and blue flag flying from Fort Picolet, guarding the entrance to the bay, that he realized that Rochambeau was trying to make a break for the open sea. He sent Capt. William Bligh [Of Mutiny of the Bounty fame] to learn Rochmanbeau's intention. Bligh found the defeated French general aboard the French Frigate *La Surveillante.* With the deadline over Dessalines threatened to sink the French ships if they didn't leave the harbor. Rochambeau had no choice but to surrender to the British. The foxy Frenchman had sought to sneak out of port but the wind was not in their favor.

While the furnace of rebellion, civil wars, British invasion and Napoléon's attempt to reestablish slavery consumed Saint-Domingue during this period, it was the kidnapping of Toussaint L' Ouverture by the French during a truce that was the catalyst which brought Generals Jean-Jacques Dessalines, Henri Christophe, Alexandre Pétion, and other Haitian rebel leaders together to defeat Napoléon's army and end French rule. Toussaint however, the remarkable black military leader, died in a frigid cell in Fort de Joux in the high Jura Mountains in France on April 7, 1803.

Revolutionary victory notwithstanding, Dessalines and his fellow generals faced a daunting task. Haiti, the first free black nation, had to be built on the ashes of the old white colony. Virtually nothing was left of the once-rich sugar and tobacco plantations. There was genuine fear that Bonaparte would try to retake the country. Thus constructing fortifications was a top priority and the defense budget weighed heavily on the new republic. Moreover, France was not the only potential danger. Not only was Haiti a black pariah in a white-dominated world; Dessalines was the Fidel Castro of that era and there was genuine fear that he might export his revolution to other slave-owners colonies surrounding Haiti.

No island—including the eastern side occupied by the Dominican Republic—has witnessed so much bloodshed. Long before the Europeans arrived the native Indian *caciques* (chiefs) fought each other. The war-prone Caribes killed the peaceful Arawaks. The devastating cross-and-sword arrived in 1492 with Columbus's discovery of the island that he named Hispaniola. On Christmas Eve of that historic year he lost his ship the *Santa Maria* on a reef not far from today's city of Cap Haïtien at a place now called Limonade. Its name is incongruous; the surrounding salt flats had little to do with the summer drink. Yet the first European settlement in the Western world, Nativity, was built by Columbus's men where the village called Limonade stands today. For building material they used the timber from the wrecked Santa Maria. The first massacre of Europeans happened at Nativity. They were left behind to man Nativity by Columbus. They were killed by the Indians. (It was in the small church at Limonade that Henri Christophe suffered a stroke and was made a partial invalid by paralysis.)

The original Spanish conquistadors worked the native Indian population literally to death in record time, and then imported African slaves to replenish the subjugated work force in search of gold.

With the division of the island of Hispaniola—Spain acceded in 1697 at the peace conference of Ryswick to the French claim to the western part Saint-Domingue—it soon became France's richest possession. The atrocities committed by Frenchmen against the slaves were often indescribable. As a disciplinary measure one favorite sport of some planters was, *"bruler de la poudre au cul d'un nègre"*. Gunpowder was placed in the anus of a slave and exploded.

———

Leaving the battlefield and dead horse behind, the guests at the independence celebration moved on to Cap Haïtien, a city around which much of Haiti's history has revolved.

The extraordinary setting for the formal dinner ending the 1954 anniversary festivities was a place so breathtaking and steeped in history and legend that one could hardly recall the lavish menu. The site was the Royal Palace of Sans Souci built in 1813 above the hamlet of Milot some 20 miles from Cap Haïtien. Guests were seated at tables set on the esplanade around the giant caïmitie tree where it was said the King Henri dispensed justice. The visitors were afforded a spectacular view of the palace ruins, still formidable-looking even after being looted in 1820 and partially destroyed in an 1842 earthquake. The baroque palace was said to be the work of a Haitian architect of the Royal Court. Spread out below were the ruins of the various Royal Ministries, print shop, library and barracks. The circular roof of the Royal chapel had been restored. Fresh water from mountain streams coursed under the Royal chambers and banquet and reception halls keeping them cool in summer and making scores of fountains dance, day and night. Christophe the hard taskmaster had thought of everything. From above the Royal chambers King Henri, semi-paralyzed and unable to face a rebellion, had taken his life with a silver bullet at age 53.

It was on this same esplanade in an effort to impress visiting Admiral Sir Home Popham, British naval commander-in-chief of the West Indies, that Christophe had played an old game. He ordered a thousand of his men to march before the admiral change their uniforms and then march again purportedly as a new unit of his army. Thirty such crossings of the terrace gave the impression that his army totaled 30,000 tall, tough disciplined fighters, when it actually numbered only some thousand palace guardsmen.

As if the historic magic of the place was not enough for the 1954 dinner, Marian Anderson, the famous African-American singer held the hundreds of guest enraptured with a repertoire of songs.

A thousand meters into the clouds behind the palace of Sans Souci was King Henri's masterpiece, *Citadelle La Ferrière.*

Perched like a gray battleship on La Ferrière, one of the three peaks of the Bonnet a L' Evêque mountain chain, this tremendous fortress was built to garrison ten thousand troops. Construction took years at a cost of countless lives and this engineering marvel included rows of five-ton bronze cannons pointing out from a lower level at the invisible enemy. The cannons and accompanying mortars covered, in their field of fire, the Plaine du Nord and neighboring mountains. The fortifications attested to the enormous amount that the new nation had found it necessary to spend on its defenses. The big guns date back to 1750s and carried the royal seals and coat of arms of their Spanish, British and French origin embossed on them. This extraordinary amount of heavy armament, which had to be hauled up the steep hills, confirm the fact that the great powers of the day were prepared unofficially to become gunrunners to a state they considered a dangerous pariah.

The next morning I awakened in a home on the Plain du Nord, once the richest plain in the world. Now, the only remnants of plantation life were huge decorative portals leading nowhere. Even the line of royal palms that led from the portals to the plantation houses had disappeared.

Cap Haïtien, renamed Cap Henri during the rule of Henri Christophe, had been destroyed in 1793 during the slave rebellion, rebuilt and again destroyed in 1802, when Christophe greeted Napoléon's army by burning down the city. Partially rebuilt it was plundered by the departing French troops. Yet in 1954 the city still exuded special charm, its streets lined by vintage two-story gingerbread homes with laced-iron balconies.

———

Back in Port-au-Prince, as part of Haiti's birthday celebrations, impressive new statues of the heroes of independence—Toussaint Louverture, Jean-Jacques Dessalines, Henri Christophe, and Alexandre Pétion dominated the sprawling park between the National Palace and the Champ de Mars. Blue lights were switched on to outline the Palace, scene of a festive ball with all the decorum that would have delighted Louis IV. Standing sentinel on both sides of the ballroom were bronze busts of Haiti's black and mulatto past leaders. It was one time they shared the same stage.

No one disputes the fact that the French revolution, and the passions it unleashed with the fall of the Bastille in 1789, had their effect on Saint-Domingue along with much of the rest of the Western World. Preceding Haiti's 150th birthday, Auguste Viatte of the Paris newspaper *Le Monde* elaborated the French point of view. The *Haiti Sun,* on Oct. 16, 1953, published a translation of his article in which he declared that for France, the loss of Saint-Domingue was "a painful anniversary, but one for which she can learn some lessons."

"Haiti, in effect, is the spiritual daughter of the French revolution," Viatte wrote. "It was the ideals of 1789, the 'French Ideals,' that gave the slaves their dream of liberty. It was at first only a question of civil liberty. Saint-Domingue could have remained French; at least what we now call an *Etat Associé* (Associated State). Proof of this from writers of this era is indisputable."

Viatte elaborated on his argument—recalling how Toussaint had not rejected the authority of the mother country. "If opinions changed it was because the colonialists had persuaded Bonaparte to re-establish their privileges by force; he sent an expeditionary corps, arrested Louverture . . . As so happens, blinded by material interests, they had destroyed the *élan du cœur* [the rebels initial impulse] and dug their own graves by persuading the blacks that only total severance from France could save them from falling under the yoke of slavery once again.

That was the first lesson and here is the second. Hardly had their independence received recognition by [France's King] Charles X, than the Haitians returned to their passionate attachment to our (French) culture. *L'idéal a regagné ce qu'avait perdu l'égoïsme.* Never, even in her darkest hours, had Haiti, the physical daughter of Africa, ever failed to recognize what she owed to France, her spiritual mother . . . truly this little country, issued from another race and freed in violence, has become a striking symbol of the universality of our Culture."

Le Monde writer Viatte's third lesson concerned the United States. "Intervening in a crisis of anarchy with a military occupation that rested heavily upon the Haitian people," he asserted, "the United States believes it to its advantage to draw Haitian youth to New York and away from Paris. The result was not what was wished. Welcomed to a Paris without color prejudice, Haitian intellectuals returned home full of enthusiasm for a civilization in which they could integrate themselves without difficulty. But in a world where the slightest pigment closed hotels and theatre doors, how could they help from returning embittered in their ethnic consciences and how could they help feeling their own misery more, faced with the overwhelming plentifulness of American living. Many became Black Racists; others, sometimes the same ones, waited for Moscow to liberate 'the proletariat' to which they were confined by blood.

The "continentalism" that the United States substituted for "colonialism", and which goes on the theory that lingual and cultural affinities should be sacrificed for the sake of geographical or economic entities, has led, on each continent, to the most dynamic nation's taking control; just as in the Far East, it has wound up by turning against its American instigators in nourishing the hostility of the weak, who have ceased to believe in the spirit of equality."

Nevertheless, Viatte concluded, " . . . France is present in Haiti intellectually more than ever before. The French Institute created by a Cultural Pact in 1944, furnishes the University of Haiti a part of its teaching staff, publishes the excellent magazine 'Conjunction,' and offers a platform for lectures much more frequently than before. Haitian students are retaking the road toward Paris. And wasn't it a Haitian delegate, *monsieur* Ernest Chauvet, who protested against the heartlessness with which the United Nations neglected our tongue in favor of English? "Black France" was the title that Michelet gave to Haiti. She Haiti repeats it with pride. If one thinks of her [Haiti's] position on the global chessboard—at the intersection of the Two Americas, one of the whites and the other of the blacks—if one recalls that she was the second Independent Nation to be born in the New World and that she remained one of the few Independent States of the African Race, one will not underestimate this attachment to our spiritual traditions."

American observers were less lyrical. Foreign correspondent Sydney Gruson of *The New York Times* wrote a curtain raiser to the 150th birthday, published on Dec. 2, 1953. "Too many people are on too little land—about 3,500,000 in an area the size of Maryland," Gruson reported, describing Haiti. "Between 80 and 90 percent of the people are illiterate and four-fifths of the land is mountainous, much of it eroded and barren." Gruson added that Haiti's "strong-man president [Paul Magloire] has achieved for the time being, at least, the political stability indispensable to economic and social development."

The *New York Times* correspondent concluded with a fundamental point: "The quality of President Magloire's leadership is perhaps best measured by his success in bridging the deeply rooted division between Haiti's pure Negroes and the mulattoes."

CHAPTER 10

Moving Ahead

N attily dressed in a double-breasted Palm Beach suit and boater straw hat, President Magloire broke a bottle of champagne on the first bucket of concrete to launch the construction of the country's most ambitious public works endeavor. Decorated with the Haitian flag the receptacle bore the sign: "First Bucket Concrete, Peligré Dam, September 10, 1954."

The 236-feet-high dam (825 feet across) would not only restore thousands of acres of farmland in the Artibonite Valley and control floodwaters; it would eventually provide electricity for the nation's capital, plagued by blackouts. The *Organization de Développement de la Vallée de l'Artibonite* (ODVA) had been set up as an autonomous entity to oversee the development of the Valley with technical assistance from the U.S.

In typical Magloire style, the ceremonial pouring of the first bucket of cement was followed by a luncheon reception and dancing for several hundred guests. There was reason to celebrate. Haiti appeared at long last to be moving ahead in the direction of economic development, boasted by the government's ambitious five-year plan.

Foreign investors began taking advantage of Haiti's liberal tax laws. For me there were business-oriented feature stories galore to file to The Associated Press in New York. A French company established a cement plant on the coast, twenty miles north of the Capital. The oil-rich Murchison Brothers of Texas built a flour-mill a few miles further up the coast and meat packing plant next to the agriculture school at Damien. Reynolds Metals Company launched bauxite mining in the hills above the port of Miragoâne.

Of all the projects, the one that garnered the most international attention was the new Albert Schweitzer Hospital in the Artibonite Valley. William Larimer Mellon, of the wealthy Pittsburgh banking family, had been literally smitten by an article in *Life* Magazine about Dr. Albert Schweitzer, who was devoting his life to providing medical help in his jungle hospital in then-French Equatorial Africa. Mellon, driven by a desire to do something more socially meaningful, decided to study medicine and seek Dr. Schweitzer's counsel on how best he could make a contribution. With a new degree in medicine Mellon, accompanied by his wife, discovered Haiti. With encouragement from Dr. Schweitzer, they built a modern hospital in Haiti's Artibonite Valley on land provided by the Magloire government. (The site was a former banana plantation.) The hospital would provide medicine and health care in the middle of the country.

Haiti had likewise regained international respect. Magazine travel editors and Freelance writers were finding the newly burnished Caribbean tourist destination fun and exotic, a rewarding place to visit. One Saturday night, a travel writer was astonished to find the president dancing the Haitian meringue at the famous Pétionville nightclub, Cabane Choucoune.

Even the summer *dead season* came alive as cruise ships flooded the capital with tourists. The visitors demand for wooden salad bowls and other tourist mementos was such a drain on Haiti's mahogany that the country was forced to import mahogany lumber from Honduras.

The Roman Catholic Church, Haiti's state religion, was delighted with President Magloire. He had officially confirmed in 1950 that *Vodou* was still outlawed. In spite of his reputation as a *bon vivant*, he was a good family man. His wife, a quiet understated person, was serious about her charity foundation and their three daughters and a son were brought up in strict Catholic schools and were known for their good behavior. The Vatican had agreed, to elevate in 1953 the country's first Haitian-born black bishop, Rémy Augustin, to Haiti's hitherto all-white French (Breton) Catholic hierarchy. Bishop Augustin became the assistant to elder Archbishop Joseph Le Gouâze. (Of the 300 Catholic priests in Haiti only a third was Haitian.) For the Haitian populace it was easy to ignore politics during that period of good feeling.

However in the Caribbean, Mother Nature has a way of reversing even the best laid economic plans. And so it was on Monday evening, October. 12, 1954, when Hurricane Hazel struck Haiti's southern peninsula with devastating force, wreaking havoc and death. The northwest also felt Hazel's fury. The hurricane was to have long-term political as well as physical consequences.

In Hazel's aftermath, towns, villages, crops, and trees appeared from the air like shredded wheat. The loss of life eventually totaled over a thousand with thousands more injured and homeless. Scores of vessels were lost around the seacoast. Disastrous flooding caused many deaths in lowlands and plateaus. Coffee and shade trees lay about on the hills like matchsticks. Every day brought news of new victims.

On Oct.12, 1954, Hurricane Hazel struck the southern peninsula with full force and left devastation and death in its wake. Having spent most of the week acting as an interpreter aboard a Marine helicopter from the USS Saipan, I was shocked by the power of the storm. Thousands were left homeless and injured. Their homes and little plantations were wiped out. Coffee and Cacao would take years of replanting to restore the region's export crops. But the human misery, in the rugged mountains was mostly hidden from view. The small coastal towns, such as Dame-Marie, above shows a church guttered by the wind. Red Cross Doctor Claude Lafontant pauses to hear the woes of an elderly victim while, in a nearby cemetery, young men prepare to bury the dead. Besides the USS Saipan that rushed to Jérémie, the British HMS Vidal also brought aid. But the damage wrought by Hazel would have a lasting effect on the country. The government would also feel the effects.

For me reporting on the aftermath of Hazel was facilitated by airlifts in U.S. Marine helicopters from the aircraft carrier *USS Saipan*. The choppers carried relief to isolated towns and villages. My information gathering was made easier by the fact that the Marines needed an interpreter.

Back in Port-au-Prince there was no such generous airlift when NBC asked me to film the remains of a mountain village called Berly. Word had reached the capital that on October 20 the mountain village had literally disappeared. A rain-soaked mountain had suddenly collapsed burying the village under tons of boulders and earth. NBC having taken note of my Associated Press dispatch on the unfortunate village asked me to photograph what remained.

Accompanied by Poet Félix Morisseau-Leroy, by no means a mountaineer, we climbed a series of sheer, rain-soaked, sponge-like mountainside to get to Berly. Fifteen miles of mountains lay between the village of Furcy, where I left my car, and the now—nonexistent village of Berly. In Haiti one is seldom alone. Even on the most distant mountain peak there are people. Morisseau required several helping hands to shore him up the mountains, which were like climbing a slippery pole. Our first night was spent in a peasant hut where we were warmly welcomed and generously given the only bed.

With a hundred followers in tow we finally gazed upon our objective. There was nothing left of Berly that would indicate that there had been a village or even houses on the mountain. Giant boulders and tons of fresh earth marked the burial place of 240 people. To illustrate my story I had a peasant point to where the village once stood and I began panning away with my Bolex movie camera. Another peasant sounded a *lambi* (conch shell, the ancient signal) as I began to film and suddenly in my frame were more than a hundred peasants all pointing to the pitiful site. I had found only color film to use and when NBC received it they commented on the beauty of the mountains, but cabled, "Where is the village?" By that time they had lost interest. It was yesterday's story. I did have still photographs with which to illustrate the enormity of the landslide in the *Haiti Sun*.

In spite of publicity surrounding the havoc wrought by Hurricane Hazel, tourism proved more durable in Haiti than coffee or sugar crops. The visitors kept steaming into Port-au-Prince. The beginning of 1955 saw some of the world's most famous people visiting Haiti. Charles Addams, the *New Yorker Magazine* cartoonist famed for his macabre humor, saw his first zombie in the Grand Hotel Oloffson gardens during carnival, or at least an individual covered with a white bed sheet. Actor Noel Coward, a drooping cigarette permanently in his mouth, with actress Claudette Colbert on his arm, opted for the upscale El Rancho Hotel while John Gielgud preferred the bohemian Greenwich Village atmosphere of the Oloffson created by Roger Coster and wife Laura who finally took over the gingerbread palace at the end of 1954. The Costers renovated the Oloffson, using 600 gallons of paint but being careful to preserve its ghosts. Pretty Laura Coster, who had been secretary to U.S. Supreme Court Justice Thurgood Marshall, sent a clipping of a feature story on the Grand Hotel Oloffson published in the *Haiti Sun* to Charles Addams telling him, "I believe this is your kind of hotel; we invite you to visit." He did. Paris-born Roger Coster, a well-known magazine photographer, offered foreign correspondents a ten-percent discount and the Oloffson quickly became a favorite of foreign newsmen.

—

Roger Coster who in 1954 turned the Grand Hotel Oloffson as one of the most popular tourist Hotels in the Caribbean. He liked to call it "Greenwich Village in the Caribbean." Coster read the future and bailed out during the early years of Papa Doc Duvalier's reign, when the Golden Age had lost its glitter.

Young tennis champions at the Bellevue Club in Bourdon

To Haitians, the next-door Dominican Republic could have been on the far side of the moon. To Dominicans, Haiti hardly existed except as a source for cheap labor. Virtually the only traffic between the two Caribbean republics, which shared the island of Hispaniola, consisted of Haitian cane-cutters bound for the Dominican sugar plantations, and a good handful of Dominican *señoritas* who staffed the "Houses of Flowers," the café-brothels on the outskirts of Haiti's Capital. Both groups were hard working and industrious, in their respective callings, but were hardly representative of their respective peoples. Though few Dominicans spoke French or Créole some Haitians spoke Spanish. It was taught in Haitian schools and there were Haitian aficionados of Mexican movies as well as the visiting Dominican *señoritas* on *La Frontière* as the red-light district was also known. (Plus there were cases of true love springing forth between Dominicans and Haitians.) Moreover the most powerful radio stations on the island were Spanish-language Dominican outlets and Trujillo's *Voz Dominicana* had the strongest signal of all in the Caribbean. It was used by Trujillo to attack Haiti and Cuba.

At the core of the political and cultural division of the island were history and racism. Dominicans recall the ill treatment meted out by Haitian invaders in the nineteenth century, while Haitians were portrayed to Dominican school children in frightening terms as backward and deeply involved in witchcraft. Dominicans tended to believe the wildest stories about Haiti. Some Dominican intellectuals had a certain respect for the French scholarship of Haitian intellectuals. But the anti-Haitian sentiment among Dominicans was the more pronounced. Haitians, for their part, saw the Dominicans as weaklings surrendering abjectly to the terror of the long Trujillo dictatorship in apparent silence. These two Caribbean-island neighbors were light-years apart.

My journalistic curiosity to know the Spanish-speaking side of the island grew with time. I wanted to see for myself the kind of grip *El Benefactor* held over the eastern side of Hispaniola. Any man with the gargantuan vanity to claim co-billing with God, "God and Trujillo," went one slogan, must have created his personal insane asylum.

The opportunity to visit Ciudad Trujillo for the first time came in March 1953, with an invitation from a friend, the daughter of the Venezuelan ambassador to the Dominican Republic. Her father, an elder general, had previously been assigned to Haiti.

The Dominican capital, then named Ciudad Trujillo (now Santo Domingo) was so clean, orderly, and organized it looked as if it was carefully sanitized daily. It had the conformed air of a cemetery. There were no visible signs of a sanguinary dictatorship. No victims hanging from lamp posts. In fact any hint of fear was well hidden or disguised. Talk politics or say anything derogatory about *El Hombre*, out loud and you were quickly whisked away. But in the privacy of their homes Dominicans hungrily feasted on *chismes,* (rumors). Traffic policemen, the majority of them black, protected by white sun helmets, stood for hours at most intersections quietly directing traffic. The only traffic violator was the dictator's son, Ramfis, and his friends who set their own speed limits in fast European sports cars.

Big Brother, in this case *El Jefe's* likeness, was displayed everywhere. Dominicans described their perpetual leader as paternalistic, a robust workaholic and, like all such men, equipped with a phenomenal memory as well as a phenomenal sex drive. Prideful of country, his own fiefdom, he had built an admirable infrastructure. Some of it however was for pure show. Such as for example a modern hospital for the handicapped erected before the entrance to the Nation's capital. It looked fine but inside there were no equipment or staff specialists.

On the Sunday of my visit, Renato Alonzo, a Mexican diplomat who had married the Venezuelan general's other daughter, called for me at the Hotel Jaragua. Acting mysteriously he instructed me to leave my camera and purchase a bottle of rum. A couple of miles from the city, on the old road to the sugar port of Haina, we stopped before an unfinished colonial-style house and went in.

We were greeted by our hostess, a thin, vivacious woman who welcomed us warmly and escorted us to the back patio. There several other guests, mostly men, were sitting and drinking. They turned out to be artists and bohemians. Lunch was being prepared in a thatch-roof *bohio*. The center of attention was a young man strumming a guitar and occasionally bursting into song. The house was tastefully furnished with French period pieces and paintings. We were introduced by first names only as was customary in subversive circles. Only when she joined us to talk did I realize our hostess's full name: Flor de Oro (Flower of Gold) Trujillo. She was *El Jefe's* eldest (legitimate) daughter, whose mother, Aminta Ledesma, had been dumped by the dictator more than a quarter of a century earlier when Trujillo climbed out of near poverty to fame and fortune.

Lively, loquacious, and slightly eccentric, Flor had once been a handsome woman. She seemed to need to unburden herself of her tormented feelings toward her family. *Negro*, her Uncle Hector (Trujillo), the current puppet president, was, she claimed, a "tight wad," and hated her because of her many marriages while he, didn't have the guts to marry his sweetheart, the daughter of a U.S. Marine. Negro, she added, was making her life even harder.

Dictator Trujillo, her father, had ordered her home from Paris, where she had been living, the year before. Refreshingly open in a tongue-tied country, she designated the most repulsive man in her father's government as the powerful Gen. Anselmo Paulino, whom she called *Mauvais Œil* (Evil Eye) in French. (Paulino habitually wore dark glasses to cover a glass eye.)

Flor de Oro had attended school in France in 1947. She laughingly told us that her sixth husband, correct sixth, was a Frenchman. Her first marriage at age 17 was to a young Dominican army lieutenant, Porfirio Rubirosa. The marriage lasted five years and helped Rubirosa, who became known as an international playboy, climb the ladder of influence in Trujillo's personalized form of government. She went on to marry a well-known Dominican physician, then an American doctor, a Brazilian entrepreneur, an American flier and a Frenchman businessman.

Flor became even more talkative as lunch progressed. A typical *sancocho* (stew) was served. There was also *arroz con pollo* (chicken and rice). The rum kept flowing. As we were preparing to take our leave Flor volunteered that her father treated her like "*mierda*" (shit) and her "poor mother fared little better."

Though she seemed politically opposed to her father her main gripe with Papa was of a personal nature. A Dominican friend later cautioned me that anyone seen talking with Flor was on dangerous ground, that El *Jefe* could be extremely mean to anyone visiting with his daughter. He had made Flor into a non-person, excluded her from society.

———

On another trip to Ciudad Trujillo (5th of November 1954), in the wake of Hazel, I paid a visit to my journalistic colleagues at the newspaper *El Caribe*. Two months earlier the publisher, Army General *Evil Eye* Paulino, had been suddenly fired and stripped of his powerful post as guardian of the Trujillo's realm. It was rumored that the general had been trying on a plumed hat in the sanctity of his home while *El Jefe* was visiting fellow dictator Francisco Franco in Spain. Everyone knew that in the Dominican Republic only Trujillo was permitted to wear a plumed hat, which he reserved for ceremonial occasions. Whether Paulino actually had such a hat was never proven but the prevailing theory was that he had become too big for his britches, or so *El Jefe* decided. Their warm 27-year friendship ended with a court's sentencing Paulino to ten years in prison along with $10,000 fine for *abuse of official power.*

At *El Caribe*, then the country's leading daily, I renewed friendship with publisher Germain Ornes, who had taken over the newspaper, and met staff members Rafael Herrera and Rafael Molina Morillo. They were good newsmen working within the bounds of *El Jefe's* rules and quirks governing the media. All praise was reserved for *El Jefe* and his government first and foremost. I wanted to know how they functioned under such a tightly run dictatorship, never dreaming that I would soon be in their position in Haiti.

From the visit to *El Caribe* I drew a lesson: Be careful what you say and what you don't say. The day following my visit a photo and story about me appeared in *El Caribe*.

I was quoted as thanking the "Dominican (Trujillo) government" for its aid to Haiti Hurricane Hazel victims when all I had done was express the Haitian Red Cross director's message of thanks to the Dominican Red Cross.

Nor was *El Jefe* beyond ordering a rewrite of an Associated Press cables to suit his own politics, I was to learn in the summer of 1955. It was only the beginning of a bizarre story *that* illustrated the extent to which Trujillo was prepared to go to even a score.

In Trujillo's Dominican Republic, with the removal of *Evil Eye* Paulino, a younger, more aggressive spy chief emerged on the scene. Johnny Abbes Garcia had no glass eye but he had a ruthless heart. He was soon to become feared as the devil incarnate. In the years that followed, I had many an opportunity to give Johnny unwanted publicity in the *Haiti Sun*.

Meanwhile Trujillo had become jealous of Magloire's popular international image. Magloire had been invited on a three-week state visit to the U.S. As noted Magloire had also made history as the first Haitian president to be honored as the subject of an uncritical *Time* Magazine cover story. The Haitian government was upset by the Dominican publication of an anti-Haitian book and President Magloire said he had no intention of visiting Ciudad Trujillo. If Haitian workers were being recruited for the Dominican sugar fields he said he would halt it. In fact as he spoke workers for the Dominican fields were being recruited at Croix des Bouquet, not far from the capital. Irked, Trujillo had gone to Spain to visit Dictator Francisco Franco. It was the only country, a fellow member of the world club of dictators, prepared to welcome *El Jefe*.

January 26, 1955. It was a red-letter day for Haiti as President Magloire departed on a state visit to Washington. The three-week-long trip would include other U.S. cities, Canada and Jamaica.

The administration of Republican U.S. President Dwight D. Eisenhower, preoccupied since the end of World War II with Europe and the Middle and Far East, had belatedly become sensitive to its neglect of its southern neighbors. Then Vice President Richard M. Nixon was preparing for a four-week trip to the Caribbean and Latin America to shoreup relations. Reaching out, President Eisenhower had invited the leader of the Western Hemisphere's only black republic and second country in the Americas, after the United States, to throw off the yoke of colonialism. Nevertheless the heavy hand of official racial discrimination was still very much in force in the U.S. when the black president of the black republic went to Washington.

No matter what Washington's motives were, Eisenhower and his wife Mamie were gracious hosts. For their part the Haitians took full advantage of the state visit to generate publicity for investment and tourism and to explain to the American audience that Haiti was not far-off Tahiti but an island nation 600 miles away. Reporter Andrew Tully in the *Washington Daily News* praised Magloire for his concern for his people's health. "When he took office more than 65 per cent of the population was afflicted with the contagious yaws disease, which is similar to syphilis," Tully wrote, adding that Magloire had asked the "United Nations for help and teams of Haitian and UN medicos treated 1,250,000 yaws cases with shots of penicillin."

It was a rare time in which Haiti reaped unparalleled positive publicity. President Eisenhower laid out the red carpet. U.S. Soldiers lined Constitution Avenue, where for a mile, Haitian red-and-blue flags flew next to the Stars and Stripes. After a White House State dinner, President and Mrs. Magloire became the first black Haitians to sleep in the Executive Mansion's Lincoln bedroom. (Magloire however was not the first Haitian president to visit the White House. In 1934 as the U.S. occupation of Haiti was coming to an end, President Franklin D. Roosevelt warmly received Haitian President Stenio Vincent at 1600 Pennsylvania Avenue. Nearly ten years later, in October 1943, President Elie Lescot was invited to stay at the White House, en route back to Haiti after receiving an honorary degree in Canada. Both presidents were mulattos.)

In his speeches at the White House State dinner and the next day to a joint session of the U.S. Congress, ex-schoolmaster Magloire gave his listeners a brief Haitian history lesson, citing his country's aid to the American Revolution. (Though Haiti was still the French Colony of Saint Domingue then, a number of Haitians who later became famous—such as Henri Christophe-took part in fighting the British at Savannah.)

"We have not always been regarded with the warm feelings of friendship which have been so evident to us here today," Magloire told Congress, and he went on to thank them for the recent Hurricane Hazel aid. Reflecting the Cold War times, Magloire expressed the theory that such assistance acted as an antidote to communism. Poverty in underdeveloped countries constituted a fertile field for the development of the "noxious germ of communism," he warned. For example, aid from the U.S. Export-Import bank "would enable the reclaiming of thousands of acres of land and raise the standard of living of the whole population of those regions, representing for us the most efficient weapons for fighting communism." Three times, Magloire mentioned the "pernicious doctrine" of communism, and then U.S. Secretary of State John Foster Dulles beamed the smile of a happy Cold War warrior.

On January 26, 1955 President Magloire departed for a state visitor to Washington. It was time in which Haiti reaped unparalleled positive publicity. President Eisenhower laid out the red carpet for the Haitian presidential couple. U.S. soldiers lined Constitution Avenue, where for a mile, Haiti's red-and-blue flags flew next to the Stars and Stripes. After the White House State dinner, President and Mrs. Magloire became the rare visiting couple to sleep in the Executive Mansion's Lincoln bedroom. The following day Magloire addressed a joint session of the U.S. Congress.

(Collection Magloire family)

Following the three-day official visit to Washington, D.C., Magloire's presidential party went on to visit the U.S. West Point Military Academy. There was also a ticker-tape parade down Broadway in freezing weather, which did nothing to dampen the spirits of the Haitians, and welcoming New Yorkers. The official visit extended to Chicago, Boston, and Nashville, Tennessee. In special ceremonies President Magloire received three honorary law degrees, one each from Columbia, Fordham, and Fisk Universities. After the 19-day visit to the U.S. and Canada, the presidential party flew to Jamaica for the observance of its 300 years as a British colony.

Magloire returned home from the three-week tour from Jamaica aboard the British aircraft carrier *HMS Triumph* and escorted by the frigate *HMS Venus*. The government estimated a crowd of 50,000 enthusiastic citizens, proud of their president were at the Port-au-Prince docks. The crowd shouted, "*Vive Papa nou.*"

New York columnist Walter Winchell in his 1955 New Year's *Broadway Digest* led off with; "Our town's new big hit is *House of Flowers* at the Alvin (Theatre). Pearl Bailey, Juanita Hall and Daihen Carroll top a talented troupe. It has the most exciting First Act we have ever seen. H. Arlen's samba and calypso score is delightfully cannibalistic." Then a week later Winchell broke the news: "The State Department cancelled Haiti's President Paul Magloire's plan to see the *House of Flowers* hit show. They feared it is too *bawdello*. This amused his (Magloire's) intimates who feel it would be the only show in town (New York) he'd howl at."

CHAPTER 11

Political Season: 1956

The January 9, 1955, elections in Haiti were encouraging. Women were finally allowed to vote, but only for municipal candidates. Special, separate polling places were set up for women. Two remarkable females, one from the ineffably named small town of Cabaret, some twenty miles north of the capital, and another from Mont Organize, in the coffee-growing northern mountains, won mayoralties. Six other women were elected to municipal councils.

The historic balloting by females was hailed by the *Haiti Sun* as the culmination of a 20-year struggle by Haitian women. The paper noted that a woman's activist group, the *Ligue Feminine d'Action Sociale* (Feminine Social Action League) had conducted a systematic civic education campaign for female voters. It had been the first such campaign on a national scale and the *Sun* expressed the hope that "it will have an influence on the entire electorate."

The other election that day, in which only men could vote, was for the Lower House of Parliament. The results, announced by President Magloire's Ministry of Interior and National Defense, were discouraging. It was as if the election returns for national deputies had been drawn out of the traditional surprise box for children, known as *la mayotte*. In the Petionville district above the capital, Boy Scout troop leader Andre Jeanty, whose popularity was confined to his family and members of his troop, had miraculously trounced the populist Deputy Daniel Fignole, darling of the area's thousands of poor constituents. In the town of Petionville itself Jeanty was given 4,507 votes to Fignole's 44 votes. In the mountainous Kenscoff above Port-au-Prince Jeanty purportedly garnered 4,667 votes to Fignole's 10 votes. In Croix—des—Mission again Jeanty supposedly won by the fantastic margin of 3,649 votes to Fignole's 39. Similarly increddible returns favoring the Boy Scout troop leader accured elsewhere. Fignole and his mass of supporters were stunned. By contrast the bourgeoisie and middleclass were relieved by the putative elimination of Fignole, a man whose populism they feared. Politicians took note. If results such as these could be conjured up by the Magloire government, they foresaw a landslide victory by Clement Jumelle, the government-backed candidate in the next presidential election, scheduled for January 1957. The obvious lesson for presidential hopefuls was that to succeed, it was imperative to gain control of the government/army machinery—an anti-democratic strategy all too familiar in Latin America.

An outcry by Fignole's partisans over the shameful results of the 1955 elections was quickly drowned out by the public enthusiasm evoked by President Magloire's preparations for his state visit to Washington, D.C. Magloire's trip completely monopolized the news. Undersecretary of State for Interior and National Defense Roland Lataillade, prior to the departure of the presidential party, gave me a timely, smiling hint: "It is not the time for negative news stories. Sorry about your friend [Fignole] losing his seat."

Brought up in a two-party, egalitarian New Zealand society in which women had obtained the vote the previous century—in 1898—I found it difficult not to sympathize with Fignole. The ex-deputy truly believed in the poor and humble. He had suffered their poverty and his voice in Parliament was needed to defend their interests.

A quick vignette illustrating Haiti's class-based society: Bernier St. Jean, a Fignolist like most of the *Sun's* employees, had learned to read and write after joining the *Haiti Sun*, working his way up from delivering the paper to collecting advertising. One day Bernier crest fallen, returned from Nadal and Company, a major importer and local agent for Delta airlines. The company's owner, Mr. Joseph Nadal, had interceded when Bernier was about to pickup the week's ads. According to Bernier, Nadal had said, "the *blan*—yours truly—had to come personally for the ad copy. "How can you send your yard boy to collect an important advertisement," Nadal reprimanded me. "He is no yard boy, but the *Sun's* advertising manager," I replied. Joseph Nadal had the good nature to laugh and apologize and was frank enough to explain that he couldn't very well discuss the political situation with Bernier. I told him that our contretemps symbolized a major problem in Haiti; the lack of communication between classes. And, furthermore, that he would have learned more about what was going on politically if he had talked to Bernier, not me.

Meanwhile it was the time of the *tarlatane*, the tight-waisted, wide-swirling skirt which was worn by stylish y oung ladies in chic circles. On the other side of Haiti's cultural divide peasant women still wore Pillsbury flour-sack dresses while men favored the long wearing *gros bleu*—denim shirts and trousers.

The country still suffered a fragile infrastructure. Trucks continued to fall into ravines off of primitive winding roads while coastal sailing vessels sank regularly with few lives saved because of the lack of safety equipment.

Tourism look as if it would surpass both sisal, coffee and cacao crops. The Southeast chapter of ASTA (American Society of Travel Agents)held its meeting in Port-au-Prince bringing all the important tourism official to examine the new tourist destination and voice their approval. The tourism official were given National palace treatment and toured the country. New hotels such as Castlehaiti, Ibo Lele, Dambala and the Riviera basked in the glow of rosy rum punches in Port-au-Prince while the Monte Joli and new Beck hotel competed with the ancient Roi Christophe Hotel in Cap Haitien.

In Port-au-Prince President Magloire inaugurated a new wing at the Tuberculosis sanatorium which tripled its capacity. Dr Louis Roy, director of the Sanatorium pointed out that,"the task of defeating tuberculosis [a major killer] is neither short nor easy . . . it has never been and can never be the exclusive work of the government, it is the task of everyone of us . . . we should join our efforts, relentlessly and without faltering so that one day we may be able to cry victory." There were plans to added TB wards to provincial hospitals.

Relations between Cuba and the Dominican Republic continued to deteriorate with General Felix Hermida, chief of staff of the Dominican Army accusing General Francisco Tabernilla, chief of staff of the Cuban army of distributing arms from fortress La Cabana in Havana to several Dominican exiles whose aim he said was: "against the person of Generalissimo Rafael Leonidas Trujillo y Molina Benefector of the Fatherland and Father is the new Fatherland, the 25th anniversary of a glorious and immaculate reign." Cubans authorities and Dominican exiles denied the charges.

Dr. Hannes Lindeman made history by sailing from Liberia across the Atlantic to Jacmel, in the narrowest craft ever to make it across the ocean. Alone in a dugout mahogany canoe made in Africa he wound up in Haiti with boils and sores on his arms and back

Senator Louis Dejoie—with straight black hair—had on Feb.9, became the first candidate to officially thrown his hat (a large wide-brimmed plantation style) into the ring for the January 1957 presidential election. He was assured the vote of fellow members of the elite. In announcing his candidacy Dejoie did not outline any program but stated, "A man's personality is the fruit of his past, and consequently, the sign of the future. From the days of my youth, my private and public life has been directed towards honest labor in order and in peace. Peace as well as order are necessary elements so that work may bring prosperity." Dejoie ended his call for an "electoral campaign our country will prove its high moral values to the whole world"

In an item in the *Sun* (Feb,19th 1956) it was noted that President Magloire on a visit to Péligre had invited "Senator Louis Dejoie, candidate for the presidency," to breakfast. "All during the meal the conversation was friendly, full of courtesy and well alloyed with irony and finest salt. The conversation was strictly between gentlemen. The president address his breakfast guest by his nickname, 'Babs'"

A trained agronomist and descendant of President Fabre Nicolas Geffrard (1859-67) Senator Dejoie liked to think of himself as a gentleman farmer. Protected from the sun by a wide brim plantation-style hat the senator traveled often to the countryside to look over his essential oil business. He also traveled to the U.S. to meet with his American business associates who had backed his entry into the Essential Oil Industry. Because he had provided jobs to peasants in areas such as Les Cayes and San Michel de Atalaye with the cultivation of vetivere, the grass from which the essential oil is produced he was assured their votes. Dejoie had a penchant for formal black-tie soirees at his residence in Port-au-Prince. High on his guest list was the current ranking U.S. embassy political officer or the Charge d'Affairs when the ambassador was absent from the country.

There were plenty of good feature stories the write about. Tourism was said to be bringing in five million dollars. Distinguished visitors kept praising Haiti as a wonderful vacation spot. Actor Van Heflin vacationing with his redheaded wife and two children hoped he could one day make a movie on the island. He recalled to the Sun that he had visited Haiti 23 years earlier as an ordinary seaman on a tramp steamer had just finished a successful Broadway play "A view from the Bridge" by Arthur Miller. (Three years earlier playwright Authur Miller and his wife, had been guests at Port-au-Prince's Hotel San Souci.) Culture was flourishing. Haiti's leading literary figures were producing like never before. There were new plays, poem and books and interesting meeting of the best minds. Roger Dorsinville's poem "Pour Celebrer La Terre", was discussed by a group of intellectuals and Lucien Montas published their comment in Optique literary review and the Sun. Participant Dr. Jacques Stephen Alexis whose novel Compere General Soleil was soon to be available in Haiti after winning high praise in Europe, noted, "I have the impression that we do not see the perspective of our people marching into the future . . ." "Lorca sang of Spain . . . Neruda of Chile, and Nazim Hirchet of Turkey. In this song present problems intervene. Does Dorsinville think that our poetic art should express the reality of our country? You have spoken of the problem of the peasant, of his production. But is that all?" President Magloire attended a performance of Jean Anouith's French adaptation of Medee at Felix. Morriseau-Leroy's amphitheater at Morne Hercule in Petionville. There was a burst of cultural collaboration between Jacques Stephen Alexis, playwright Frank Fouche and Morriseau-Leroy on a Creole play, "Rossignol mange Corrossol" that seemed to promise great things to come.

As the year progressed Felix Morisseau Leroy launched, "La Cabrite Litteraire" (Literary Goat on the green) at his Morne Hercules theatre. He considered the literary gathering the greatest thing since his translating Sophocle's Antigone from the original Greek into Creole. He followed it with Shakespeare's Macbeth turning the witches into Haitian zombies. All the literary lights found their way to the "Literary Goat." Judy Ross, professor of Literature (Brookyn College, New York), on her second trip to Haiti describing it as "the last stronghold against the Aspirin Age in the twentieth Century." There was nothing derogatory in her remarks and she raved: " . . . life in Port-au-Prince is the closest surviving reflection of life in eighteen century France: a life of gracious leisure, unhurried and serene, but operating at a fever pitch of social and intellectual activity." "The life of the mind, both in old France and in modern Port-au-Prince, seems never to stagnate; be it confident or groping, successful or not it simmers and seethes in many quarters, erupting now and then in a play like Morisseau-Leroy's "Anatole" or a painting by Wilson Bigaud at the Centre d"Art . . . . Ms Ross liken Sunday's literary Cabrit as completely assuming the aspects of "the French Literary Salon in the best eighteenth century tradition of Madame de Rambouillet herself, but in a way, the scene outshone the original De Rambouillet model, for the pastoral setting under a clear Haitian sky put the musty Paris drawing room to shame. Under the flamboyant trees of Morne Hercule, surrounded by tropical bloom in a cosy clearing gathered a band of Haitian writers, actors and musicians . . ." Ms Ross went on to describe at length the various poets, writers and playwrights and disussed their works.

Author Jacques Stephen Alexis who had written the foreword for *Anatole* was honored the Sunday before he departed in early July on the Hamburg-American steamer Caona en route to Paris for the publication of his new book, *Les Arbres Musiciens.*

A committee had already been formed in February to prepare a series of events to mark in October the 80th birthday of Dr. Jean Price-Mars, rector of the University of Haiti. The star-studded career of the venerable scholar known as the "Prince of Haitian Intellectuals," was credited with bringing honor and respect to Haiti. Dr. Price-Mar's accomplishments were too numerous to list and it was noted that in the domain of sociology, ethnology, diplomacy, writing, teaching and field work in history and medicine he had won international honors and recognition. The quiet spoken son of Grande Riviere du Nord was the most revered personality in the country.

The *Haiti Sun* considered Dr. Price-Mars' address to the graduating class of 1956 delivered at the Faculty of Medicine in the presence of President Magloire of such importance that we carried a summary of the speech as an editorial. It was as if he had a premonition that the future of the University might one-day be in jeopardy. Which it was.

Addressing staff members and students of the faculties of medicine, science, ethnology, arts, school of agriculture, music conservatory and Roman Catholic Major seminary, Dr Price-Mars noted, "A building to house our services—temporary or permanent—no matter how beautiful it may be, is only and can only be an envelope, the outer form of its contents. But what is the quintessence of such contents?—It is the culture that we provide for the youth who enter our portals with confidence, and for whom we are responsible by State commission.

The Rector pointed out that of the two definitions of culture (1) advanced intellectual training. (2) The expression of a collective 'facon d'etre' which incorporates knowledge, customs and beliefs, the latter definition fits what he refers to as "Haitian culture", which is the function of the various faculties of the university, for an increasing number of students. "Are these faculties aware of their duty," Dr. Price-Mars asked. "I dare not say."

He stressed the danger of over-specialization on the part of certain categories of teachers—they often forget the practical relations between the subject and civic objectives. Teachers, first of all, should exemplify professional probity, which is as important as the technical information they impart, the speaker warned. In support "Has it not been said that Kant was so punctual in delivering his lectures at the Koenisberg that the day that he arrived a few minutes late, it was surmised that some serious world event must have taken place. Indeed it had—the French Revolution had just broken out blazing the trial to a New World.

"The great German philosopher conformed to his own well-known motto: "Act in such a manner that the maxim of your action may be erected by your will power into a universal law."

"Appealing to his fellow professors, he pointed out the gravity of non-moral instruction. He said that if a teacher were a liar, amoral and corrupt person, his teaching would be purely negative. It would produce that type of warped intellectual, fond of paradoxes and craving after nihilism—and equally dangerous in private and public affairs. But you would not have formed the genuine, moral values which are the honor and glory of any community," Dr. Price-Mars contended.

He exhorted the graduating students to be devoted and patriotic citizens, warning them that they should be ever on guard against demagogues who might seek to deviate them from the straight path of professional duty.

He counseled them; "True knowledge begins with gradual, patient and personal integration and assimilation of ideas based on experience. In the final analysis it is perceived that the more one knows the more one see revealed before him the intangible mirage of the vast unknown and perhaps the unknowable. For this reason w should be cautious and humble."

In conclusion, Dr Mars reminded the graduates that they were now well prepared to enter the vast and confusing arena of life, and ready to answer the call of the country, which sooner or later, will entrust them with the reins of command. "Remember," he urged, that there is only one maxim of the honest man—*bien faire tout ce que l'on fait.*"

The OAS meeting in Ciudad Trujillo to formulate policy regarding national sovereignty over natural resources in the waters adjacent to coastal states *El Jefe* ordered the distribution of an anti-Haitian book. The book, *la Isla Iluminada* written by a Colombian J.A Osorio Lizarazo and been re-printed on *El Caribe* presses in 1953. When Haiti's foreign minister heard that the anti-Haitian book was being distributed to delegates he ordered his delegation to walkout. Correspondent Paul Kennedy reported the story for the *New York Times*, which had renewed interest in Trujillo's fiefdom since the disappearance of Dr. Jesus Galindez, Columbia University lecturer from New York on March 12. Both the *New York Times* and *Life Magazine* had asked me to learn what I could from the Dominican Republic about the missing Basque teacher who had once worked for Trujillo. Travelers from the Dominican Republic whom I interviewed at the Port-au-Prince airport knew very little.

The *New York Times* revealed that the Inter-American Association and The League for the Rights of Man meeting in New York had offered a $10,000 for information leading to the arrest of those responsible for the "abduction or murder" of the Spanish scholar. Norman Thomas, chairman of the post-war World Council read notes of an address before the Inter-American Association for Democracy and Freedom that the missing scholar had prepared. Trujillo rule, he quoted Galindez as stating, "is a daily drama which silenced lips and oppressed hearts."

The Basque writer also whose thesis on the Trujillo regime was soon to be published had also stated that,"Trujillo has succeeded in completing a period of dictatorship—which marks the complete submission of a people, the destruction of all civic spirit and the most ironic parody of democratic institutions that can be imagined." All fingers pointed to Trujillo as responsible for the disappearance of his enemy in New York. But it took time to unravel the kidnapping plot.

—

The Political season opened with a bang on May 17, 1956. News reached the Sun's office that hot and humid morning that students at the Lycee Toussaint Louverture were going to take to the streets. For days the Haiti Sun had been inundated with anti-Magloire leaflets. These subversive mimeographed sheets signed "Comite Revolutionnaire" argued that Magloire's term of office ended May 15 and called on the students to go on strike. The anti-government movement began in the traditional manner with attempts to frighten marchands (market women) from delivering their produce to the capital. Word was spread around Port-au-Prince market places that "loup-garous," those mystical werewolves so real to the country folk, were on the loose. The difference from earlier times was that the werewolves were said to be motorized. Riding around in the pre-dawn darkness they were said to be kidnapping market women, plucking them from their donkeys laden with produce for the markets, to cut off the city's food supply.

With no radio, television, or smoke signals, news was spread on the teledoil.

Over the years in Haiti, I had learned that it was impossible to rely on eye-witness reports because no matter how sincere the witnesses were not only did the chaos and panic distorted their account but their fertile imaginations were colored by hallucinations. The politically motivated saw what they wanted to see.

Arriving on the scene I found the Police in their familiar black and white police wagons endeavoring to restore order. (The public had baptized the police wagons "smoking" after the tuxedo so common to palace and private club balls) Students at Lycee Toussaint Louverture on St Anne Square were in the process of erupting, smashing chairs and desks and taking to the streets shouting slogans—they had not as yet found a catchy slogan and they were shouting different things. Several shots were fired. A student was wounded and 15 were injured including one policeman. But the Louverture students failed to force other schools to join them in the streets. The Lycee located in the middle-class district in which many of them had grown was fertile ground for the new "revolutionaries." The following day the number of casualties was multiplied by the teledoil.

President Magloire and police chief, Col. Prosper both spoke up and the official version of what had happened made page one. In fact only the police chief made the front page of the Haiti Sun because what he said was the most intriguing. The parliament had met and voted a state of siege, a modified form of martial law curtailing certain constitutional guarantees.

Magloire's powerful police chief, as corrupt as he was tough, a diamond as big as an acorn on his finger and another in his tie, in a rare 1,300-word prepared statement published in the form of an interview in the newspaper Le Matin, on May 25,1956, stated rumors of students being killed were untrue that one student had been wounded by a policeman who had been threatened by a mob of students.

At the time Col. Marcaisse Prosper's charges appeared as a simple police report but it also appeared as a crafty worded declaration that gave Dr. Duvalier the public notice he so desperately needed, in fact in his statement he launched Dr. Francois Duvalier's presidential campaign.

The police chief stated that among a group of plotters who were members of a Haitian Revolutionary Committee, "are known for their attachment to Dr. Francois Duvalier, who happens to be still in hiding, undercover for more than a year, afraid to show himself, notwithstanding the presidential clemency." He named, names and said that the police were unsure for what candidate Windsor K. Laferriere and Alex Dominique worked but speculated it might be Dejoie. Two members of the Revolutionary Committee arrested were Paul Blanchet and Jacques St. Lot.

Prosper's declarations could have been scripted by Duvalier himself. "He (Duvalier) is trying to make people believe that with the support of the American personnel of SCISP (where he worked) he is certain to accede to the presidency, as if that was admissible. He (Duvalier) also maintains that he is the 'successor' of the political doctrine of the late president Estime, and that in this capacity all the partisans and friends of the ex-chief are duty-bound to support his candidacy . . . the students of Lycee Toussaint Louverture seem to have been driven to white heat by the partisans of candidate Duvalier."The stuttering police chief was politically cautious and very astute.

President Magloire' speech on the other hand, which the *Sun* ran inside made no mention of Duvalier listing the "veritable acts of terrorism" committed by those now opposed to his rule. The President stated, "the reason advanced for justifying these subversive maneuvers is that my mandate, contrary to the provisions in the constitution of 1950, the Supreme Law of the land and our supreme guide, expires May 15, 1956, instead of May 15 1957. I will not delay in emphasizing the illogicism of such an assertion, above all that those who have expressed it allege their respect of the constitution, and, they say, have no other fear than that of seeing me myself violate it at the expiration of my mandate."

The following week police arrested Windsor K. Laferriere and Alex Dominique publishers of the mimeographed *Le Souverain*.[They considered themselves an independent radical political movement.]

President Magloire flew to Panama to represent Haiti at a two-day (July 21-22) meeting of 19 chiefs of state of the Americas (President Hector Trujillo was absent.) Magloire took his seat next to President Eisenhower, who assured his fellow chiefs of state they need no longer have fears of the United States as a colossus of the North . . ." Never will peace and security be sought at the price of subjecting any nation to coercion or interference in its internal affairs."

Ceremonies marking the 22nd anniversary of the "Haitianization" of the *Armee d'Haiti* and the August 1, 1934 when the last U.S. Marine occupation unit left Haitian soil were celebrated as never before. The program was long and colorful and a sign that the armed forces were devoted to their commander-in-chief.

There were inaugurations. A new army barracks in the town of Petit Goave along with a surgery pavilion to the hospital and a new Lycee Fuastin Soulouque. President Magloire protested in the Southern city of Les Cayes that he favored all Haiti not just the North.

Yet in spite of the official explanation of the causes of the political unrest there were skeptic who believed it was all a plot by the government to hold onto power. They didn't believe the fact that former partisans of President Estime were now activists and directing their proselytizing to schools, the army and the police department. Their target was the small neglected lower middle class from which they had sprung. Some of the tough sadistic detectives of the Criminal Research Bureau designated to search for Doc Duvalier when he went underground were already converts to his cause, and they later filled the first ranks of Duvalier's civilian goon squads, the infamous *Tontons Macoutes*.

———

Finally Duvalier quietly resurfaced in August 1956 ending 22 months in the *maquis*. Magloire, secure and confident, had offered guarantees that the fugitive physician-politician would not be arrested.

On September 5th, 1956, no longer driving the taptap but at the wheel of a shiny, gray Buick, Henri Jean-Baptiste drove up to the office of the *Haiti Sun* proud of his single passenger. It was my first meeting with the 49-year old Duvalier. He was wearing a thick serge suit and a bow tie. Speaking French he addressed me by surname and explained he was only making a courtesy call in preparation for announcing his candidacy for presidency of the Republic. He sat with his hat on looking through prism-thick glasses and asked the questions. We were alone in my little air-conditioned office. He seemed preoccupied about, "what do the Americans think of me?" By Americans he meant the U.S. embassy. It was important to have the Americans on your side ever since the 1915-34 Marine Occupation. The Embassy, he appeared to think, could be an obstacle to an ambitious Haitian politician. Despite his early anthropological writings and earlier career in politics and service in the Estime government, Duvalier's style had not brought him great public notice. He smiled revealing a gold tooth when he heard that the Americans working with Point IV's Inter-American Cooperative Public Health Service, (known by it's French abbreviation initials,SCISP) were known to speak well of him. I admitted that I was not privy to the Embassy thinking. What I did not say and he probably already knew as it was no secret that the U.S. Embassy looked kindly on the candidacy of Louis Dejoie. The Senator had actively courted the U.S.embassy with his with his upper-class sophistication and charm.His chic soirees had paid off. Duvalier on the other hand had trouble with newspapers misspelling his name. Le Jour and I must admit, the Haiti Sun followed up by spelling his name as Duvallier. I found it impossible to get him to discuss his own childhood or personal life. He gave no hint or clue to his origin. Not even his close associates could furnish any details of very private life.

Watching him being driven away that day seated alone in the back seat of the Buick, I could not help thinking that while he had none of the charisma of Fignole, none of the expertise of Jumelle and none of the flamboyance of Dejoie or other minor candidates but he had a confidence and quiet determination about him. Although he hardly seemed presidential material, he did have a small corps of fanatical backers.

When ex-President Estime died during the summer of 1953 in New York exile, (as no one dies a natural death in Haiti it was rumored that Estime had been poisoned.) Magloire saw that he was brought home and given a national funeral. Dr. Francois Duvalier's life suddenly changed. He accelerated his own maneuvering to become Estime's political heir.

His family saw little of him for the next 22 months as he remained undercover plotting against Magloire. It was during this time Duvalier established his credentials as a credible opponent. Clement Barbot, a native of Gonaives, whom Doc Duvalier had helped get a job, was one of the tight little group of supporters who had organized themselves into a multi-tiered political organization that was to later included a terrorist bombing arm. One of those who went underground with Duvalier was Lucien Daumec, a dapper and talkative intellectual with an infectious laugh. Daumec was a graduate of Haiti's small ethnology school and became a member of its faculty. He had been on the staff of *La Ruche* in 1946 and active in Lescot's overthrow. He joined the Haitian Communist Party that year and was among those who agreed to dissolve the party when Estime became president to avoid any embarrassment for the new chief of state. Like Duvalier he had become an Estimist. During their sojourn underground, Daumec wrote anti-Magloire tracts which he signed "Revolutionary Committee," and began a role as one of Duvalier's speechwriter.

These were lean times for Mrs. Duvalier and her four children. The Jumelle family, established member of the black bourgeoisie from the town of St Marc, close neighbors on Rue Capois and Ruelle Roy were among those who came to her aid. Clement Jumelle had been one of Duvaliers assistants in the Department of Labor and had helped him write a new labor code but Jumelle remained in the government and collaborated with Magloire. His reasoning was that Haiti needed a civil service and not a system that forced officials into retirement every time a president changed and the new palace occupant handed out jobs as political patronage. Jumelle with a master degree in economics from the University of Chicago eventually became Magloire's Finance Minister while his older brother Ducasse, the venerable leader of Haiti's main masonic lodge became Minister of Interior and National Defense, the key cabinet post. As a cabinet minister Duvalier's only known business venture had been to purchase a station wagon. With hired driver, Henri Jean-Baptiste, at the wheel Duvalier entered the taptap business—taptap being jitney buses in Haiti that carry people around for a modest fare. When Magloire's police arrested Driver Jean-Baptiste the Jumelles had him quickly freed and the taptap returned.

The cash flow from the jitney's seven-cent fare was the money that kept the Duvalier household together while Papa was in hiding. The Jumelles also used their influence to keep his father Duval on the government payroll.

Duvalier used a series of hiding places, and at the beginning he took the utmost precautions. Moving to one hideout he disguised himself as a woman. In Father Jean-Baptise Georges's house Duvalier was required to fold up his cot and sit in the shower stall while the priest said Mass. Father Georges, who later became Duvalier's first education minister, ultimately went into exile and became a dedicated anti-Duvalierist who tried more times to mount invasions and plots to overthrow Duvalier than any other Haitian. Duvalier, Father Georges recalled in an interview with the author in Santo Domingo in 1964, was not a troublesome boarder. Because of diabetes, he ate no sweets and neither smoked nor drank alcoholic beverages. He spent much of his time working on what would become of his first law on illiteracy and laying the groundwork for a school of international studies. One of his companion books was Machiavelli's The Prince.

While he hid at the home of Colbert Bonhomme, close to the police headquarters Duvalier would go out at night, and once he even visited the newspaper Le Nouvelliste across the street from the National Penitentiary in broad daylight. But he had a powerful protector Police Chief Marcaisse Prosper. In a show of rare gratitude years later, Duvalier purchased Prosper's home which became the government guest house in Bourdon, and sent the million dollars purchase price to the exiled Prosper in Jamaica. Prosper had escaped into exile when the Magloire government had collapsed. At Colbert Bonhomme's home Duvalier kept himself busy with his host drafting a constitution. Bonhomme was a lawyer and judge.

It was years later that I learned that the day Duvalier left the *marquis* he went immediately to visit Estime's widow and met with her at the large family home on Avenue N. Jean Fouchard was there and he recalls, "His hair was long and it made him look top-heavy, he was not a big man. I said, You can't remain like that to begin your campaign, He replied, 'I have no money', As I had that day sold a little land in Bolosse I had $200 and gave it to him, 'It's too much money,' he said. He had absolutely no notion of money. Even at the end of his rule he had no idea of money. (Later when he became president he had money stuffed in his desk drawer and to one woman who asked for six hundred dollars he gave $6,000. I gave him $200 and he said it's a lot. Antonio Andre, head of the National Bank, had given Duvalier a checkbook when he became president. To his amazement Duvalier quickly overdrew his account. He told Duvalier, ' I see you have written a lot of checks but president you have spent too much.' ' No, there are still a lot of checks left in the book,' he replied.)"

The main reason Duvalier remained an enigma was his early political style. He broke with tradition. Any premature display of political ambition, he reasoned, was fatal to such a career. This tactic suited his introverted character. Speaking extemporaneously he found a difficult chore and he never succeeded in mastering it. A fellow cabinet member in the Estime government, Antonio Vieux, whom Duvalier later imprisoned and killed, used to complain that during cabinet meetings Duvalier never opened his mouth to say anything. "You never knew where he stood and he was infuriatingly dull," explained Vieux. It was the same during his years working with the Americans who often mistook his quiet polite manner as a sign that he was dumb. Yet this tactic contributed more to Duvalier's election than any other single factor. It enabled him to win the campaign support of able and clever Estime supporters who skillfully managed his campaign, steering him away from controversy and seldom if ever mentioning his earlier writings. Some of these men who formed his brain trust and laid the strategy for his campaign believed Duvalier would become their instrument of power. He encouraged their dreams. They were unable to penetrate his. Duvalier's secretive style also contributed to the growth of a million myths. A mythical man is often more dangerous than a real man who at least is a known entity. While this quality caused Duvalier at first to be underestimated, it later helped to blow his mythical image out of proportion.

El Jefe's Long Arm

Before the CIA crept into the Caribbean and became a fixture in the hearts and minds of the political establishment, there was a far more frightening and similarly insidious secret service. It was the very long arm of Rafael Trujillo's SIM, *Servicio Inteligencia Militar* (Military Intelligence Service). Not only was the SIM used as an arm of repression at home; its agents, part of a vast international network, were posted around the Caribbean, especially concentrated in Havana and Mexico City which were havens for many anti-Trujillo Dominican exiles. *El Jefe* harbored a particular fury against those who he felt had betrayed him. He was prepared to go to any length to settle his score with perceived traitors, a SIM officer told me years later. For Trujillo it was like a game of chess outwitting his myriad *enemies*. At stake was nothing less than many a human life.

One case which illustrated *El Jefe's* vindictiveness and his long arm of retaliation— made for exciting reporting for the *Haiti Sun* during the dog days of the summer of 1955 in Port-au-Prince. Two Dominicans, Ulises Sanchez Hinojoso and Rafael E. Graffer, had fled across the border into Haiti and their trial in Port-au-Prince caused a sensation. It was difficult to squeeze into the old Palace of Justice courtroom as the case reached its climax. The wooden benches and narrow aisles were packed, mostly with students. However my camera assured me a front-row seat.

Raising a hand now and then to stress a point, Haiti's Public Prosecutor (*Ministère Public*) Alphonse Racine, the folds of his black gown giving him the appearance of a barrister in London's Old Bailey, laid out his case of asylum for the two Dominicans elaborating on his argument that their families had been forced to publicly denounce them.

Taking the stand in the sweltering courtroom refugee Sanchez Hinojoso told his story. He related that as a Dominican army officer with the rank of captain, he had been assigned to manage one of *El Jefe's* private business concerns. Sanchez then went on to list some 200 private businesses and industries that were owned by Trujillo. Sanchez's defense lawyer, Ernest Sabalat, displayed a sheaf of papers all containing the name of what he said was the largest Dominican property owner, Trujillo. The papers were proof, Sabalat declared, and that the Dominican dictator basically "owned the country."

For his part witness Sanchez recounted that when he had complained of being tired of doing Trujillo's private business work on an army officer's salary, he was arrested and imprisoned. It was his "very good friend, Anselmo Paulino, who interceded and had me set free." Once freed, Sanchez continued, he had fled to the U.S. where he joined a band of Dominican exiles. One day the Dominican consul in New York contacted Sanchez saying that Trujillo had asked him to return from exile. It was only after Paulino visited him and promised to guarantee his safety that Sanchez finally agreed to return to the Dominican Republic. However, he took the precaution of obtaining an American passport for his U.S.-born daughter.

Back home, Paulino got Sanchez a job as supervisor of a tax office and later assistant national police chief. But Sanchez' refusal to betray his former fellow exiles and name those he had associated with in the U.S. resulted in a three-month prison sentence. On Sanchez's release, Paulino sent him to FADOC, a shoe-manufacturing company owned by Trujillo, and from which Sanchez was accused of stealing $5,000. He denied the charge declaring that the company owed him much more than that from unpaid 5 % commissions which he had earned as a shoe salesman. When Paulino fell from power, Sanchez fled to Haiti. He had crossed the border in a private car with his cousin Rafael Graffer, and given himself up to Haitian authorities.

When Judge Joseph Salomon finally pronounced the Haitian court's decision— rejection of the Dominican dictator's official request that the two Dominican refugees be extradited as "common criminals"; it drew long and lusty applause. A key point in the case was the supposed disowning of Sanchez by his own family as published in the infamous *Foro Publico* column in *El Caribe*, interpreted by the defense as indicating unconscionable political pressure.

Indeed, the denunciation of Sanchez by his own family, to prove Trujillo's allegations that Sanchez was a common criminal, was a common feature of *El Jefe's* technique of lies and intimidation. The purported disowning of Sanchez by his own relatives was published in the *"Foro Publico"* (Public Forum) column of *El Caribe*. Dominicans read *"Foro Publico"* with dread. They all knew when it came from *El Jefe*!

Sabalat, Sanchez's Haitian lawyer, repeatedly attacked the "known policy of forced immorality employed by the neighboring Republic." Ultimately the two refugees, Sanchez and Graffer, were granted political asylum in Ecuador. End of story? Not quite. It was not difficult to visualize Trujillo's rage at these men, who had dared list his private businesses, and at Haiti which had allowed such a public display against him. He could be expected to react. Departing Haiti under police protection the two exiles stopped off in Havana with the intention of applying for visa to the United States. I had a feeling the story was not over.

Meanwhile I had made arrangements to fly to nearby Santiago de Cuba ($25.00 round trip by Cubana de Aviacion airline) with a group of Haitian friends for Carnival and to enjoy the fiesta of Cuba's patron saint, the *Virgin de la Caridad del Cobre*. Without a doubt Santiago de Cuba's Carnival was among the most colorful anywhere with competing Afro-Cuban dancers and bands. Cuba's leading breweries fueled visitors and the infectious dancers in their traditional garb handed down from slave times. Some were descendants of slaves brought by their French owners to Cuba's Oriente province when they fled the anti-colonial rebellion in Saint Domingue. *El Marinero* (The Sailor) was the popular Carnival song and I felt right at home.

But even in Cuba, Trujillo's intrigue, and Latin America's volatile politics, followed us. It had been only two short years since a band of anti-Batista rebels under the leadership of a youth named Fidel Castro had made an abortive attack on the city's Ft.Moncada. One evening when I returned to my room at the old Casa Grande Hotel on Cespedes Square I discovered an envelope slipped under my door that contained photographs of gruesome, bloody bodies. "Victims of the tyranny," a note attached to the pictures stated. The author or authors obviously knew that I was a journalist. It was not clear whether the pictures were of the victims of the 26 of July 1953, Moncada attack or new victims of the Cuban dictatorship of Fulgencio Batista. (I returned to Haiti with them but as the bodies were not properly identified the Associated Press explained they could not use them.)

One night during the carnival parade a fat, saber-bearing army trooper snatched a mask resting on top of my head and the elastic snapped back with a welt to the ear. "No masks in this carnival," he ordered. A Cuban friend who worked for the *Cubana* airline suggested that it might be prudent not to sit in the official stand during the festival. I began to understand that there was a dark side to Santiago's carnival. Not only could no masks be worn for fear of anti-Batista rebels infiltrating; some carnival dancers were checked for bombs before they reached the reviewing stand.

As for the long arm of *El Jefe* in the Dominican Republic, when the reaction to Sanchez Hinojoso's disloyalty did come from Ciudad Trujillo, it was chillingly ominous. In its August 12 edition, *El Caribe* published a note tucked away in a corner of the last page. The brief paragraph under the heading, *"Reintegrase a filas de Policia Nacional."* ("Returned to Police Ranks") stated: *"El señor Ulises Sánchez Hinojoso* returned last night by Delta from Port-au-Prince and Havana after intelligence work, and resumed his police post."

Back in Port-au-Prince I checked Delta's August 11 passenger list. There was no trace of Sanchez, having passed through Haiti en route from Havana to the Dominican Republic.

It all appeared to be a typically devious Trujillo plot. The next news of Sanchez Hinojoso was another small note in *El Caribe,* which appeared the same week, reporting that the policeman was suffering from a minor ailment and therefore had been confined to his home. In *El Jefe's* Dominican parlance that could mean only one thing: Sanchez had been or would be terminated.

Sanchez' story was made even more frightening by the news item from Havana reporting that on August 8, a Dominican exile named Jose (Pepe) Hernandez Santana had been stabbed to death at the site where the new Havana Hilton was being constructed, and where Hernandez worked. One man had held him while another stabbed him in the back.

There were of course other intriguing dimensions to this period of my Caribbean experience. One had to do with a fellow New Zealander, Ted Scott. During visits to Havana I became acquainted with Ted, whose visible means of income was as a columnist on the English-language *Havana Post*. We quickly agreed to exchange information on the Sanchez Hinojoso saga. The *Post* would work the Havana end of the story; the *Haiti Sun* would provide background from the trial in Port-au-Prince and the reaction in Ciudad Trujillo. (There was nothing that Ted Scott relished more than intrigue and espionage. A legend in Panama where he was for many years editor of the *Panama-America*, Ted had been a British agent during World War II and it was said he had terminated a Nazi operative in Central America. Given special training in Canada during that period, Scott had worked under the directions of Sir William Stephenson, Winston Churchill's key operative in New York during World War II, who among other duties oversaw British espionage in the Western Hemisphere and especially subversion against German interests in the Americas. Scott and Stephenson remained friends after the war and had a reunion in Bermuda before Stephenson, the "quiet Canadian" died a natural death of old age.)

Scott, who was also an ex-prizefighter who carried pugnacious features from his years in the ring back in New Zealand, Europe and Panama (His manager fled with his winning and left Scott stranded in Panama) was described by British writer Norman Lewis as the man on whom Ian Fleming had based his James Bond character. Though the portly, pink-faced Scott hardly resembled Sean Connery or any of the other dashing males who have portrayed Agent 007 on the screen.

Nevertheless Scott was every bit the womanizer and gambler. (I once refused to loan him money in a Havana casino when he lost). He had reported for the former United Press (now United Press International) in 1948 while fighting alongside Costa Rican President Jose (Pepe) Figueres against the Communists. Ted would think nothing of filing a dispatch to UP, then picking up a machinegun to battle the *Commies*.

A loyal subject of the Queen, Scott once got into an argument with Ernest Hemingway in Havana and challenged the author in Havana to a duel with pistols, 45 calibers. Hemingway in anger (surreptitiously taped by Scott) on the telephone declared he had proven himself in war and peace and wasn't going to get into a duel with a mere colonial. Scott retorted that Hemingway had learned that he (Scott) was a crack shot with a pistol.

While Cuban Dictator Fulgencio Batista was still in power Scott attempted to recruit me for an assignment in the Dominican Republic. It involved in locating the two hired killers suspected of killing the Dominican exile Jose (Pepe) Hernandez. Ted handed me a codebook, which on the surface was simply a well-known biography of Dwight Eisenhower. The code was simple but time-consuming. The message was to be sent in numbers and in an order that gave the page, paragraph, and key words in the Eisenhower book, of which Scott had the corresponding copy. Ted wouldn't listen to my protests that it need not be a cloak and dagger affair that if I found the hitmen in the Dominican Republic I would first publish the story in the *Haiti Sun*. I didn't know for whom he was working at the time. I agree to take the book home to Haiti interested in what it might produce. When Ted did send a coded message from Havana by mail it proved out-of-date. Shortly after this communication an Argentine diplomat spied the Eisenhower book on a shelf at my home and asked to borrow it. During later years when as a radio reporter for NBC Ted worked the same stories as I in the Caribbean, he never mentioned my failure to become his sub-agent.

While we didn't share the same political leanings, Ted was right-wing and loyal to the British monarchy, our friendship lasted his lifetime. He died in 1985 at age 86 at his retirement home in Coco Beach Florida where he fished and watched launchings in nearby Kennedy Center.

—

It took until the end of August to be able to pick out the *Haiti Sun's* largest typeface and run the front-page headline: "Sanchez Not Secret Agent: Trujillo Got Him!" Our story went on to report: that Trujillo had dispatched the exile's mother and a brother, Emilio, to Cuba to plead with Sanchez Hinojoso to return to the Dominican Republic. Emilio promptly fell victim to a suspicious accident; stepping out of the Havana airport he was knocked down by a car and seriously injured. The driver fled. A photographer was on the scene and a Cuban newspaper published Emilio's picture with the fact that he had been interned in Havana's Calixto Garcia Hospital. When Ulises Sanchez Hinojoso saw his brother's picture in the newspaper he rushed to the hospital. Trujillo's agents were waiting. He, his mother, and injured brother were whisked off to the airport and onto a one-way flight to the Dominican Republic. Trujillo's agents carried diplomatic passports and it was speculated in the Cuban media that these same agents had been responsible for killing Dominican exile Jose (Pepe) Hernandez.

In a letter to the *Haiti Sun* from Havana, Ulises Sanchez Hinojoso's fellow Dominican exile, Rafael Graffer Andujar, reported that *El Jefe's* agents had warned Sanchez that if he did not return, his two young daughters in the Dominican Republic would disappear. In his letter Graffer lauded the Haitian people and lawyer Ernest Sabalat and thanked them for their generosity as well as the *Haiti Sun* for devoting its resources to the two exiles' story.

—

Neither did I escape Trujillo's wrath. The effects of Hurricane Hazel were still being felt in Haiti a year later. Dr. Louis Roy, head of the Haitian Red Cross, after a visit to the affected region in the southwest, drew a graphic, tragic picture of some 40,000 people, including children, facing starvation and disease because of the destruction of their crops.

Haitian Methodist Pastor Alain Rocourt, working in the devastated area, sent his own reports and pictures of starving children, which the *Sun* published.

The situation was critical and the story I filed to The Associated Press was based on Dr. Roy's eyewitness account. *El Caribe,* in Ciudad Trujillo ran the story with my byline, but there was a conspicuous difference in what *El Caribe* published in Spanish and the story I had sent to New York. Dr. Roy was quoted by *El Caribe* as saying, "Up to now nothing has been done towards the solution of these grave problems." The Associated Press in New York confirmed that neither such quotation had been in my original dispatch nor was it put on the wire to newspapers around the world. It was part of a familiar pattern. The Trujillo-controlled press and radio had been sniping at the Magloire government ever since the Haitian court's decision in favor of the two Dominican exiles.

—

The famine story was indeed serious and damaging to the Haitian government which had been caught napping. "40,000 in Grave Peril Need Medical Aid Now: Doctors Must Be Mobilized," was the *Haiti* Sun's headline on Aug. 7, 1955. "Starvation in the south has reached the stage where nothing less than immediate and extensive mobilization of medical teams can save thousands from death, Dr. Louis Roy reported after a survey of the stricken area. Supplies of beans and rice are no longer enough", the doctor declared, "many thousands of children, and almost as many adults, are so ravaged by hunger and privation that vitamins, proteins, food and milk; and in some cases transfusions and plasma are the only means of staving off certain death."

The *Sun's* story added: "Forty thousand adults and children are in peril from starvation and tuberculosis, Dr Roy told this newspaper on his return to Port-au-Prince following the two week, 2,000 kilometer trek through the Southern peninsula. Dr. Roy who also directs the Tuberculosis Sanatorium in Port-au-Prince said that the Grande Anse and neighboring regions have been hotbeds of tubercular infection.

'I am primarily concerned with the problems of health that the deplorable situation offers, the physician stated, 'as I think that there are already enough competent people to grabble with the other problems."

"Dr Roy revealed that he had prepared a full report setting forth the conditions prevailing in the southwestern peninsula to President Magloire. One member of the inspection party described one stretch of the devastated area as the *moon.* The trees that used to supply masts for coastal shipping industry now stand dead and stark against the sky, while nothing grows. The people are starving and have just enough energy to drag themselves out of the blazing sun, or pelting rain (as the drought had broken), into little lean-to shelters too small to hold a standing adult. The children have become so affected by starvation that their stomachs are inflated, while the skin sags on their bones. The grown men and women, whose bodies have more strength reserve, are still only in the emaciated stage: they may live for a year or two, prey to misery and disease, but the children will probably die within the next six months if nothing is done. Mothers have no milk for their babies. Their breasts are flat and dry."

Dr. Roy suggested to the government using the new doctors who had just graduated from the University of Haiti, about 40 in number, to work with government nurses to staff existing dispensaries that could be enlarged. He also proposed that temporary shelters be set up to gather children together for emergency treatment.

—

Angered by The Associated Press story on the front page of *El Caribe*, President Magloire ordered members of his Cabinet to hold a press conference. Called suddenly to the National Palace (in my office I kept a suit and tie for such emergencies) I found myself on the hot seat. Dr. Roy was also invited to attend. Commerce Minister Marcel Fombrun conducted the conference and he was clearly distressed. Much of his anger was directed at me. He grudgingly accepted my explanation that *El Caribe* had purposely distorted my story to the AP. In an acid tone he asked, "What was the source of your information *Monsieur* Diederich in reporting that a starving girl had salvaged a morsel of a dead rat for food?" Dr. Roy replied on my behalf and read the section of the report he had sent the President dealing with the incident. (Observing Dr. Roy organizing relief after Hurricane Hazel I had told his wife, also a relief worker that what Haiti needed was a compassionate doctor to run the country. I had Dr. Roy in mind. Little did anyone know then that Haiti would soon have a medical doctor as chief of state, the infamous "Papa Doc" Duvalier and that Dr. Roy and his family would be living in exile in Canada.)

Fombrun was still glaring at me as we left the palace. Minister of Health Roger Dorsainville pulled me to one side and said, "You did well. Those people will certainly get the help they need now." Two weeks later Magloire sacked his cabinet. Only Finance Minister Clément Jumelle remained.

Magloire's government quickly dispatched medical teams to organize relief efforts. Even Mrs. Paul Magloire, who oversaw a humanitarian foundation, flew to the south to see for herself.

—

That same week I was invited by Illinois Governor Adlai Stevenson to accompany him to Cap Haïtien to visit the Citadel. En route back to Port-au-Prince after our Citadel visit in the Reynolds Metal president's DC-3, the pilot suddenly announced that the plane would be landing in Ciudad Trujillo. Looking somewhat apprehensive I asked, "Can I have a parachute, please?" We were still over Haitian territory. It turned out to be a great joke. Governor Stevenson after reading an article in the *Sun*, which also carried the story of his arrival in Haiti, had been briefed on the problems between Haiti and Trujillo. The Governor and accompanying family members of Richard Reynolds (President of Reynolds Metal) understood that I would not be welcome in the dictator's lair. There were peals of laughter at my expression of dismay. Adlai Stevenson was not enamoured of dictators, especially of Trujillo's ilk.

Fifty years old at the time he had been beaten for the presidency by Eisenhower in 1952 but appeared to be a shoo-in for the Democratic Party's nomination in 1956. He refused to say whether he would be a candidate or not. I needed a positive news story I told him. He laughed and told me to wait.

It was shortly before Vice President Richard M. Nixon's early March visit to Haiti in 1955, Nixon was gradually working his way through nine nations in Central America and the Caribbean on a month long trip, when I had happened to spot Adlai Stevenson at Port-au-Prince's Bowen Field airport in transit section, which consisted principally of a bar facing the tarmac. It was then that he had described his longing to one-day visit King Henri Christophe's Citadel. When I invited the Governor to stay, he said, "I would be delighted to, but some other time. I hear you have another invited guest (Nixon) about to arrive." Laughing he boarded the airliner and continued his trip to San Juan.

When he returned to Haiti seven months later, in early September 1955, with his son, daughter-in-law and members of the Reynolds family I was there to greet him. Stevenson's visit became my exclusive story.

On horseback on the steep, winding trail leading up to the Citadel, fit and relaxed in open-necked shirt, the Governor confessed that he was truly happy about his thirty year old dream come true. U.S.politics was rarely mentioned on the climb but Stevenson's questions showed he was well read on Haiti. An excellent horseman, Stevenson was halfway up the rugged climb when the girth of the old saddle broke and he dismounted. The Governor declined offer of my horse," I can brag when you become President that I gave you my horse," I quibbed. "I'm not a declared candidate yet, so you better keep your horse," he replied as he plodded up the verdant trail asking the names of the various tropical fruits.

Suddenly the magnificent Citadel appeared like the prow of a giant ship riding the clouds. He stood in silence. The rest of his party caught up interrupting his thoughts. When the military attendant at the Citadel presented Stevenson with a small ancient cannon ball, he held it and joked, "Do I use this to bowl over the Republicans?" (Haitian Army Adjutant Edouard Paul, who accompanied us on our visit, asked me to take his picture with the Governor. The next picture I saw of Paul was of him tied to a stake before a firing squad in the Haitian border fort at Ounaminthe. He was executed on "Papa Doc" Duvalier's orders.)

Meanwhile Trujillo's war of words would continue. In subsequent months El *Caribe* declared that the SIM had uncovered a Communists *junta* in Haiti and listed, as one member defense lawyer Ernest Sabalat. The Haitian attorney denied the charge and in a long letter published in the *Sun* explained why Trujillo had branded him a Communist. Also included on the list were well-known Dominican exiles. As for Haiti, "The list of Haitian Communists is rather long and will be published in installments," stated *El Caribe*. It was a laughable propaganda line that was one of *El Jefe's* choice weapons. Yet in the Cold War atmosphere of late 1955 it was still a cause of concern for one to be labeled a Communist, even by a tyrant like Trujillo.

By publishing *El Caribe's* report on the so-called Communist *junta* in Haiti, *Le Matin* accused the *Sun* of "causing annoyance to the government." *Le Matin* called upon the Minister of Interior to take action against me, (i.e.expell the foreigner). While the *Sun* had dismissed in an editorial *El Caribe's* story, curiously *Le Matin* stated, " . . . among the names cited there are some who have no communist attachment." *El Caribe* didn't publish the rest of its so-called list.

—

U.S. Vice-President Richard Nixon and his wife Patricia had arrived from Ciudad Trujillo during the first week of March 1955. The three-day visit to Haiti was the last stop on their month-long tour. They were lodged in President Magloire's brand-new villa in Turgeau which only the week before, had been blessed by the Vatican's papal nuncio, Msgr. Luigi Raimondi, with a liberal sprinkling of holy water. In suit and tie in the warm tropical clime, Nixon said all the right things, calling for open trade with the region, which would allow its countries, including Haiti, to sell more produce in the U.S. In signing a commercial treaty with Haiti, Nixon announced that it was his first treaty signing and that he was happy it had taken place in Haiti among old friends.

Vice President Nixon and his donkey.

As to Port-au-Prince, Nixon described it as a "beautiful city" and when the mayor made him an honorary citizen of the Haitian capital and handed him the symbolic key to the city, Nixon stated that he would accept the key only if he was correct in presuming that citizenship entailed the right to stay in the city indefinitely. "I hope to return and take advantage of my rights," he added.

His busy schedule included a tour of the Artibonite Valley, a visit to the Péligre dam construction site and a flight over the Citadel. An astute politician, Nixon, apart from all the pleasant platitudes, did see a little of the other side of Haitian life. He frequently ordered his limousine driver to stop and with interpreter in tow visited with peasants in their mud huts. He learned that most of them ate but one meal a day of "*piti mi*" (guinea corn).

The Nixon press conference winding up the trip was called for 7 a.m. at the Magloire villa. Most of the foreign correspondents covering the vice president were doodling, with little anticipated news in sight. Suddenly a Haitian ex-senator, Alphonse Henriquez, who published a newspaper, *Le Justicier,* bounced to his feet and demanded to be heard. Paul Kennedy, the barrel-chested, no-nonsense *New York Times* correspondent, came alive, asking me, "Who is this guy?" "There is no freedom in Haiti," declared Henriquez in English before astounded Nixon aides and Haitian government officials. Henriquez's tirade lost its force however when he also complained that he was having trouble getting his senatorial pension. A U.S. embassy official escorted Henriquez from the room as he endeavored to dominate the conference. Nixon commented that he was confident he had seen both sides during his visit and emphasized, "Haiti has grave economic problems and it is essential to find a way to increase national productivity, which would raise the standard of living."

There was one moment on the vice president's trip that illustrated just how literal or otherwise an official interpreter can be. On a five-mile return trip after visiting a fish farm at Damein Agriculture School, Nixon stopped his official car, breezily waving Secret Servicemen away, and visited huts and with passing peasants, cross-examining them concerning their lives. He halted a milkmaid and caressed her donkey, which she reigned in at the sight of this man in suit and tie speaking a strange language. Shaded by a large straw hat, the milkmaid who was returning to her Cul de Sac home after delivering milk to the city was not happy with having her trip interrupted. Her children were waiting for her.

Through the Haitian interpreter, Nixon tried to break the ice by asking the donkey's name. "You are crazy. It has no name. Its *bourrique* (donkey)". The Haitians now crowding around told her to give any name to the darn donkey. Her replies were supposedly being translated into English but the translation bore little relationship to her answers. At one point she referred to the distinguished visitor as a *cocoyer* (coconut), and it was translated as, "She is happy to meet the Vice President of the United States." No, she was not married, but she had to get home to her children. The translator said she was not married but was *fiancée.*

When Adlai Stevenson saw the *Haiti Sun's* photograph of Nixon, the donkey, and the milkmaid with both her Créole responses and some of the interpreter's free-style English translation, he said, "I'd like a copy." He got more than one copy.

There was another footnote to Stevenson's visit. He had wanted to visit a *Vodou* temple but finally it was his son Adlai Stevenson II and his wife, who went in his stead while he visited the Reynolds bauxite mines in the hills above the seaport of Miragoâne. We went to Croix des Bouquet and I introduced the young couple to *oungan* Rémus Balan. The stocky, graying Balan, a notable in the town who apart from his priestly duties owned extensive real estate, was only too pleased to give the young couple an extensive tour of his elaborate temple. When he heard that Adlai Stevenson II was the son of next year's possible Democratic candidate for the presidency of the United States, Balan begged to be kept informed, as he wanted to be of assistance to the elder Stevenson's campaign. When Adlai Stevenson Sr. did declare his candidacy the following year, *oungan* Balan said he needed to travel to Washington to be close to Stevenson for whom he would give vital assistance in a manner known only to a superior *Vodou* priest. This was important because the New President would then help Haiti, he explained. Unfortunately I didn't have the means to help Balan. When he heard the news that Stevenson had lost his bid against Eisenhower he came to my office. Balan looked at me knowingly and threw up his hands. He should have been in the U.S. capital, he indicated. He was certain he would have made a difference.

Haiti Sun, Sunday October 9, 1955: "It was at Jérémie and on a Sunday morning that F. Morisseau-Leroy, whom we asked to interview Emile Roumer, met his co-religionist and colleague. We are happy to afford our readers an audience in the conversation of the two most solid pillars of contemporary Haitian literature though the medium of Créole, more so as Roumer is going to publish very soon a volume of Créole poems entitled *Coucourouge* and Morisseau-Leroy has finished writing a drama in three acts which unfolds against the turgid background of Rara. Another important detail: the two poets have been keeping up a correspondence in Créole for the past two years.

"Only the Haitian writers who have lived for a long time in France can produce a literary work of international value," Roumer thinks. He adds: "Let us be left to ourselves with the thesis of isolation the little stories written in an approximation of French are read by nobody. And what can they do to make us known abroad? Only the great writers manage to make themselves known. The chances of being a great writer in the French tongue are minute. It is possible to be a small and bad writer in Créole too. But those who participate actively in the creation of a literary language and who, as we are, are convinced of the riches of Créole will make a certain contribution to international literature".

"Now this contribution may be of interest to the entire world, if the writer who borrows from the infinite resources of the collective mind of the people is powerful enough to present in all their strength and their originality the extraordinary qualities of the Haitian people."

"Roumer does not doubt the possibilities of Créole as a literary language if Créole does not imply the lack of talent that would have made the writer mediocre in any other language. To illustrate his point, he often tells the story of a big boy whom he met at the Y.M.C.A. in London and who spoke seven languages correctly yet remained stupid in each of the seven tongues.

"To write, it is naturally necessary to know your language. All the same, it is necessary to know to write.

"Emile Roumer continued, citing several popular songs where the choice of words and the arrangement of phrases have put the illiterate composers above our *poètes de salon*.

"The fear heard here and there that Créole will replace French in Haiti draws from Roumer one of those bursts of laughter that are stronger than all arguments. How many of us speak French? How many speak Créole? The method of teaching French to young Haitians as their maternal tongue has been at fault. It is necessary to try another method, to face reality. It is a *lèse-intelligence* (crime) to wish to be ignorant of such a string of facts which are so obvious.

"The celebrated author of poems of Haiti and of France further believes that his Créole work is more important than French-expressed poetry and that half-dozen talented writers could create a veritable revolution in our national literature. Will this revolution influence the liberation of expression in Haiti? To this question, Roumer replied: You define it. Liberation of expression. Liberation of the intelligence imprisoned by a foreign language. He who reads and writes Créole does not injure his study of French. He will learn it more easily and more rapidly than someone who knows neither to read nor write. Only people of bad faith find today the means to rise against so lucid a point of view.

"Roumer is also bitterly opposed to the Lauback spelling as well as to all linguistic methods which tend to deform the Créole words taken from the French vocabulary.

"The public awaits with impatience the Créole poems of the author of *Marabou de mon Cœur* and of *Prends garde*. And young scholars of literature think that *Coucourouge* will be a definite stride forward in the important movement of Haitian literature through the medium of Créole."

In Sept. 1955 Illinois Governor Adlai Stevenson invited the editor to accompany him to Cap Haïtien to visit the Citadelle. The Governor was accompanied by his son and daughter-in-law and Walter L. Rice, Reynolds company Vice-President. The 50-year-old Democrat had been beaten for the presidency by Gen. Dwight Eisenhower in 1952 but appeared to be a shoo-in for the Democratic Party's nomination in 1956. Governor Stevenson refused to say whether he would be a candidate. I needed a positive news story, I told him. He laughed and told me to wait.

Returning from the climb to the Citadelle: Cap Haïtien Tourist authority Eric Etienne, Lieut. Edouard Paul (Later executed by Duvalier). Adlai Jr and wife before the ruins of King Henry Christophe's Sans Souci palace. King Christophe's famous Citadelle as seen from the air.

The Governor and his daughter-in-law before the tomb of King Christophe.

Editor of the *Haiti Sun* welcoming Governor Stevenson.

Oungan Remus Balan of Croix des Bouquet who sought to help Stevenson win the presidency of the United States.

CHAPTER 12

The Autumn of the General

As if the summer of 1955 were not hot enough I got carried away celebrating press freedom. As polemics were a celebrated tradition of Haitian newspapers I overstepped myself and foolishly decided to cross-pens with Georges Petit, a veteran newspaper street fighter. The muzzled media in Trujillo's fiefdom during my visits had had a profound effect on me, and there was that year a sense, as the scheduled end of President Magloire's term drew near, that the Haitian media, which had already lived a perilous existence, might once again be stifled.

Georges Petit, like so many of his generation, had won his journalistic spurs opposing the U.S. Marine Occupation and spent time in jail because of the government's draconian press laws. I expected more from Petit and his current newspaper *L'Indépendance*. In a ridiculous, if utopian, frame of mind, believing that constructive criticism was needed as never before, I quixotically took Petit to task, also in part because the *Sun* had become a target for his xenophobia.

Press Freedom Is a Sacred Heritage Not to Be Abused by Sensationalists
L'Indépendance; An Example of Irresponsible Journalism.
So ran the *Sun's* lead headline on Press Freedom Day, Tuesday, June 6, 1955. Expressing our gratitude to the pioneers who blazed the trail to present-day press freedom, and to the editors and journalists whose integrity and restraint have helped to maintain the tradition of a free and responsible media the *Sun* held forth as follows:

> Exultant newsmen across the free nations of the world will hail the anniversary of the day which commemorates the unleashing of a tremendous force in the molding of public opinion. They will also, no doubt, reflect on the equally great responsibility, which is the heritage of those who prepare news for the eyes of the large number of men and women who base their opinions upon what they read in the newspapers.

This responsibility is not to be taken lightly. The greatest threat to the freedom of a nation is a shackled, corrupt or irresponsible press. In our own country (Haiti), journalism has made rapid steps forward during the past half century, since the founding of the first major newspapers. Today, we can boast a competitive Press, expressing the uncensored opinions of the public—as the reporters and editors interpret them. Unfortunately, the vital spirit mirrored in the latter-day editions of *Le Nouvelliste*, or *Le Matin* is balanced by a totally irresponsible faction whose mouthpiece is *L'Indépendance*

The *Sun's* disquisition continued:

The patriotism of Haitians is acclaimed throughout history. The free, independent spirit that has defied the oppressor's lash and kept our shores free from invasion is, and always has been, more praiseworthy because it does not stoop to chauvinism. Foreigners were welcomed in the time of Christophe and they played an important role in the development of his great kingdom. Today, our government realizes the continued importance of technical aid from countries which are older, larger and are therefore scientifically more advanced than Haiti. But the disgruntled chauvinists who slap together the four-paged bi-weekly have the gall to christen their brainchild Indépendance, parodying the most sacred word in this republic's vocabulary with their biased and destructive criticisms of everything progressive. Independence implies progress. There can be no freedom if we are subject to poverty, disease, malnutrition and illiteracy. Even the most diehard critics of the Magloire administration must admit that tangible results have been produced in the field of progress. New roads, new schools, new industries, and most important of all—new ideas.

This means nothing to the ***Indépendance.*** Having once scrawled the word in disgracefully printed characters above the equally messy front page, the editors proceed forthwith to prejudice the opinion of all that will listen. Snapping at the heels of the government has become the set policy of the financially honest, but misguided newspaper. But that is not enough. Erratic and unprovoked attacks are made on everyone and everything that appears for a moment in the spotlight. Evidently disappointed in personal ambitions of their own, the men who write and support the newspaper are furious at the popularity of anyone else. But there is an old Haitian saying, 'The dog barks while the carriage passes,' which accurately sums up the effectiveness of their criticism.

The concern for unimportant, unworthy details shown by the editors was illustrated in the last issue of the newspaper. Milton Barrall, U.S. ***chargé d'affaires,*** gave a luncheon last month for the Press. The major newspapers of the capital, including the Sun, were invited to send representatives, and assigned reporters or editors to the event. Probably owing to the fact that the embassy (in common with the majority of the Haitian reading public) is unaware of the existence of ***L'Indépendance,*** the publication was not included.

This was cited by the bi-weekly (which devoted 1/3 of its news coverage to drooling over the luncheon) as an example of the favoritism shown the *Haiti Sun*, the only weekly included in the invitations. Mr. Barrall reportedly invited to 'his' lunch the members of the daily press, yet he saw fit to make an exception in the case of the *Haiti Sun* because he is American, even if by naturalization, declared ***L'Indépendance.*** The editor of the *Haiti Sun* is nearer to being a Haitian than an American, although he travels on a New Zealand passport, but the editors of the little bi-weekly did not take the trouble to check their assumptions before printing them.

This is precisely the kind of irresponsible and inaccurate report that is expected from *L'Indépendance.* **Reminiscent of the now-forgotten** *L'Action Sociale,* **the newspaper is evidently controlled by would-be mob-rousers who are infuriated because the Haitian people have too much common sense to become aroused by the ranting of a disappointed demagogue. Though capable of doing little harm to the country, the journal distracts those who try to do anything constructive for the country, with its constant nagging.**

No constructive criticism ever appears within the sloppily printed pages of ***L'Indépendance.*** Facts are not accurately presented, opinions not honestly formed; in sum, the newspaper is fast building a reputation for all the characteristics which good, responsible journalism abhors. ***L'Indépendance,*** therefore, may not be directly responsible for harm to Haiti, but it certainly is responsible for a great deal of harm to other newspapers. The journal undermines the reputation of the Press as a body, contaminating its ***confrères*** with the stigma of its own ill health. The tradition of trust and of integrity which the Press, here and elsewhere, has struggled against all odds to maintain, is threatened by the sensationalists who scream before they investigate.

And the *Sun* had more to say, viz.:

In two weeks of international and local events ***L'Indépendance*** could find nothing better to print than an assortment of scurrilous and trivial occurrences, most of them containing some minor detail which could be built up into a case against foreigners. The front page warned darkly of the dangers of sodomy, or the perilous state of our commerce; complained about Hasco (The Haitian-

American Sugar Company); snapped at the *Sun*; and in general painted a dark picture of Haiti with the foreigner as the root of all evil. The foreigner is the 'piece de resistance' of the newspaper's critical feast apparently. Anytime, on any, or no, pretext the foreigner is the target of the gentleman (and one lady, Mme. Therese G. Petit) who run *L'indépendence*

The *Sun's* critique concluded:

Another strange deviation from generally accepted journalistic principles is the method of 'reporting' employed by the journal. No newsmen ever represented *L'Indépendance*, at state ceremonies or wherever news usually is made. The complete source of all the facts printed in the newspaper is the collective press of the capital. It appears that *L'Indépendance* merely skims through a copy or two of the daily newspapers, then checks off the items that can be turned around to attack foreigners.

This is obviously a dangerous practice. No newspaper should be allowed to flourish, with all due respect to the sanctity of press freedom, in such overt disregard of all the principles that form the backbone of journalism. Especially in a pioneer country such as Haiti, destructive criticism should be limited. But this should not be necessary from outside sources. The members of the press should regard it as their personal responsibility to uphold the good name of their fraternity and not to injure their country, their people or their profession by wanton disregard of the fundamental principles of journalism. Now, when the government is spending vast sums annually to sow the seeds of a future tourism harvest, the unprovoked attacks against foreigners may one day undo much of the careful work being achieved. The Central American republic of Guatemala recently provided an example of what happens to tourism at the first hint of political instability. [A reference to the CIA-backed overthrow of the leftist Guatemalan government of Col. Jacobo Arbenz.] If the irresponsible accusations of *L'Indépendance* were read by prospective tourists, Haiti could expect a sharp decline in an industry which is fast rising from second to first place in the economy.

Publisher Petit was understandably hopping mad. In a banner headline, with the largest set of hand type he possessed, he counter attacked not in one edition but in half a dozen editions. In the third attack he finally got the spelling of my name right. He called upon Minister of Interior Adelphin Telson to revoke my *permis de séjour* that allowed me to work. (The demand was ignored.) It was all a sad lesson. This was the way it was and would remain. Haitian journalism was a special kind of journalism, too poor and too weak to help build a nation. I always regretted the amount of space Petit devoted to criticizing me, when my objectives were the opposite. And I also had a soft spot for Petit, who later became another victim of Papa Doc. Duvalier ordered his arrest and he died shortly afterwards. (Ironically, in 1929 a little known Francois Duvalier had made his newspaper debut writing in Georges Petit's combative publication of the times, *Le Petit Impartial*.) Haiti enjoyed a restrictive kind of freedom of the press under Magloire. Since the major newspapers relied on government financial support in the form of official advertising from the various ministries, tended to blunt their criticism. The conformist media was nicknamed, *musicien palais*, meaning they played only the music that was agreeable to the palace. The *Sun's* policy, to which we strictly adhered, was no financial support from the Haitian or any foreign government agency. This allowed the *Sun* freedom to publish what we wished. And because the *Sun* was in English, we were generally tolerated by the authorities as no threat.

In Haiti there was no such thing as investigative journalism, and for understandable reasons. It was a costly and perilous specialty of journalism. Apart from being high risk physically, it required that a newspaper be financially independent. Corruption remained a taboo subject. The opposition political media, for its part, was very small and ill equipped. Opposition leaders had to rely on job-printing their publications and press owners took no risks. Mimeographed leaflets, known as *tract*s in Haiti circulated clandestinely carrying attacks against the regime in power and accusations of corruption. However everyone knew the obvious; they didn't have to see it in print. Haitians understood what was going on and corruption was a standard subject of gossip.

With the paltry presidential salary of a thousand dollar a month, plus an expense account and allotment for a security entourage, Magloire managed to have a tasteful villa built in the capital city on a steep hill in residential Turgeau, plus a summer home in the cool mountains of Laboule.

Police Chief, Col. Marcaisse Prosper, a stickler for well-creased uniforms (it was said he had to be hoisted into his pants in order to preserve the cease), built a lavish villa surrounded with terraced gardens. The villa stood out on the busy road to Pétionville as a highly visible monument to questionable gotten gains. Expensive European furniture was imported to adorn the villa along with huge, ornate, gold-leaf-framed Italian period paintings.

A popular meringue at the time was *Twa Bébé Soti Leogan,* a catchy, *risqué* tune that told the story of three *babes* (gals) leaving the town of Léogane for Port-au-Prince where they would seduce the young fellows of the capital. The song survived efforts at censorship and when three neat bungalows sprouted in Turgeau, said to be built for the Magloire family as insurance against the general's old age, they were quickly referred to as the *Twa Bébé.*

Nothing was too good for the feared police chief. He became arguably the richest man in the regime on a colonel's salary of $250 a month. Neither he nor President Magloire had won the first prize of the Haitian national lottery, the *Gros Lot,* which amounted to paltry $20,000.

The optimum Haitian dream is to own a big house, and as big as possible. This is doubtless in response to the fact that the vast majority live in urban hovels and rural mud huts. Moreover in a country in which mortgages were then unknown and Italian moneylenders on the *Grand' Rue* asked extraordinary interest rates for a loan, building a house required cash!

In Port-au-Prince's tree-shaded Bois Verna, only a short distance from the National Palace, the most important bourgeois (elite) families lived side by side in lovely gingerbread mansions. They were also conveniently close to the foreign diplomatic missions in case political asylum became necessary. Gradually the bourgeoisie had also begun to move up into the cool mountains. The mountainward drift had accelerated with the availability of the automobile. The poor had followed in the elite's wake, erecting makeshift homes in the ravines. As for Haiti's stunted middle class, their small homes, in which families were packed together, even in the 1950s lacked most modern amenities such as running water and indoor toilets and showers. Cooking was done in a back shed over charcoal braziers.

In spite of the indulgence of the top men of the Magloire regime, and that included the President's brother Arsène, who while minister of public works became wealthy, at least economic and some social development was being pushed. Finance Minister Clément Jumelle, a bright, University of Chicago trained technocrat, was attempting to put together a competent national planning board, something the country lacked. It was already a well-known secret Jumelle had been anointed to succeed Magloire when the general's term ended.

A *gran nèg* or a person with power, the right name, or the right pigmentation, enjoyed privilege. He or she could order a policeman about and expect respect. One morning a close relative of President Paul Magloire ordered Lieut. Jacques Laroche of the Criminal Research Bureau to throw a houseboy into prison. Laroche foolishly asked why and on what grounds. What was his crime? Stupefied by Laroche's reaction, the personage went to Colonel Prosper's corner office, was quickly received by the police chief, and complained of being insulted by Laroche. The sympathetic police chief ordered the impertinent Laroche to Fort Dimanche, not for duty but as a prisoner. Taking the incident philosophically, Laroche used his two weeks in detention at the old fort to study for his final law exams. When I visited Lieutenant Laroche at the ancient Fort Dimanche it had none of the bloody mystery that it later acquired as Papa Doc's gulag. Laroche later became a fervent follower of Papa Doc, who rose to power championing the black middle class, to which Laroche belonged.

---

*   (Years later Dr. Francois (Papa Doc) Duvalier purchased exiled Colonel Prosper's villa with a million dollars in state funds turning it into a government guest house, *Villa d' Accueil.* In the post Duvalier era it became the headquarters for the first election and much later served as the residence of the Prime Minister.)

——

Meanwhile the *Haiti Sun* had the good fortune of recruiting Haitian as well as foreign-born contributors to brighten the guest columns. The foreigners included Bernie Kalb, then working the night shift at the *New York Times*. He later made his name as a foreign correspondent with CBS News in particular and had an infectious sense of humor.

Wise and Otherwise was a column by resident expatriate T.J. Grant, who had arrived in Haiti with the Marines had stayed on and raised a family. T.J. Grant, with his weird stories seldom concluded but always hilarious, developed a large following but not all were friendly. A prominent Haitian dentist took T.J. to task accusing him of being rude to his wife and beat him up. Grant defended himself admirably at age 75.

Other contributors treating more serious topics included Maya Deren, who had arrived in the winter of 1947 on a Guggenheim fellowship to study Haitian dance and eventually authored a classic book on *Vodou, Divine Horsemen*. David Holden, of the *London Times* Washington bureau wrote about tourism for the *Sun* during his stay. Another English newsman, George Ward Price, who had interviewed Adolf Hitler and Benito Mussolini for the *Daily Mail* of London, was an expert on dictators. However his book on the Axis leaders had been deemed too soft on them and the British ambassador in Port-au-Prince snubbed him. For the *Haiti Sun*, Ward Price contributed advice on how not to write about dictators.

In terms of local news, Haiti was rife with man-bites-dog-stories. Typical was the one about a man, a wealthy farmer, who built his own above ground tomb, quite a large affair. He found it so comfortable that he added doors and windows and moved in to live in it. The *Sun* published a photo of the live-in-tomb (To understand how such a thing would be true, one must understand that some well-off Haitian peasants scorn cemeteries and build their own tombs in the backyard particularly in south Haiti).

There was also the economy-minded and definitely non-conformist American woman tourist who decided to go to the airport with two rented *bourik*—donkeys, one carrying her, the other for her luggage. The spectacle of the *blan* with two donkeys was too much for the Haitians; many locals abandoned their work and followed in throngs, laughing their heads off. Guinea hens caused a near riot in the crowded open air Croix des Bossales market when they escaped their cage and had scores of market women raced around hunting them. A rhythm-loving peacock that danced the meringue whenever it was played made the paper. And who would have guessed that the Yellow Room of the National Palace, in December 1955, would be the scene of a serious, five-day debate on Emmanuel Kant, marking the 150th anniversary of the German philosopher's death. Dr. Camille Lhérisson, former Minister of Health, was the organizer of this spirited exchange among Haitian and German intellectuals.

And there was the folksy Ohio-born American ambassador, Roy Tasco Davis, who, when he presented his credentials to President Magloire in 1953 at the palace, recited from memory a Wordsworth poem on Toussaint Louverture.

It was a country of surprises. The *Haiti Sun* sponsored an essay contest on the topics *Who was Audubon?* ; The famous ornithologist and naturalist painter, John James Audubon, who was born in the southern Haiti town of Les Cayes in 1785. The winner of the contest was one Anthony Saint-Cyr of Les Cayes, who proved to be a descendant of the famed Audubon's brother Belloni Fougère, and thus a relative of John James Audubon. The *Sun* could find no known relative of Alexandre Dumas, though the people of Jérémie, in Haiti's southern peninsula were proud of the fact that Alexandre Dumas had been born a few miles from their town in 1762, the son of a handsome black woman and an aristocratic French plantation boss. The first Dumas had entered the French army as a youth and climbed to the rank of general in France. He fathered Alexandre Dumas the Elder (author of *The Three Musketeers* and *The Count of Monte Cristo*) who in turn fathered Alexandre Dumas the Younger. For that reason the main square in Jérémie is called *Place des Trois Dumas* (the Plaza of the Three Dumas.)

The *Sun* noted just how deep German penetration of Haiti was in the old days with the item about how the infamous German airforce chief was nearly Haitian born. "One of the leaders of the Third Reich, Marshall Herman Goering, who after years of unlimited power ended in prison where he poisoned himself, was conceived in Haiti and was almost born here. In 1891, Dr. Henrick Ernest Goering, the Marshall's father was named Consul General and resident Minister for Germany in Port-au-Prince. He took his second wife Franiska to Haiti and their son was conceived here. But the Prussian diplomat did not wish his child to be born anywhere but in Germany, so he rushed his wife home for the birth."

The *Sun's* *Sans Blague* column pointed out to readers that it doesn't pay to be too critical of folk. Dr. W.C. Cumberland, financial advisor and general receiver of customs in Haiti in the 1920s said some strong things: "Haitian have a diarrhea of words and a constipation of ideas," the American stated. In loving memory of Dr. Cumberland, Haitians got an idea. They devised a method of diverting electric current to their homes in order to balance their family budget at the expense of the American owned electric company. They named this manner of theft of electricity the *Cumberland*.

The *Sun* tried to be optimistic. The water falls of Saut Mathurin in South Haiti, we announced, would be harnessed soon for hydroelectric power. That was in 1953. It took another 30 years to happen. Still in good humor and optimism often went begging as a time of change was rapidly approaching—and the most dangerous political period in the country's history.

———

Like the preliminaries in a cockfight (Haiti's national sport) when the cocks appear to be strutting and sizing up their adversary, Haitian politicians move slowly and carefully into the ring. But like the cocks they eventually fly at each other in all-out combat. It became obvious that Haiti was approaching dangerous crossroads even though Magloire's term was still more than a year away. Interior Minister Alelphin Telson found it necessary to issue a communiqué on Oct, 21, 1955, declaring there was no cause for alarm, that there was "no political movement active in the country that could disturb the peace and quiet of the families."

"During last week, shots fired in the night in some quarters of town (Port-au-Prince) prompting police investigations which have led to the arrest of some suspects," the communiqué stated. "The investigations are still underway and will certainly end with the arrest of the authors and accomplices of this atrocity."

The communiqué added, "Agitators have, however, profited by this to create a certain amount of confusion, to seek asylum in several foreign embassies and legations pretending that their lives were in danger." The Interior Minister vowed that the government would continue to guarantee the life and property of people living in the republic.

The *Sun* began receiving new opposition underground leaflets known as *tracts*. It was Fern Baguidy, who worked for Pan American World Airways at their Rue Pavée office, who told me of *Doc* Duvalier being a man to watch. As Dr. Francois Duvalier was in hiding I could only listen to his few supporters. Baguidy would pull me into a corner of the airline office, as I checked the passenger lists for flights to and from Miami and a new direct flight to New York for tidbits for the *Sun's Beachcomber* social column and insist that I keep a watch on the ephemeral *country doctor*. In fact I later learned that during that period Duvalier was literally hiding around the corner not far from police headquarters.

The fateful year of 1956, all years were fateful from then on in Haiti, began with Magloire's making the traditional presidential speech to the nation on January 2, the *jour des Aieux* (Day of the Forefathers). The address was brief and he alluded to the end of his regime. Said Magloire: "We are proud on this morning when all the church bells ring in unison to celebrate the glory of our heroes and . . . to ask of those who in 17 months will succeed us, to continue the task that we have undertaken, to impress on hearts and minds the need for renewing the discipline and sense of moral value which will give to our birth and life as a people a halo of grandeur and immortality."

However, there remained the problem of when the presidential term ended. The 1950 constitution stated: "The President of the Republic, Citizen Paul E. Magloire, elected on October 8, 1950, will begin his functions on December 6, 1950 and his term shall end on May 15, 1957." Nevertheless the growing opposition, mostly the *outs* of the urban middleclass, claimed that Magloire's term should end on Dec. 6, 1956.

Meanwhile social life continued in spite of a downturn in the economy. Politics was left to the politicians. Private clubs were as active as ever. President Magloire had been invited to the Bellevue Club to celebrate its 50th birthday. Of all the clubs Bellevue prided itself in counting as members the *crème-de-la-crème* of local society. Until the Magloire regime the only gentlemen with dark skin at Bellevue were waiters. The Turgeau Tennis Club was also exclusive. The Port-au-Princien was a social club with mostly businessmen as members. Its site next to the American embassy enjoyed a splendid view of the Champ de Mars Park from its open second-story balcony. The American Club was principally for wealthy expatriate Americans. Its membership consisted mostly of a small group of American businessmen who had succeeded in Haiti during the occupation and preferred to socialize with each other and play tennis or golf. The American Club was situated in an exclusive section of the Port-au-Prince suburb of Bourdon, across from the U.S. Ambassador's residence, in a most spectacular setting. The club boasted an Olympic-size swimming pool below an airy clubhouse, and a golf course that sloped down the actual side of a mountain turning players into sure-footed goats.

Provincial towns also had their private clubs. The best known was the Union Club in Cap Haïtien where President Franklin D. Roosevelt had met with Haitian President Sténio Vincent in 1934 at the end of the U.S. Marine occupation. In the town of Jérémie there was a literary club that was as selective as any of those in the capital. There were also Masonic lodges; even King Henri Christophe and other pioneer leaders were members of Masonic Lodges. Early French colonists had brought masonry to the island.

Emanuel Freedman, the foreign editor of The *New York Times,* informed me that a new man had joined my beat and would be covering Haiti, the rest of the Caribbean, and Central America out of Mexico City. "Work with him, you'll like Paul Kennedy." During Nixon's visit I had already met Paul Kennedy. An impressive, tough newsman, Kennedy possessed strong journalistic vigor and even stronger vocal cords. Though born in New York Paul had attended the University of Oklahoma and had tangled with Dictator Francisco Franco of Spain and other dictators on his far-flung beats and would do the same in Haiti.

Those last months of a presidential term in Haiti were days of suspense. By the closing days of the term all those in the government bureaucracy who owed their jobs to loyalty to the president knew they were facing unemployment if another regime took office. As Haiti had no civil service, there was heavy pressure on the president to stay in office. And as Haiti's presidents tended to believe that they were the only ones capable of governing, they usually didn't need much pressure.

In early January 1956, Paul Kennedy flew in from Mexico to learn Magloire's political intentions. Driving Kennedy into Port-au-Prince from the airport to the Grand Hotel Oloffson, I was doing my best to explain how delicate the situation had become, with Clément Jumelle, the minister of finance, waiting in the wings to succeed Magloire and the president's newspaper *Le National* calling on Magloire to remain at the helm. It was a very tense time, a time of real suspense. "The only suspense here," Kennedy suddenly burst out, "Where is in the damn rum? What kind of stringer are you anyway?" (From then on I invariably met Paul on arrival with a bottle of Barbancourt. He swore it was the best rum in the world.)

Magloire received reporter Kennedy on January 7. I had briefed my visiting correspondent and accompanied him to the interview. Wearing his handsome smile the president received us warmly in his National Palace office. Kennedy lost no time in asking him the big question: "Are you going to succeed yourself?" Magloire's answer produced the lead for Kennedy's *New York Times* story. "President Magloire reaffirmed today that he would not succeed himself next January."

Kennedy's dispatch continued: "In the last month, pressures have been growing to influence the president to have the constitution amended so that he could serve another term. Such pressures are especially interesting to politicians here in that they center in the newspaper *Le National* in which the president has a controlling interest."

During the interview I was ready to believe that the president was sincere until Magloire stated: "Some want to give the impression that *Le National* is an official paper but it is not". From that point on I had the creeping feeling that he had not yet made up his mind and that he would take the country down to the wire. Magloire went on "*Le National* expressed its own opinion, but the opinion of *Le National* cannot cause me to go back on the word of a soldier."

"*Le National* had said editorially that the people of Haiti "demanded "that the president continue in office. The paper indicated that he was "indispensable."

General Magloire disclaimed his "indispensability" and said, "I only hope that the man who succeeds me will be able to do more for my people than I have done."

"He described his role in the presidential elections the forthcoming January as that of a "good citizen". He said he would cast his vote "for the man who has my sympathy and who assures me he can do more for the people than I have done.

"The president noted that under "the Haitian political (constitutional) system" he could not campaign actively for any group or candidate. His sole role, he asserted, was to see that "everything goes off in perfect order."

Paul Kennedy's *New York Times* story continued: "The pressure is enormous for him (Magloire) to continue in office or to select his successor, inasmuch as in Haiti virtually all positions of prestige stem from the government and those now in office would automatically be replaced if an anti-Magloire candidate should win. Thus, with a year to go before the elections, an abnormal degree of political heat is developing."

As we left the palace Kennedy asked me what I thought."Good story, good intentions," was my answer. To which the veteran responded, quoting the old saying, "the road to hell is paved with good intentions."

During nearly a decade Paul Kennedy would cover Haiti and his name would become synonymous with newsman. He would be expelled by Magloire and later by Duvalier. Kennedy became my boss and mentor. I couldn't have asked for a better friend. Meanwhile, Haiti's national suspense drama deepened.

The last caudillo, General-President Paul E. Magloire hitches up his pants in a symbolic gesture in 1956 to show he is wearing his "iron Pants" prepared to deal with those he calls "vagabonds".

(Collection Maud Wadestrand)

Professor Daniel Fignolé

Clément Jumelle

Senator Louis Déjoie

Dr. François Duvalier

CHAPTER 13

Sunset of an Era

The *Haiti Sun* received a full-page advertisement for a newly developed tranquilizer called Equanil and for those who could afford this anxiolytic medication, it had arrived just in time. A new national Senate was to be elected in January of 1957 and a new Haitian president the following April. Thus the fight for the presidency was about to begin in earnest and anxiety was already running high.

On the afternoon Sept. 6, 1956, Clément Jumelle, 40, beaming a winning smile for our camera, finally announced his long-expected presidential candidacy at a press conference at his new home in *Montagne Noire*, above Pétionville. Jumelle had resigned the week before as finance minister and already his new house, which he said was paid for with his own funds, was raising eyebrows. (Actually Jumelle did not own the house, the Banque Nationale d'Haiti had a mortgage on it and also on a house in Obléon. Both houses were later repossessed and sold.) To be president a candidate was required by law to be a property owner. Louis Déjoie rented a comfortable home in Babiole, a hilly section of Port-au-Prince; as an industrialist, (considered an astute businessman by his *students*) he claimed that the returns on his business investments were far better than the ownership of a home. Despite the property ownership clause Francois Duvalier didn't own a home. He rented a small house on Rue Capois, a short distance from the National Palace. Daniel Fignolé's wife owned the house-school in which they lived.

Jumelle was universally believed a shoo-in as Magloire's anointed successor. As a technician with a good grasp of the country's myriad problems Jumelle carefully laid out a detailed platform of government, stressing the urgency of addressing the country's challenges without delay. He did appear to be the only candidate with a clear vision of the country's needs.

Joining the *fearsome foursome,* as some called Jumelle, Déjoie, Duvalier and Fignolé, were two minor candidates who could be assured a consolation prize: diplomatic posts abroad, for their efforts, by the new president.

If anyone at that time believed that Magloire would backtrack on his promise to step down when the time came, Magloire firmly restated his promise to call it quits in an interview with the *Reader's Digest*. Eugene Lyons, the magazine's senior editor wrote in his August article, "Presumably the President will have the deciding voice in the nomination of his successor. But his authority is by no means absolute, and many groups and individuals are already jockeying for the power of the National Palace." Lyons ended his story with, "It is almost certain that President Magloire's successor will be, like the overwhelming majority of the people, a '*noir*,' a Negro, and that, like the present incumbent, he will ignore color shades in ruling this proud little republic." (This brought a howl of protest from the mulatto candidate, Louis Déjoie.)

Ernest Chauvet, Haiti's ambassador to the United Nations, interviewed Magloire for his own newspaper, *Le Nouvelliste*. In a laudatory article Chauvet quoted the president as saying, "I am renewing this promise (to step down at the end of his term) again today and as the *Generalissimo* of Haiti's army." Magloire added that his pledge to relinquish his office was "important to assure stability for the new president who will be elected by the people next April. Without this stability, no government will be able to make this country progress." The president's gesture, Chauvet wrote, "Is perhaps unique in Haiti's history, and will immortalize Paul E. Magloire."

President Magloire decided in early September 1956 that he needed some cooler weather and flew to Philadelphia with the excuse that he needed a medical checkup at the Temple University hospital. The Parliament granted him fifteen days' leave. After being certified fit and healthy he and Mrs. Magloire with the rest of their entourage visited Niagara Falls and Atlantic City, and finally sailed home from New York aboard the Cristobal, a passenger vessel belonging to the Panama Canal Company. Rested and relaxed after 22 days abroad Magloire included some remarks in his homecoming speech that raised questions as to whether he had in fact decided to dump Clément Jumelle as the President's designated successor.

During his trip, Magloire said, he had been asked (by Americans) about the candidates. He commented first on Senator Louis Déjoie, praising him as an industrialist and businessman but noted, "Concerning politics, however, I must confess that I was somewhat reticent. In my opinion . . . he is considered an industrialist . . . in a country such as ours, political ability is of primordial importance for a statesman."

As for Dr. Francois Duvalier, Magloire stated that "this candidate is reputedly the candidate of the Americans working in the country, and apparently counting on their influence and that of the SCISPA staff to win the coming election."

"Mr. Duvalier, without doubt, has never collaborated with my government," Magloire said adding, "but he has no enmity against me. I believe him to be too great a patriot to connect him with playing on the American strings in order to ascend to the presidential seat."

"As to our friend Daniel Fignolé Magloire concluded, "He had not declared his candidacy before my departure for the U.S. so I cannot be very precise on his candidacy."

Magloire added that although Fignolé "has rarely been in accord with me on politics and while he is known as *intransigent* I have to admit, in all truth, that if he has his shortcomings he has, on the other hand, many fine qualities."

And as to candidate Jumelle, Magloire said that in New York, "he is said to be a racist, a *mangeur de mulâtres,* (mulatto-eater, meaning anti-mulatto). I emphasized that Jumelle had several times been minister during my presidency . . . I believe him to be a good technician . . ." He went on to compliment Jumelle for his expert work during Hurricane Hazel.

Magloire's backhanded compliments fooled no one. And the question Haitian politicians were asking was why had he branded his own candidate, Clément Jumelle, as a racist? Sensing that Jumelle might not be a shoo-in after all, and that the field might be open, the three other leading candidates were energized and began campaigning in earnest. It was the first presidential campaign in Haiti in which the candidates actually stumped the countryside and went to the people with their promises. In a less-admirable sign that the competition was indeed serious, partisans of rival motorcades showered their opposition with verbal insults and rocks.

The *Haiti Sun,* in an effort to keep its sense of humor, advertised a new service: *The diagnosing and interpreting of rumors.* Readers were reminded that no modern communication system could compete with Haiti's *télédjol,* which with the opening of the electoral campaign was overloaded with rumors. The fact was that Haiti had few working telephones and thus no means of mass communicating other than by mouth. "It (the rumor)outstrips everything, streaks past us like a bat out of hell, and emits the belligerent odor of a dead caiman exposed to the sun," declared the *Haiti Sun.* "Nothing is more difficult to overtake than a rip-snorting, odoriferous, jet-propelled rumor fired from the most effective of all launching platforms; your best friend's lungs. Bring your rumor to the *Haiti Sun* offices. We'll diagnose it, shake it free of mud, or put a leash on it."

The editor of the newspaper *L'Indépendence,* Georges Petit, went to jail for publishing material considered injurious to the person of the President of the Republic. When our Haitian Journalists Association protested to the Ministry of Interior, Petit was released.

However, Magloire's human rights record on the whole was considered fair. One cloud that did hang over his regime was a horrible crime committed in March 1953 at Martissant on the southern edge of the capital and which became known ever after as the Martissant crime. Ludovic (Dodo) Désinor, an accountant in the Ministry of Public Works, though badly wounded by machete and gunfire, managed to survive. His family was not as fortunate; his wife and children were killed. The unidentified attacker or attackers set fire to the family house after the murderous rampage. The charred ruins of the Desinor house at Martissant stood as a chilling reminder of the worst crime to take place in Haiti during the Magloire presidency. Because the President's brother, Arsène Magloire was Minister of Public Works at the time, and Désinor worked for him, suspicions arose that the Ministry might have somehow been involved. However Désinor gave no hint as to who his attackers might have been. When he recovered he left the country, having been appointed to the post of vice-consul in New York City.

In a March 1953 radio speech following a reshuffling of his cabinet, from which his brother Arsène was dropped, President Magloire did mention the Désinor case stating:

> Certain rumors have found some acceptance in the public mind. More than one of them maneuvered to put a political character on the crime at Martissant. A favorable ground for the spread of these rumors was created by the search for the criminals by police working in perfect cooperation with the Department of Justice. What it is necessary to remember is that such crimes are committed everywhere and that it is always difficult for the police to put their hands on the guilty party . . . I am convinced that detectives will soon deliver the authors and accomplices of the odious crime at Martissant to the hands of Justice.

During an interview for my book *Papa Doc*, at his exile quarters in New York, Magloire said that while the crime had never been solved, he felt that Duvalierists who sought to embarrass his government might have committed it.

Then in June 2000, Charles Dupuy a columnist for *Haiti Observateur*, a New York City Haitian weekly, picked up the old story. As reported by Dupuy the guilty party was Désinor himself who had murdered his own family and inflicted his own wounds. He had confessed and had been interned in a New York mental institution.

Ex-President Elie Lescot, 73, Haiti's last mulatto chief of state, overthrown in 1946, returned from eleven years in exile, vowing to remain out of politics and fade away, surrounded only by his grandchildren. Lescot did however bring home with him his tombstone; custom made in Europe, which he explained was for the family vault in Cap Haïtien, his native city. He died a few years later to be buried in the family vault under his own headstone.

—

As Cuba began to heat up politically the neighboring Caribbean island suddenly became front-page news in Haiti. Foes of the Batista dictatorship had machine-gunned to death the Cuban chief of military intelligence, Col. Antonio Blanco Rico, as he left the Montmarte, a fashionable Havana nightclub. The shooting had touched off a crackdown of suspected opponents of the regime. On October 29, 1956, after receiving a report that four Cubans had entered the Haitian embassy that morning, Batista's national police chief, Gen. Rafael Salas Canizares, quickly surrounded the embassy in the Havana suburb of Miramar. Then in an action seldom witnessed in Latin America Gen. Salas, ignored the traditional sanctity of political asylum and violated Haitian diplomatic territory. The general personally led his men into the embassy and paid with his life. He was fatally shot. However his police killed all ten Cubans refugees in the embassy. Six of the dead had been Cubans who had been in the embassy for three months and were awaiting their safe-conduct passes to leave the country. The other four had entered the embassy that morning. The Cuban police had completely ransacked the embassy premises.

Haiti was outraged. The Foreign Ministry sent protests and university students took to the streets of Port-au-Prince to demonstrate before the Cuban embassy, demanding reparations for the violation of Haiti's national honor.

———

The return of candidate Louis Déjoie from the U.S. brought out a throng of backers, most of them mulattos, who crowded the little Port-au-Prince airport. There was a heavy police presence as trouble was expected, and when some of the most passionate followers began shouting "*Vive Déjoie,*" *Vive la Liberté,* and "*A bas Magloire*" the police responded by breaking up the crowd with brute force, pushing and shoving. With the exception of some leading mulatto businessmen who had a close association with Magloire, most of the elite were enthusiastically flocking to the Déjoie banner.

In a November 18 interview with *Le Matin*, Port-au-Prince Police Chief Col. Marcaisse Prosper, stated that he "sincerely regretted the trouble at the airport, although the nature of the cries uttered by Déjoie supporters was judged by the police on duty as being seditious". Though he could use a gracious tone as reflected in the *Le Matin* interview, Prosper was an organized man and no one doubted his toughness. The police chief warned:

> The police will not tolerate any electoral rally degenerating into a subversive manifestation against public order. Nor will it be tolerated that insults be addressed to the person of the President of the Republic or any other top-ranking functionary. If criticisms must be made against their public acts, that can pass, but insults, defamatory remarks such as those flung about during the meetings, for example in La Saline, or the rock-throwing against the cars of candidates on their passage through the streets, like Bel Air last Thursday, will not be tolerated by the police.

Asked by *Le Matin* his opinion of the tendency of certain groups to resurrect the divisive question of color, Prosper responded: "I must admit that the reports from the police which I have consulted signal, in fact, this tendency on the part of several groups." Emphasizing "the danger that all exaggeration in this direction presents," Prosper added; " . . . If President Magloire has been able to realize so many things during his term, it was because he based his policy on a true national union in connection with which he has always been strict in maintaining his policy for the best of us all."

On the 24th of November the *Bureau d'Inscriptions* officially opened voter registration offices throughout the republic. All citizens over 21 years of age could register up until

December 24 in order to be eligible to vote in Haiti's national elections. Balloting for 21 senators was to take place on January 13, 1957. The presidential election was scheduled for the following April. Women were to vote for the first time.

In the United States, Gen. Dwight Eisenhower had been reelected president, defeating Adlai Stevenson despite the long-distance assistance of *Vodou* priest Balan of Croix des Bouquet. In Haiti, Andre Roosevelt, a cousin of U.S. President Teddy Roosevelt died at 69 ending a chapter in Haiti's hotel business. Andre Roosevelt had launched *Le Refuge*, a resort hotel in the mountains; later managed the *Ibo Lélé Hotel* in Pétionville and had recently opened the *Marabou* Hotel close by the Petionville Plaza. Another hospitality pioneer, Mrs. Wilhelm Oloffson, who had founded Port-au-Prince's legendary Grand Hotel Oloffson, had died that same week at age 79.

An early pre-winter tourist, who arrived on Nov. 14, 1956, was British author Graham Greene. He returned this time with a lovely lady, whom he introduced only as Catherine.

Greene appeared oblivious to the raucous din of Haiti's first, seemingly open, presidential and senate campaigns as he showed off the country to his Catherine. Greene's first visit two years earlier had turned him into a fan of Haiti. He had enjoyed his ten days enormously even observing his friend, theatrical producer Peter Brook, adapting Truman Capote's 1947 short story *House of Flowers* into a Broadway musical. There was no doubt that the celebrated Graham Greene had become another victim of Haiti's charms. In his words visiting the country was a "delightful voyage of discovery." (He still liked to recount his second brief landing in Haiti after U.S. authorities in Puerto Rico barred him entry, even in transit back to England, on grounds that as a student he had once been a member of the Communist party.)

Graham and Catherine was a charming couple. They seemed to be enjoying themselves immensely, doing things that tourists in Haiti don't normally do such as riding in the little taptap buses and trekking into the interior. When Graham arrived, we renewed our friendship (He had obtained his tourist visa at the Haitian embassy in London and as the tourist office in Port-au-Prince had been advised of his arrival. I had been also alerted.) I was excited about getting to know a little more about one of my favorite authors and invited Graham and Catherine out, careful not to intrude too much on their holiday together. Catherine's presence made Greene much more open and friendly. They were fun to be with and it was for me a welcome interlude from the Haitian political storm that was beginning to gain strength.

When two dozen top U.S. women journalists who covered Washington suddenly checked into El Rancho I thought tourist-hater Greene would go through the Spanish— tile roof. (The group included Helen Thomas of United Press who later made a name for herself covering the White House.) Graham and Catherine retreated to a corner with their Scrabble board whenever they were in the hotel grounds.

Realizing how allergic Greene was to other tourists and how ill at ease he was when they were around, I suggested they could escape the "maddening tourists" (Greene's words) by moving to Roger Coster's Grand Hotel Oloffson. Coster was prepared to hold a room for Greene and Catherine even though the hotel was full. Graham was undecided, as he didn't wish to displease their genial host, El Rancho owner Albert Silvera. But after visiting the Oloffson and sampling Laura Coster's kitchen and Oscar's rum punch, both Graham and Catherine were smitten. They put aside the last two days of their visit to savor the Oloffson, which they did indeed enjoy.

Both Graham and Catherine displayed a keen interest in the Haitian art movement. One afternoon I drove them out to visit *La Galerie Brochette* in the village of Carrefour. Enchanted by the paintings Catherine wanted to arrange a showing in London. On the last night of their eleven-day stay Dewitt Peters' director of the Centre d'Art invited the couple to a cocktail party. Earlier we had spent an evening visiting the *Houses of Flowers*. During the day flaming bougainvillea identify the *Houses of Flowers* and at night the café-brothels come alive like a Christmas tree with a profusion of colored lights. Graham displayed admiration for the beauty and grace of one young fille *de joie* dancing with another girl. Catherine pretended to be offended by his glowing description of another beautiful Haitian girl, offering to take a taptap back to the hotel so we boys could enjoy ourselves. It was all a joke and neither of us males required anything but a good rum punch. (Graham and Catherine's visit to the red-light district is recounted in this author's book, *Graham Greene: Demons and Dictators* . . .)

For Graham and me his 1956 sojourn in Haiti was the beginning of a long friendship that lasted until his death in 1992. Catherine, I regret to say I never had the occasion to meet again. Be that as it may, the couple was front-page copy in the *Haiti Sun*.

Graham and Catherine gave no hint that they were nearing the end of their affair. (Graham had already written about their romance in his novel, *The End of the Affair* more recently made into a motion picture.)

Nor did Haiti show signs that its so-called golden years were fading fast and that the end of an era was about to plunge the country into its darkest night of dictatorship, the regime of Francois (Papa Doc) Duvalier.

CHAPTER 14

Magloire's Hat Trick

On launching an Anti-Cancer fundraiser the first week of December 1956, Haitian doctors painted a grim picture of the disease. Members of Haiti's Anti-Cancer league stressed, in interviews in the *Sun,* that cancer was not exclusively an infirmity of the rich. The poor were also victims but seldom knew it because of the expensive tests needed to learn about the inroads of the disease. Tuberculosis and malaria were well known killers in Haiti, and after decades the fight against the terribly disfiguring disease known as yaws had finally yielded results, thanks to penicillin. Yvonne G. Sylvain, M.D., one of the country's early female physicians, reported an astounding statistic. Of "one hundred people gathered today twenty-three would be struck by cancer," she declared. To help fund its activities the league had organized a charity ball under the patronage of Mrs. Paul E. Magloire, the President's wife. The ball was scheduled to take place at *Cabane Choucoune,* Petionville's popular nightclub, on Wednesday December 5.

But that very same Wednesday bombs exploded in various sectors of the capital, heralding the beginning of yet another tragic political crisis. A market woman was badly wounded when a time bomb shattered the concrete table at which she was seated in Port-au-Prince's famous Iron Market. A man reported to be carrying a shoeshine box was blown to bits when the box, which actually contained a bomb, exploded prematurely in residential Bois Verna. Horrified spectators who had rushed to the scene stood staring at the man's entrails hanging from an almond tree. An explosive device sabotaged a water reservoir at Bolosse.

The following day President Magloire did what he had promised he would never do. He did however what most Haitian presidents did do. Only the manner in which he did it was novel. He simply changed hats and retained power. Whether it was his Petite *Junte* the group of young, army officers who served as his kitchen cabinet, who formulated the plan, or whether it was inspired by the bombs that Magloire feared might unravel the nation, his action united the country against him. Whoever or whatever motivated his political hat trick Haitians considered it an insult to their intelligence. The common consensus at the time was that Magloire himself was responsible for the bombs, as a pretext for his *auto-coup d'état*. (Much later the authors of the bombings were identified as members of candidate Duvalier's underground force, who had carefully planned and executed the terrorist acts that brought much better results than they had expected.)

In a radio announcement on Dec. 6, 1956, Magloire declared that he had accepted the opposition's interpretation that his six-year term had ended that day. Then he dropped a bombshell. He had stepped down as President and assumed the title of *Chef du Pouvoir Exécutif* (Chief of the Executive Power) and commander-in-chief of the Army with *extra legal* powers.

Gen. Antoine Levelt, the Army chief of staff, went on the radio to explain the fanciful scenario: When the President had stepped down the chief justice of the Supreme Court, next in line, had refused his constitutional prerogative to rule. Interim power was then offered; General Levelt elaborated, to the vice-president of the Supreme Court, then the oldest judge of the court. He too had refused. General Levelt, as Army commander, had then asked Magloire to retain the power. Once again, Levelt intoned, General Magloire had agreed "to sacrifice himself for the fatherland."

The auto-coup would have been laughable had it not been accompanied by a decree ordering the immediate roundup of the political leaders. Presidential candidate Louis Déjoie was imprisoned in the National Penitentiary along with Duval Duvalier, the father of candidate François Duvalier who had managed to disappear. Several opposition senators and deputies were also jailed. All were accused of subversive activities. A communiqué issued on Dec.7 announced that the 58-member Parliament and the Government Council, composed of senators and deputies, had been dissolved.

So scandalized was the country by what they considered to be Magloire's bald-faced ploy to retain power that a spontaneous general strike erupted the following day. The strike snowballed with amazing speed and totality. The capital was soon a ghost town as stores and other businesses, many of whose owners were Déjoie partisans, pulled down their storm-and anti-riot shutters and went home to wait out the strike. Typewritten protest flyers appeared in the form of chain letters requesting each recipient to type and distribute ten, more producing an endless supply of tracts. Students who used their notebooks to copy and pass on the anti-Magloire message circulated a separate manifesto. In it they declared they would not resume classes until Magloire renounced power. Others called on the Supreme Court judges to assume their responsibility, declaring: "We the people are behind you."

The *télédjol* worked overtime in an effort to destabilize the regime, spreading wild rumors of government abuses and intimidation. Though the rumors heated up the political still more, the strikers were however careful not to provoke Magloire any more than necessary. The close-down was completely non-violent. *Radio Commerce*, * spewed

---

*   (The powerful radio station was a birthday present from the businessmen to Magloire during
      better days.)

out official communiqué after official communiqué. In filing stories to the *New York Times* and the *Associated Press* I was careful to be circumspect, and to quote the communiqués in order to avoid having the censor kill my cables.

The coup became a major story in the U.S. and the rest of the world, not least because of the progressive record which Magloire, up to that point, had compiled. His naked bid to hold onto power caught the U.S. embassy by surprise. Washington recalled its Ambassador, Roy Tasco Davis, for consultation. It was evident that no country was in a hurry to recognize the new Magloire regime, certainly not the United States.

One of the first staff correspondents to arrive was *The New York Times'* Paul Kennedy. Flying in from his Mexico City base on Saturday December 8, he was delighted when I met him at the airport, with the customary bottle of Barbancourt, which I had not forgotten. (The rum was from my own stock as the shops were all shuttered.) Former war correspondent, Relman Morin, one of the top staff correspondents of *The Associated Press*, also arrived, as did Harvey Rosenhouse, a Mexico City based veteran correspondent for *Time Magazine*. Rosenhouse was making his second trip to Haiti in three years. Bearded Jim Cunningham of United Press arrived from Cuba where he had been covering anti-Batista rebels in the mountains. It was good to have such distinguished "big foot" companions.

At the Oloffson Hotel I briefed Kennedy and showed him a copy of *La Phalange*, the Catholic daily which had appeared that morning with a declaration signed by Supreme Court Justices Joseph Nemours Pierre—Louis, Rodolphe Barau, and Lélio Vilgrain. The judges had clarified their position. They had refused, they said, to accept the Executive Power from the Army because of the conditions requested of them. The Army had demanded that they agree to unconstitutional *extralegal* powers.

Driving around town the next morning Paul Kennedy and I witnessed a rare sight indeed, at least in Haiti. Several hundred women, many of them from the elite class and thus fanatical supporters of Louis Déjoie, were marching on the prison where he was held. They had attended Sunday mass and were reciting their rosaries and chanting: *Je vous salut Marie,* as they marched. At the ancient National Penitentiary, as the guards looked on amazed at the unusual spectacle they continued to pray and chant. The women circled the high, buff-colored walls three times before dispersing.

Back at the hotel, Kennedy hammered out his first story on his battered typewriter. His dispatched was a fine report outlining perceptively Haiti's political situation. Kennedy handed his typed article to the RCA cable office attendant, happy to have been able to make the *Times'* Monday edition deadline. An Army officer reached over and took Kennedy's cable dispatch from the RCA man. The officer was the government censor, explained the RCA attendant. After slowly reading the file, the Army officer returned the copy to Kennedy. A robust and vigorous reporter, Kennedy insisted on a responsive answer as to what part of his file the censor found objectionable. I knew Kennedy was losing his patience. Finally the officer said, "All of it," and turned his back. Kennedy, who did not suffer evasiveness lightly even during interviews, stood there with his chest heaving and a look of incredulity, which I feared was about to turn to rage. He banged the cable office counter with a fist, and exclaimed, "Shit!" Fortunately I was able to persuade him to depart without further antagonizing the Army censor, and we left.

I suggested we try some artifice at the international telephone office, the place to communicate overseas by telephone. At the little West Indies Telephone Company Haiti office, which occupied a very small structure on the seafront near the mouth of the Bois de Chêne canal, Kennedy squeezed his brawny chest into one of three stiflingly hot telephone booths. He got through to New York, but no sooner had he begun to dictate his story to the *New York Times* foreign desk than the communication was cut. As Kennedy demanded an explanation from the pretty operator Josseline Bazelais, a large fat censor in the uniform of Haiti's small Navy squeezed his way to the counter scowling and simply gave us the thumbs down sign. As we left the building Kennedy gritted, "What a bunch of idiots. We'll have to find a way." It was Magloire who the next day would furnish Kennedy with a way to bypass Haiti's military censors.*

On Monday morning I drove Paul Kennedy around the city which we found completely shuttered. Kennedy had still not found a way to file his story and we had decided to give the copy to a passenger leaving Haiti by air. It so happened, General Magloire was also making a personal tour, and had stopped at La Belle Créole department store and ordered Elias Noustas its owner to keep his store open. A heavy force of well-armed police officers accompanied Magloire.

One of the police officer flagged down my car and asked, "Is that Kennedy?" Told that it was, the police officer said, "Mr. Kennedy you have six hours in which to leave the country. Then to me the officer added: "Make sure he leaves." "Ask him on whose orders and why?" Kennedy said to me. When the officer left us without replying the tough Oklahoman uttered some choice curses.

A short while later we were lunching at the Grand Hotel Oloffson before I was to drive him to the airport when two other police officers arrived. One said: "Mr. Kennedy, you are supposed to be at the airport. You have not made a plane reservation to leave." Kennedy waved to his suitcase and portable typewriter next to the table. "As you can see I'm packed and I don't usually pack for lunch," he replied. Then he added, "Here is my ticket you can make the reservation if you like." The officers took seats at another table and waited until Kennedy had finished his lunch. He took his time, ending the meal with a shot of his favorite rum.

During the lunch we discussed the possible reasons why Magloire had singled Kennedy out. It was difficult to rationalize Magloire's action in expelling Kennedy except that the General must have feared the reporter. In the correspondent's most recent interview with Magloire, when asked whom he saw as his successor, the President had made a sweeping gesture with his arms from a palace window, asserting that every

---

*   (At that time Haiti had two cable offices, the RCA and All Americas Cable, besides the West Indies Telephone Company. Each evening they closed and Haiti was completely cut off from the rest of the world.)

Haitian over 40 aspired to his job. After that age, he explained, they had a more elevated objective than simply running for a seat in the country's Senate. After that interview which I attended I told Kennedy I believe it was probably one of Magloire's more profound statements. The president for example was now a rich man and it was not because he banked his meager salary. Indeed some Haitians likened the presidency to winning the lottery, winner takes all.

There was also Kennedy's story on the Péligre Dam. The construction under Magloire of the Péligre Dam, which was to facilitate irrigation of the Artibonite Valley, which in turn was visualized by planners as Haiti's future breadbasket, was treated by the political opposition as a domestic scandal even though the contractors, Brown and Root were American from Texas. The original cost of the dam had been estimated at $14 million. However when additional irrigation and canal costs were added, the total outlay reached $28 million, a 100 % overrun, and equal to the nation's small government budget at that time.

It was hard to prove allegations of kickbacks in highway construction funds from an American company that tar-sealed the main highway from Port-au-Prince to Cap Haïtien with such cheap material that it washed away with the first tropical downpour. Moreover, a percentage of the $7 million dollars cost to face-lift Cap Haïtien's waterfront allegedly found its way into official pockets.

However corruption was only partly the cause of the now-burgeoning national crisis. It was that old and seemingly endemic malady of Haitian chiefs of state, endeavoring to prolong their sojourn in the National Palace, which had inflamed passions once again.

I offered to drive Kennedy to the airport, and the police officers said they had their orders and escorted us and watched him board the plane for Puerto Rico.

Several fellow journalists, myself included, had tried to get the order expelling Paul Kennedy rescinded, pointing out that it would further dramatize the Haitian political situation and indicate that the country had no freedom of the press. Our efforts were to no avail.

The expulsion of Kennedy, however, resulted in a fine irony. The action allowed the correspondent the luxury of filing a long, front-page story for the *New York Times* from the San Juan, Puerto Rico, and office of Western Union that same evening. The result, the *Haiti Sun*, pointed out in an editorial was "The facts, only slightly delayed, came out as they inevitably do, and the censorship futile as always was defeated as it inevitably must be." General Magloire was making all the mistakes.

Tuesday evening thirty-two leading merchants of Port-au-Prince's 300 commercial and industrial enterprises were summoned to the National Palace. A communiqué stated that the businessmen had agreed to reopen the following morning. On Wednesday morning, however, all stores remained closed.

The traditional tendency among Haitians political leaders to blame foreigners for the country's ills came in another government communiqué in which foreign companies and organs of the American government were blamed as fomenters of the general strike. "The closing of the foreign companies constitutes a serious foreign intervention in the affairs of the country," General Magloire's communiqué stated, adding that a formal protest would be lodged with the U.S. government.

The public was unmoved. One leaflet, reflecting what many considered an insult, criticized Magloire for insinuating that the *blans* were behind their effort to oust him. "The descendants of Dessalines and Pétion don't need the *blans* to help them get rid of a dictator," the leaflet declared.

Magloire's long-hoped-for capitulation finally came on the afternoon of Wednesday, December 12. The strongman announced in a radio speech that he was stepping down. The non-violent general strike had succeeded. There was bitterness in Magloire's voice. He reiterated his accusations that "foreign powers" were attempting to destroy Haiti's national sovereignty. "Americans were at the bottom of this nefarious attitude," he charged. Magloire went on to warn that civil war was at "our door" and stirred the delicate domestic matter of class and color prejudice, in a last jab of bitterness.

Army chief of staff, the dapper General Levelt declared that the Army had accepted Magloire's resignation and that, in conformity with the Constitution, the title of chief of state and all executive power had been vested in Chief Justice Joseph Nemours Pierre-Louis. In the radio broadcast the old judge was then heard accepting the office of provisional president. His first official act was to release all political prisoners.

General Levelt then resigned and Col. Léon Cantave, who had been placed under arrest several days earlier accused of rebellion against Magloire's regime, was named in Levelt's place.

Nevertheless, on Thursday morning, December 13, the capital was still strike—bound. Pro-Déjoie women again congregated at the Roman Catholic cathedral, many of them accompanied by their children. The women circulated their *mot d'ordre*, "Continue to strike until Magloire quits the country."

Tipped that Magloire was indeed leaving, I drove to the airport in the afternoon with Harvey Rosenhouse of *Time* Magazine. We managed to take up positions in the Bowen Field control tower, which provided an excellent view of the neighboring military airport terminal. It was at 6:30pm that General Magloire, his family, and his close aides climbed aboard the government-owned C-47 bound for Jamaica and exile. As with so many of his predecessors it was an unhappy and all too familiar ending for Magloire. He had fallen into the same power trap and his actions, as much as any other factor, led to years of disintegration and dictatorship.

Military armored vehicles patrolled the access road to the airport. One of the vehicles, I noted, was commanded by Lieut. Philippe Dominique who was later to return to Haiti in the strangest invasion of them all.

In the control tower as we waited to make sure the plane departed, which it did, Rosenhouse asked me to become a "stringer", non-staff local correspondent, for *Time* Magazine. I wasn't sure I wanted to work for the magazine. "It is very conservative and known as a WASP publication," I recall telling him. "It seems to denigrate the *natives*. They are always *barefoot*". Rosenhouse laughed. "I'm a liberal, more liberal perhaps than you," he rejoined, adding, "And hell, Haiti is no big policy story. You can call the shots, put shoes on the *natives*." I accepted and six months later a story I reported for *Time* got me expelled from the country. But putting shoes on the natives was easier said that done. In the first post-Magloire story *Time (Dec.24)* was at it again. The story read:

> Informal in a beige camel's hair jacket, candidate Louis Dejoie pressed his presidential campaign last week in the south Haitian town of Jacmel. Pretty quadroons rushed up to kiss him; black, barefoot peasant women in red bandannas jumped ecstatically and shouted in Haitian Créole: Vive Papa mwe (Long lives my Papa)! Starting his speech in French, Déjoie switched as a crowd pleaser to Créole.The Haitian throng cheered.
>
> The happy ending of Haiti's revolution-by-passive-resistance thwarted deposed President Paul Magloire's plan for putting off elections, and the campaign started right up again. Déjoie promptly took to the field. Also back in the running was Dr. Francois Duvalier, a respected but unassertive physician with a considerable backing among Haiti's lower middle class. Since one or the other was the indicated heir to Haitian political power, Déjoie and Duvalier, cooperating closely, demanded and got their supporters named to the Cabinet of the provisional government that took over from Provisional President Joseph Nemours Pierre-Louis who further promised the candidates that he would call and election soon, probably setting it around the original date of next April.
>
> As the campaign resumed, Déjoie was clearly the man to beat. A 61-year-old agronomist and self-described millionaire plantation owner, he talked frankly about his wealth, the most practical kind of guarantee that he would be immune to the national penchant for corruption in office. He tells crowds that he is a "production engineer" rather than a politician, offers a country-manager program that would apply his farm know-how towards raising the national agricultural output, particularly in sugar, and thus brings greater prosperity to Haiti."

Paul Kennedy was warmly greeted on his return to Port-au-Prince on December 15 after having been on hand in Jamaica to enjoy the delicious irony of covering the arrival of Magloire and his family in exile. Magloire refused to talk to the media.

The *New York Times* in a December 14 editorial called for "Three cheers for Haiti," declaring,

> "Haitians have once again shown their remarkable capacity for taking things in hand and setting them to rights in their democratic way. It is not our way, but when Gen. Paul Magloire seized power by a crude *coup d'état* last week-end he was reckoning without the good sense and essential civic discipline of his people. There, was no armed uprising. Haitians employed one of the most powerful weapons in the armory of modern times—the general strike . . . the

people shouted for joy in Port-au-Prince yesterday and we can all say, "Three Cheers" with them."

But when the cheering stopped, the dam of recriminations burst. From love to hatred is but a short passage in Haitian politics. Magloire was deemed a dictator, he had been corrupt, and all even imaginary crimes were attributed to him. Bureaucrats were literally chased from their jobs. Several homes of Magloire aides were pillaged. Roland Lataillade's house was set on fire and he lived out the rest of his life in Jamaica, helped by friends from falling into poverty. President Joseph Nemour Pierre-Louis called for an end to free-for-all demonstrations of so called *popular justice*, groups.

Georges Petit devoted most of his newspaper to criticism of Magloire and ended with a warning, "Let everyone be vigilant! The same acolytes of Magloire are busy at work. The Magloire type of danger is in the air . . ."

While he was in jail, Senator Louis Déjoie's popularity had soared to such heady height that some of his political aides believed he should march directly from prison to the palace and assume power. Déjoie wisely did not attempt it. Instead, he believed, naively, that he would be elected on the strength of his own personality. He became infatuated with his role and pompously thought he would win no matter what. In this he was to be proved wrong. His principal supporters, Haiti's mulatto elite, also labeled the bourgeoisie were actually a tiny minority of the populace. Moreover, Déjoie's candidacy made color and class a prime issue and he and his followers exacerbated it by their attitude and arrogance, obscuring the larger problems.

During a difficult nine-month pre-electoral gestation period following Magloire's fall, five provisional governments came and went as the four leading candidates sought to control the official machinery and the Army to ensure victory at the polls. No other Haitian election campaign had been contested with such fury. At times it appeared a life-and-death struggle, which for many, in retrospect, it was. It was also the first election in 153 years in which all Haitians over 21, including women, were eligible to vote.

The mulatto establishment, the middle-class, and even poor families were torn apart by the bitter electoral battle. Some never recovered. Friends became mortal enemies. Except for Daniel Fignolé's MOP, Workers and Peasants Movement, there were no real political parties. Each candidate created a *party*, which was more like a personal *coterie*, and jockeyed for power to fill the vacuum left by Magloire's ouster. Each candidate tried to convert each of the five provisional governments into a vehicle to reach the presidency. When a candidate decided that a provisional government was favoring a particular opponent, he made common cause with other candidates to overthrow the regime of the moment. The situation made for near-anarchy and strange political bedfellows.

It was the end of an era.

The streets of Port-au-Prince were deserted as a general strike paralyzed the capital. The strikers call for President Magloire's departure.

Paul Kennedy, in jacket waiting for his flight after being ordered out of the country by Magloire. He is surrounded by Pan American Airway employees. The large man next to Kennedy is Maurice Duchatelier who was later killed by Papa Doc.

Oungan Ti Couzin's grave by the old road near Carrefour Dufort. Ti Couzin had it built long before he died.